The Temptress

by

William Le Queux

Double 9
BOOKS

The Temptress
by William Le Queux

Copyright © 2023

All Rights reserved.

ISBN: 978-93-59955-08-7

Published by

DOUBLE 9 BOOKS
2/13-B, Ansari Road
Daryaganj, New Delhi – 110002
info@double9books.com
www.double9books.com
Tel. 011-40042856

ABOUT THE AUTHOR

Anglo-French journalist and author William Tufnell Le Queux was born on July 2, 1864, and died on October 13, 1927. He was also a diplomat (honorary consul for San Marino), a traveler (in Europe, the Balkans, and North Africa), a fan of flying (he presided over the first British air meeting at Doncaster in 1909), and a wireless pioneer who played music on his own station long before radio was widely available. However, he often exaggerated his own skills and accomplishments. The Great War in England in 1897 (1894), a fantasy about an invasion by France and Russia, and The Invasion of 1910 (1906), a fantasy about an invasion by Germany, are his best-known works. Le Queux was born in the city. The man who raised him was English, and his father was French. He went to school in Europe and learned art in Paris from Ignazio (or Ignace) Spiridon. As a young man, he walked across Europe and then made a living by writing for French newspapers. He moved back to London in the late 1880s and managed the magazines Gossip and Piccadilly. In 1891, he became a parliamentary reporter for The Globe. He stopped working as a reporter in 1893 to focus on writing and traveling.

CONTENTS

Chapter One
Handfast

"May she ever imitate the holy women of former times, and may the Evil One have no share in her actions."

The nuptial blessing was droned monotonously in French by a stout rubicund priest, who wore soiled and crumpled vestments.

The scene was strange and impressive.

Upon a tawdry altar, in a small bare chapel, two candles flickered unsteadily. The gloomy place was utterly devoid of embellishment, with damp-stained, white-washed walls, a stone floor, dirty and uneven, and broken windows patched with paper.

Over the man and woman kneeling at the steps the priest outstretched his hands, and pronounced the benediction.

When he had concluded a gabbled exhortation and premonishment, they rose. The weary-eyed man regained his feet quickly, gazing a trifle sadly at his companion, while the latter, with a scarcely perceptible sigh, got up slowly, and affectionately embraced her newly-wedded husband.

As the bride placed her arms about her husband's neck, he bent, and, lifting her black veil slightly, gave her a fond, passionate caress.

Turning from the altar, the priest grasped their hands, wishing them health and happiness. What bitter irony! what a canting pretence of humanity! As if either could be obtained in New Caledonia, the malarial island to which the French transport their criminals. The ill-timed sarcasm caused the statuesque warders to grin, but a tear stood in the eye of more than one of the bridegroom's comrades in adversity, even though they were desperate characters, hardened by crime.

"We thank you heartily for your kind wishes," he replied, "and trust that your blessing will render our lot less wearisome."

The convict's bride remained silent, gazing about her unconcernedly.

"Come," exclaimed the officer, rising abruptly, "we must not linger; already we have lost too much time."

After the register had been signed, the husband again kissed his wife. As she raised her lips to his, he whispered a few words, as if to reassure her, then said aloud—

"Farewell, dearest. In seven years I shall be free. Till then, *au revoir, sans adieu!*"

"*Sans adieu!*" she echoed in a low voice, apparently unmoved.

He shrugged his shoulders, and turned towards his stern guards.

"I must apologise for detaining you, gentlemen," he said. "Let us go; I am ready."

The bride, who was young, was dressed very plainly in black, yet with Parisian taste. Perhaps she was handsome, but the thick veil concealed her features. The husband's appearance, however, was decidedly unprepossessing. He was undergoing a term of ten years' hard labour and lifelong banishment.

Tall, bronzed, and bearded, with a thin face wrinkled by toil, although still retaining traces of good looks, he remained for a moment motionless, contemplating with loving eyes the woman who was now his wife. His attire was scarcely befitting a bridegroom, for he had no coat, and wore the soiled and ragged grey shirt and trousers of a miner, while the chains that bound his wrists seemed strangely out of place.

Yet the spectators of this odd ceremony were as strikingly incongruous as the principals themselves.

There were but eight persons. Five were fellow-prisoners of the husband, comprising the labour gang in which he worked, while close behind them sat an officer and two sinister-looking warders in faded military uniforms, the butts of their loaded rifles resting on the floor. The convicts were watching the ceremony interestedly, frequently whispering among themselves, and ever and anon, as either stirred, the clanking of their chains formed an ominous accompaniment to the hastily-gabbled formula, as if reminding them of the dismal hopelessness of their situation.

Neither replied. The warder who held the chain to which the five prisoners were manacled stepped forward, and locked it to the bridegroom's fetters.

For a few minutes, while before the altar, the latter had been allowed comparative freedom, but now, the ceremony over, he was compelled to return with his gang to the atrocious tortures and dispiriting gloom of the copper mines—that monotonous, toilsome existence of French convicts; a life without rest, without hope, with naught else beyond hard labour, brutal taskmasters, and the whining homilies of drunken priests.

At a word from the officer the men filed slowly out, a dismal, dejected procession. Notwithstanding the uniform grey dress and closely-cropped heads, the difference in their physiognomy came prominently out. It was easily distinguishable that the husband belonged to a higher social circle than the others, who, from their ferocious, forbidding aspect, had evidently given the rein to their evil passions, and were undergoing their just punishment. Through the narrow door they passed in single file, the warders following immediately behind with their rifles upon their shoulders.

The officer paused at the door, and turning, lifted his cap politely to the bride, saying—

"Forgive me, madame, for thus taking your husband from you, but, alas! I have orders which must be obeyed."

"No apology is needed, m'sieur," she replied, with a slight sigh. "My husband's honeymoon has been brief indeed, but, as one convicted of a serious crime, what can he expect? We must both wait. Nothing further need be said."

"And you have followed him here—from Paris?"

"Yes."

"Ah, what devotion! Madame, truly yours is a cruel separation, and you have my heartfelt sympathy. Adieu."

"Thanks, m'sieur; adieu," she said brokenly; but the officer had already passed out, and was beyond hearing.

Drawing herself up suddenly, and bowing stiffly to the priest, she left the chapel without deigning to thank him.

Outside the furnace heat of sunshine was intense.

The fierce, glaring sun reflected upon the unruffled surface of the Pacific Ocean, and beat down mercilessly on the white road that stretched away for a mile or so to Noumea, the chief town of the penal settlement, which is altogether a curious place, where society is composed chiefly of *recidivistes* and warders, and where in the Rue Magenta, one rubs shoulders with murderers, thieves, and notorious conspirators, the scum of French prisons, who, having completed their term of hard labour, have developed into colonists, respectable and otherwise.

Hesitating on the threshold, undecided whether to return to the town or take the road which led up the steep hill to where the black shaft and windlass marked the mouth of the convict's mine, she quickly resolved upon the former course, and, strolling leisurely down to where the waveless sea lazily lapped the shingly beach, continued her way under the welcome shadow of some great rocks overgrown by tropical vegetation, and rendered picturesque by palms, acacias, and giant azaleas in full bloom.

The landscape, though arid, was beautiful.

Away across the bay, the cluster of white houses, embowered in branches, stood out in bold relief against the more sombre background of forest, and behind rose mountains denuded of their foliage, but clothed by the sun and air with a living garment of constantly changing colours, which sometimes hid their loss, sometimes more than atoned for it. Into the far distance the long ranges stretched away in undulating lines of ultra-marine and rose, while in the centre the snow-capped summit of Mount Humboldt glistened like frosted silver. Not a breath of wind stirred the sultry atmosphere. The very birds were silent, having sought shelter from the terrible heat; and the calm waters, shut in by coral reefs, seemed to reflect and even increase the intensity of the sun's rays.

Suddenly she halted, and looked back contemplatively along the road the convicts had taken.

Words escaped her. They were scarcely vapid sentimentalities.

"Bah! even the warder pities me, the imbecile!" she exclaimed in French, breaking into a nervous, discordant laugh. "I have obeyed you, my elegant husband, merely because I am helpless; but my fervent wishes for your welfare are that you will descend yonder mine and never return to the light of day—that your taskmasters will crush the life out of you long before the expiration of your term. You think you have ingeniously strengthened the tie by making me your wife, but you have yet to discover your mistake. You have yet to discover that you are dealing with one who can hold her own against the world!" Motionless and silent, she stood for a few moments with fixed eyes and hands tightly clutched. Then she continued—

"Seven years must elapse before you return to civilisation. Meanwhile much can be accomplished. *Sacre!* I hope you'll die the death you deserve, and rot in a criminal's grave before that, curse you! Your wife—*ma foi!*—your victim!"

Hissing the last sentence with bitter contempt, and stamping her shapely foot vehemently, she added—

"Why should I barter myself? By going through the ceremony I have effectually closed his mouth for at least seven years, yet I still have freedom and the means whereby to enjoy life. Shall I calmly submit, then, and pose before the world as a social outcast—the wife of a notorious convict?"

The words were uttered in a tone that clearly demonstrated her intense hatred of the man to whom she had bound herself.

After pausing, deeply engrossed in thought, she exclaimed resolutely —

"No, I will not."

In a frenzy of passion she tore the ring from her finger, and with a fierce imprecation flung it into the water as far as her strength allowed.

"And so I cast aside my vows," she muttered between her teeth, as she watched it disappear.

Then, without a second glance, she turned upon her heel, and, with a harsh, discordant laugh, resumed her walk towards Noumea.

Chapter Two
The Charing Cross Mystery

Two years later. A frosty evening, clear and starlit—one of those dry nights in early spring so delightful to the dweller in London, too familiar with choking fog, drizzling rain, and sloppy mire.

In the vicinity of Charing Cross the busy stream of traffic had almost subsided. At ten o'clock the Strand is usually half deserted—the shops are closed, foot passengers are few, and the theatres have not yet disgorged their crowds of pleasure-seekers anxious to secure conveyances to take them to the suburbs. For half an hour previous to eleven o'clock the thoroughfare, notwithstanding the glare of electricity at theatre entrances and the blaze of garish restaurants and public-houses, assumes an appearance of almost dismal solitude. Boys who have hitherto indefatigably cried "special editions," congregate at corners to chat among themselves, the few loungers stroll along dejectedly, and cadgers slink into doorways to await the time when they can resume their importunities among returning playgoers.

A similar aspect was presented this calm, bright night, as one of the omnibuses plying between the Strand and Kilburn slowly crossed Trafalgar Square, mounted the short incline to Charing Cross at walking pace, and, turning into Duncannon Street, pulled up before the public-house which at that time was the starting-point for that route.

The driver, facetiously adjuring his colleague on the 'bus, which was just moving off, to get "higher up," unfastened his waist-strap, and, casting aside his multifarious wraps, descended. Stamping his feet to promote circulation, he was about to enter the bar. Suddenly he remembered that the conductor, after collecting the fares, had left the vehicle at the corner of the Haymarket for the purpose of walking the remainder of the journey—a proceeding not unusual in cold weather, when one's hands become numbed, and a walk proves a welcome exercise.

It occurred to him that some one might still be inside. His surmise proved correct for, ensconced in a corner in the front of the conveyance, sat a well-dressed, middle-aged man. His fur-trimmed overcoat was unbuttoned, his head had fallen forward upon his chest, and he was apparently slumbering soundly.

"Charin' Cross, sir," shouted the plethoric old driver, peering in at the door.

The man showed no sign of awakening.

Sleeping passengers, who at their journey's end awake irate and in great consternation at finding themselves a mile or two past their destination, are the daily experience of every omnibus conductor; and it is a remarkable fact that the rattle, combined with the rocking of the vehicle, is conducive to slumber.

Chuckling at the unconscious man's probable chagrin, the driver entered the conveyance, and, grasping his shoulder, shook him violently, exclaiming in a loud voice—

"'Ere y'are! Charin' Cross, sir. Wake up, guv'nor, please."

The passenger did not stir. His arm dropped inertly by his side, and as the driver relaxed his hold, he swayed forward, and, before the mishap could be prevented, fell heavily upon the cushions opposite, and rolled upon the floor.

"He must be ill," the driver exclaimed to himself in alarm.

Then stooping, he seized the prostrate man round the waist, and with some difficulty succeeded in dragging him to his feet and replacing him upon the seat.

As he did so he felt his fingers come into contact with some wet, sticky substance. Holding his hand against the dim oil lamp, he examined it closely.

"Blood, by God!" he gasped.

Glancing quickly down at the feet of the inanimate man, he noticed for the first time a small, dark pool, beside which lay a white handkerchief.

In a moment the terrible truth dawned upon him.

Vaguely apprehensive of foul play, he pulled aside the overcoat, and placed his hand upon the heart of the prostrate man.

There was no movement.

"Hullo, Teddy, what's up? Any one would think you were robbing the chap," shouted a voice jocosely at the door.

The driver started, and, looking up, saw his conductor who, having taken a shorter route than the omnibus by walking along Pall Mall, across the north side of Trafalgar Square, and entering Duncannon Street from the opposite end, had just arrived.

"Bill," replied the driver in an awe-stricken tone, his face wearing a scared look, "there's something wrong here. I believe the gent's dead."

"Dead?"

"Yes. Come here."

The conductor grew pale, and got into the conveyance beside his companion.

"Look! that's blood," the latter said, pointing to the floor.

"You're joking," the other replied incredulously, bending down to examine it.

"'Pon my honour I'm not. There's some on my hand here. Besides, his heart doesn't beat."

Leaning hastily forward, the conductor pressed his hand to the passenger's breast. He quickly withdrew it, admitting that such indeed was the case.

"But what can be wrong with him, Ted? He looks like a gentleman," he added in amazement.

"I can't tell. In this 'ere light it's impossible to see."

Striking a vesta, the conductor held it close to the man's coat. As it shed its light in fitful gleams, their eager eyes at once discerned a small hole in the breast, from which blood was slowly oozing.

Both drew back in dismay.

"He's been stabbed?" the man who held the match exclaimed in a low, terrified voice. "See, the overcoat must have been opened first, as it isn't pierced."

The victim had been wounded in the heart, struck by a steady hand, and evidently with great violence.

They stood aghast at the horrifying discovery.

"What do you think of it, Bill?" asked the old driver timorously.

"Murder, without a doubt."

"I wonder whether this will give any clue to the murderer?" the elder man said, picking up the handkerchief.

It was a lady's—a small square of fine cambric with a delicate border of lace.

"Let's look," exclaimed his companion, taking it in his hands, and holding it to the lamp.

"Any mark on it?"

"No, nothing," he replied. "There's some funny scent on it, though," he added, placing it nearer his nose.

"Good heavens, Bill, what shall we do?" ejaculated the driver, thoroughly alarmed at the startling discovery.

"Call the police at once. Wait here a minute, and I'll fetch a constable," the other replied, getting out of the omnibus, and running to the corner of the Strand, where an officer is constantly stationed on point duty.

Already a small crowd had collected, for the cabmen from the shelter opposite had quickly discerned that something unusual had occurred, and, on learning of the crime, grouped themselves around the vehicle in a state of great excitement, and eager to obtain a glimpse of the corpse.

A minute later the conductor returned with two constables. These were immediately followed by a detective-sergeant, who chanced to be passing, and another constable. The detective himself was astounded, although he had been present on more than one occasion when bodies had been found.

The circumstances having been briefly explained, he despatched one of the men to Agar Street for the hospital ambulance, and gave other orders, which were executed with obedience and promptitude.

"Do you know the gentleman by sight?" asked the detective of the conductor, as they both stood gazing upon the body, awaiting the arrival of the ambulance.

"No, I've never seen him before," the man replied; "and the strangest part of the affair is, that when I got off at the Haymarket corner he wasn't inside. There were two gentlemen in the 'bus."

"They got out at Spring Gardens," interrupted the driver. "I stopped for them."

"Then he must have entered immediately afterwards," remarked the detective thoughtfully.

"Yes, that's the only way I can account for it."

"It is certainly an extraordinary case," the officer said, bending down and re-examining the dead man's wound. "From the time he got into the 'bus until you discovered him dead could not have been more than six or seven minutes?"

"Not so much," replied the driver. "I generally reckon it takes four minutes from Dent's to the corner here, including the stoppage in front of the lions."

"But you didn't pull up there to-night?"

"No, because I was not aware I had any fare inside."

"Ah?" exclaimed the detective confidently. "The murder was evidently cleverly planned, and the assassin has got away very neatly indeed."

"It couldn't be suicide, could it?" suggested one of the constables.

"Impossible, for the knife has disappeared. But here's the ambulance; we must remove the body and disperse the crowd."

At that moment a hansom, which had turned from the Strand towards Pall Mall, was compelled to pull up owing to the throng of eager onlookers which had now become so augmented as to reach across the road.

Pushing up the flap in the roof with his walking-stick, the fare, a well-dressed and rather handsome young man, whose face bore that frank, good-humoured expression which always impresses favourably, asked — "What's the fuss, cabby?"

"Can't exactly make out, sir," replied the man. "They say a murder's been committed."

"Somebody murdered!" he exclaimed in surprise. "By Jove, a crime in a 'bus isn't a sight to be witnessed every day. Wait over there, cabby, opposite the church. I'll go and have a look."

Alighting, he quickly made his way through the excited crowd. As he edged in towards the omnibus, two constables, who had just lifted the body out, were placing it carefully upon the stretcher, for a doctor had already made an examination and pronounced that death had been almost instantaneous.

In the brief moment while the constables arranged his head the light of the gas lamps outside the public-house shone full upon the pale, bloodless features, revealing a man of about thirty-five, whose face was well moulded and refined, with closed eyes, very wavy hair, and short, pointed beard. That he was a gentleman was evident. His hands looked soft and white, his finger-nails showed that attention had been bestowed upon them; a large diamond glittered on his finger, and in his scarf was another valuable stone. His attire, too, was the reverse of common, for his overcoat was lined with sable in a style which only a West-End tailor could produce, and his other garments were of the best quality and latest fashion.

"Poor fellow—he looks as if he's asleep," exclaimed a woman sympathetically, at the young man's elbow.

"Ah," remarked another, "he'll never wake again. Whoever killed him accomplished the deed very effectually."

"He's a thorough gentleman, too," commented a cabman, who was eagerly watching with several of his companions. "I wonder what the motive could have been?"

"They'll call Teddy Mills's 'bus the hearse, now," said another cabman; but his companion replied—

"G'arn, 'Arry, it ain't no laughing matter."

"Well, it's a bold stroke, at any rate," rejoined the man addressed. "Why, he couldn't have been seated in the 'bus a minute before he was killed."

"Is it such a mysterious affair, then?" asked the young man who had alighted from the cab, turning to them.

"Mysterious? I should rather think it was. It all happened between the corner of Pall Mall and here. The victim must have entered the 'bus as it was going along, but whether the murderer was inside or whether he followed, nobody knows."

"Pass along, please; pass along!" two constables commanded.

The body, which had by this time been placed on the ambulance and lightly covered, was being wheeled away, and the police were busy dispersing the ever-increasing crowd.

"By Jove, it's terrible! Such sights are enough to give one the blues," the young man exclaimed aloud, as he made his way towards his cab. "I wonder who the Johnnie is? The face seems familiar, yet for the life of me I can't recollect where I've seen it before. But, there, it isn't any use making oneself glum over the troubles of others, and, goodness knows, my own cursed luck is hard enough."

He sighed, and, springing into the hansom, shouted—"Drive on, cabby, as fast as you can make that bag of bones travel."

The man laughed at his fare's humorous cynicism, and, whipping his horse, drove rapidly away.

Chapter Three
In Bohemia

"Look here, Hugh, what is the cause of this confounded gloominess?"

"Nothing that concerns anybody, except myself," was the morose reply.

"Well, you needn't snarl like that at an old friend. Come, out with it, and let's have no secrets."

"There's not much to tell, old fellow, beyond the fact that I'm ruined."

"What!" exclaimed John Egerton, open-mouthed in amazement. "Ruined?"

"Yes."

"Are you really serious; or is this another of your confoundedly grim jokes?"

"It's too true, alas!" the other replied, with a sigh. The artist, laying his palette and mahlstick aside, turned and faced his visitor, exclaiming—

"Sit down and relate the circumstances; we must see what can be done."

"Nothing can prevent the catastrophe. I've considered the problem long enough, and can find no solution."

"Well, don't knock under without a struggle, my dear old chap. Men work for fame and fortune, but expect happiness as a gift. Confide in me, and perhaps we may arrange things."

The other smiled sadly, but shook his head.

It was the afternoon following the events related in the previous chapter. The two speakers who were in such serious conversation stood in a shabby studio in Fitzroy Square gravely contemplating one another.

John Egerton, the owner of the place was a successful artist, whose works sold well, whose black and white illustrations were much sought after by magazine proprietors, and whose Academy pictures had brought him some amount of notoriety. His success was well deserved, for, after a rather wild student life on the Continent, he was now exceedingly industrious. Art was his hobby, and he had but little pleasure outside the walls of his studio.

Though discarding a collar, and attired negligently in a paint-besmirched coat very much the worse for wear, a pair of trousers much bespattered, and feet thrust into slippers, yet his face spoke of genius and indomitable perseverance, with its deep grey eyes, firm, yet tender mouth, and general expression of power and independence.

His visitor, Hugh Trethowen, was of a different type—handsome, and perhaps a trifle more refined. A splendid specimen of manhood, with his fine height and strongly-built frame, well-cut Saxon features, and bright colouring, with laughing blue eyes, the earnest depths of which were rendered all the more apparent by the thoughtful, preoccupied look which his countenance wore.

A young girl, undeniably beautiful, with a good complexion, stood watching them. She was dressed in a bright but becoming costume of the harem, and had, until the arrival of Trethowen, been posing to the artist. Upon the easel was a full length canvas almost complete—a marvellous likeness, representing her laughing face, with its clear brown eyes, and her bare white arms swinging the scimitars over her head in the undulating motion of the Circassian dance.

Besides acting in the capacity of model, Dolly Vivian was the artist's companion, critic and friend. Among the brethren of the brush she was well-known as a quiet, patient, unobtrusive girl, who, with commendable self-sacrifice, had supported her mother and invalid sister by her earnings. Egerton had become acquainted with her years ago, long before he became known to fame, at a time when his studio was an attic in a street off the Edgware Road, when he used frequently to eat but one meal a day, and had often shared that with her. She was his friend and benefactor then, as now. When times were hard and money scarce, she would give him sittings and accept no payment, or, if she did, she would spend the greater portion in the necessaries of life, which she would convey to his sky parlour on the following morning.

This platonic friendship, which sprang up in days of hardship and disappointment, had been preserved in affluence. From her model the rising artist had painted most of the pictures that had brought him renown, and he acknowledged the debt of gratitude by making her his confidante. It was not surprising, therefore, that at his studio she conducted herself as if thoroughly at home, nor that she should be well acquainted with such a constant visitor as Hugh Trethowen.

When, however, the two men commenced so momentous a question, she felt that her presence was not desired, so busied herself, with a good deal of unnecessary noise, with the teacups which stood on a small table beside the easel.

Suddenly she raised her handsome head, and, looking at Egerton, said:

"If you are talking of private matters, I will go and rest until you are ready to recommence."

The artist glanced inquiringly at his friend.

"There is no necessity for leaving us, Dolly," said Trethowen. "We are all three old friends, and my purpose in coming here this afternoon is to spend an hour with you for the last time."

"The last time!" she echoed in dismay. "Why—are you going away?"

He did not answer for a moment. His eyes were fixed upon the girl's face, and his lips trembled a little under the shadow of his fair moustache. Could he really muster up courage to tell them of his intention? He hesitated, then he replied, firmly enough:

"By an unfortunate combination of circumstances I am compelled to leave all my friends. I much regret it, but it cannot be avoided."

The men had seated themselves, and the pretty model was pouring tea into three dainty little cups.

Egerton frowned impatiently.

"This sort of talk isn't like you, Hugh, and it sounds bad. Surely you don't contemplate leaving us altogether?"

"I must—I cannot remain."

"Why?"

"I've already told you. I'm ruined."

"Ruined—good God—you're joking! But even if you are—confound it—why should you go? Other men have got on their legs again."

"I never shall," Trethowen replied sadly. "It's impossible."

"If you'll tell us about it," said the artist persuasively, "we can judge for ourselves."

"Well, briefly told, the facts are these, old fellow. You are aware I'm only the younger son, and that on my father's death my elder brother, Douglas, with whom I've not been on friendly terms for several years, succeeded to the estate."

The other nodded acquiescence.

"My father undoubtedly meant well," Hugh continued, "for he left me some property yielding nearly five hundred a year. Upon this I lived for five years, but—"

"And what more could you expect?" interrupted his friend. "Surely that's enough for a bachelor to live upon?"

"It would have been, I admit," he replied despondently. "Unfortunately, I have been compelled to dispose of the property."

"Why?"

"To temporarily satisfy my hungry creditors."

"Are they numerous?"

"Numerous! Why, they're so plentiful that, by Jove, I've never troubled to count 'em."

"But how have you become so entangled?"

"The usual method is responsible, old chap—tempting fortune," he replied bitterly. "The fact is, things have been going wrong for a long time past, and I've disposed of all I'm worth in an endeavour to settle up honourably. It's no use, however—I've sunk deeper and deeper into the mire, until the only means by which to extricate myself is to go right away. Dunned on every side, with county court summonses descending in showers, the Hebrew Shylocks who hold me in their accursed clutches seem to be taking a delight in crushing me out of existence."

The artist was mute with astonishment. He had always considered his friend very lucky in having ample means at his command, and had never imagined he was in such straits.

"Then, as I understand, you've had to go to the Jews, and they've foreclosed," he said, after silently contemplating the canvas before him.

"Exactly," Hugh replied. "Think. What can a fellow do when he's about town like I've been? He must necessarily follow the example of others on the course and in the clubs, if he doesn't wish to be ranked with outsiders. As an instance, I lost over the St. Leger a clear eight hundred."

"Whew! If that's the case, I'm at a loss to give advice," exclaimed Egerton gravely.

"It would be of no assistance," he said. "Like an ass, I've run through all I possess, with the exception of a bare couple of pounds a week. I must therefore drag out an existence in one of those dismal old continental towns that seem to be provided as harbours of refuge for unfortunate fellows like myself. I'm truly sorry to leave you both, but needs must when the devil drives."

"Why not remain here? If you are hard hit, I can see no reason why you should bury yourself," contended the artist thoughtfully.

"No, Mr Trethowen," added Dolly, gazing into her teacup in a vain endeavour to hide the tears that stood in her eyes, "don't leave us. Why, Mr Egerton would not have half the spirit for his work if you didn't run in now and then and make him laugh."

"I—I cannot remain," he replied hesitatingly. "You see, I'm utterly incapable of making a fresh start in life, for I've no profession. Besides, there's a much stronger reason for my departure. It's absolutely imperative."

His face was lined with pain and sorrow, as he drew a deep sigh, the index to a heavy heart.

"What's the reason?" demanded his friend, glancing sharply at him.

"Because, if I don't get away almost immediately I shall find myself arrested."

"Arrested?"

He nodded, but for a few moments no words escaped his lips.

"Yes, Jack, old fellow, I'm in a terrible fix," he replied in a gloomy tone unusual to him. "I'll confide in you because I can trust you. Three months ago I was hard pressed for money, and seeing a dishonest way of obtaining it, I yielded to the temptation of the moment. I imitated a signature, and drew a thousand pounds."

"Forgery!" the artist exclaimed, dumbfounded.

"Call it what you like. The bill is due the day after to-morrow, then the fraud will be detected."

He uttered the words mechanically, his head bowed upon his breast.

Jack Egerton bit his lip. He could scarcely realise the grave importance of his companion's words.

"Are there no means by which I can assist you, Hugh?" he asked presently in a sympathetic tone.

"None. There is room enough in the world for everybody to stretch himself. You understand my departure is inevitable. It is either arrest or exile, and I choose the latter."

"I'm afraid it is; but, look here. Have a trifle on loan from me—say a hundred."

"Not a penny, Jack. I couldn't take it from you, indeed," he replied, his voice trembling with an emotion he was unable to subdue. "With finances at the present low ebb I could never repay you. Perhaps, however, there may be a day when I shall require a good turn, and I feel confident of your firm friendship."

"Rely on it," the artist said, warmly grasping his hand. "You have my most sincere sympathy, Hugh; for bad luck like yours might fall upon any of us. In times gone by you've often assisted me and cheered me when I've been downcast and dispirited. It is, therefore, my duty to render you in return any service in my power."

Hugh Trethowen rose, listless and sad. The lightheartedness and careless gaiety which were his chief characteristics had given place to settled gloom and despair. "Thanks for your kind words, old fellow," he exclaimed gravely. "I really ought not to trouble you with my miseries, so I'll wish you farewell."

The handsome girl, who had been silent and thoughtful, listening to the conversation, was unable to control her feelings, and burst into tears.

"Don't cry, Dolly," said he in a sorry attempt to comfort her. "Jack and yourself are old friends whom I much regret leaving, but don't take it to heart in this way."

Raising her hand reverently to his lips he kissed it, with a murmured adieu.

She did not reply, but, burying her face in the rich silk robe she wore, wept bitterly.

For a moment he stood contemplating her, then, turning to the artist, he said:

"Good-bye, Jack."

"Good-bye, Hugh," replied Egerton, wringing his hand earnestly. "Remember, whatever happens, I am always your friend—always."

A few brief words of thanks, and Hugh Trethowen snatched up his hat and stick, and, drawing aside the heavy plush *portière* before the door, stumbled blind out.

Chapter Four
The Nectar of Death

Slowly and solemnly the clock of St. James's, Piccadilly, chimed nine.

In his comfortable chambers in Jermyn Street, Hugh Trethowen sat alone. The graceful indifference of the Sybarite had vanished, the cloud of apprehension had deepened, and with eyes fixed abstractedly upon the flickering fire, he was oblivious of his surroundings, plunged in painful reverie.

The silk-shaded lamp shed a soft light upon the objects around, revealing that the owner of the apartment had debarred himself no luxury, and that, although a typical bachelor's abode, yet the dainty nick-nacks, the cupboard of old china, the choice paintings, and the saddle-bag furniture — all exhibited a taste and refinement that would have done credit to any drawing-room. Upon a table at his elbow was a spirit stand, beside which stood a glass of brandy and soda; but it was flat, having been poured out half an hour before.

Suddenly he tugged vigorously at his moustache, as if in deep contemplation, and, rising, crossed the room and touched a gong.

His summons was answered by an aged male servant, the venerable appearance of whose white hair was enhanced by his suit of spotless black and narrow strip of shirt front.

"Anybody called, Jacob?"

"No, sir; nobody's called, sir," replied the old man in a squeaky voice.

"You may close the door, Jacob, and sit down. I want to have a word with you."

The aged retainer shut the door, and stood near the table, opposite his master, fully prepared to receive a reprimand for having performed his work unsatisfactorily. "Sit down, Jacob; we must have a serious talk." Surprised at these unusual words, the old man seated himself upon the edge of a chair, waiting for his master to commence.

"Look here, Jacob," said Trethowen; "you and I will have to part."

"Eh? what? Master Hugh? Have I done anything wrong, sir? If I have, look over it, for I'm an old man, and—"

"Hush, you've done nothing wrong, Jacob; you've been a good servant to me—very good. The fact is, I'm ruined."

"Ruined, Master Hugh? How, sir?"

"Well, do you ever take an interest in racing?"

"No, sir; I never do, sir."

"Ah, I thought not. Fossils such as you do not know a racehorse from a park-hack. The truth is, I've chucked away nearly every farthing I possess upon the turf and the card-table; therefore I am compelled to go somewhere out of the reach of those confounded duns. You understand? When I'm gone they'll sell up this place."

"Will the furniture be sold, sir? Oh, don't say so, Master Hugh!" exclaimed the old servant, casting a long glance around the room.

"Yes; and, by Jove, they'd sell you, too, Jacob, only I suppose such a bag of bones wouldn't fetch much."

"You—you can't mean you are going to leave me, sir?" he implored. "For nigh on sixty years, man and boy, I've been in the service of your family, and it does seem hard that I should remain here and see the things sold—the pictures and the china that came from the Hall."

"Yes, I know, Jacob: but it's no use worrying," said Hugh, somewhat impatiently. "It cannot be avoided, so the things from the old place will have to travel and see the world, as I am compelled to."

"And you really mean to go, Master Hugh?"

"Yes; I tell you I must."

"And cannot I—cannot I come with you?" faltered the old man.

"No, Jacob—that's impossible. I—I shall have no need of a servant. I must discharge you, but here's fifty pounds to keep you from the workhouse for the present. I'd give you more, Jacob, but, indeed the fact is, I'm deuced hard up."

And he took some notes from a drawer in his escritoire, and handed them to his faithful old servant.

"Thank you very kindly, sir—thank you. But—hadn't you better keep the money, sir? You might want it."

"No," replied Hugh, with a sad smile. "I insist upon you taking it; and, look here, what's more, the basket of plate is yours. It is all good stuff, and belonged to the dear old governor; so sell it to-morrow when I'm gone, and put the money into your pocket. Take anything else you like as well, because if you don't others will. And, by the way, should you ever want to write to me, a letter to the 'Travellers' will be forwarded. I—I'm busy now, so good-night, Jacob." Grasping the venerable servant's bony hand, he shook it warmly.

"Good-night, Master Hugh," murmured the latter in a low, broken voice. "Good-night; may God watch over you, sir."

"Ay, Jacob, and may this smash bring me good luck in the future. Good-night."

The old man tottered out, closing the door noiselessly after him.

"Poor old Jacob," said Hugh aloud, as he stood before the fireplace with his hands thrust deep in his pockets in an attitude of despair. "It must be truly hard for him to leave me. He was my father's valet when he was a young man; he has known me ever since I could toddle, and now I'm compelled to throw him out of doors, as if he were a common drudge who didn't please me. He's been more than a servant—he was the friend and adviser of my youth. Yet now we must part, owing to my own mad folly. Some people carry wealth in their pockets, others in their hearts."

With a sigh and a muttered imprecation, he paced the room with deliberate, thoughtful steps.

Suddenly he noticed the evening newspaper that had been placed upon the table by his servant. Anxious to know the result of a race, he took it up mechanically, when his eyes fell upon the head-line in large capitals, "Mysterious murder in the Strand."

"Good heavens!" he exclaimed in surprise. "Why, I had really forgotten that strange incident last night. It must be the man I saw taken from the omnibus. By Jove, that was a curious affair; I wonder what the paper says about it?"

Reseating himself, he commenced to read the column of elaborately worked-up sensation with which the journal regaled its readers.

It certainly was an extraordinary case, inasmuch as the crime must have been committed with a swiftness and dexterity that was little short of marvellous. As far as the representative of the journal had been able to ascertain, the body was still unidentified, and, after advancing an extravagant theory of his own, the enterprising scribe terminated with the stereotyped phrase, invariably used on such occasions, declaring that the police, "though very reticent upon the matter, were prosecuting diligent inquiries."

"Remarkable!" ejaculated Trethowen, when he had finished reading this account. "I wonder who the victim is, and what object anybody could have had in murdering him? So daring, too—in a public conveyance in the very heart of London. There was some motive, I suppose; but evidently the person who committed the crime was no novice, and went to work with swiftness and caution for the purpose of baffling the police. I've been thinking so much of my own affairs to-day that the remembrance of last night's tragedy had entirely gone out of my head. Yet, after all, why should I puzzle my brains over a case that will require all the wit and cunning of skilled detectives before the guilty person is revealed?"

He cast the paper aside, and passed his hand wearily across his aching brow.

"No," he continued, after a brief silence. "I've got too much to think of with my own affairs. Here am I, ruined irretrievably, with no hope beyond that of dragging out a miserable existence in a poverty-stricken sort of way, while my friends laugh over my misfortunes, and make themselves fat upon what they've won from me by foul means as well as fair. Bah! I've been a downright consummate fool, and deserve all this punishment; by Heaven I do!"

And he sprang to his feet, and again paced the room.

"What is my punishment?" he asked of himself, after some soliloquy. "Social ostracism, perpetual poverty, interminable despair. Yet, after all, what have I done to deserve it? I've not been more wild than other fellows during the sowing of my wild oats, as old fogies term it. No; the simple reason for it all is merely because I'm a younger son. My brother has enough to keep him in luxury, whereas I had but a pittance at most, and upon it was expected to keep up appearances and spend it like other fellows. I've done so, and now am doomed to pay the penalty of poverty. Even death would be preferable to the life before me."

He halted, suddenly impressed by the idea. His face was pale and haggard, and in his eyes was a strangely intense look.

"Death! Why not?" he repeated in a hoarse whisper. "I have no longer any interest in life, therefore death would be the easiest means to end my difficulties. It would be all over in a moment."

Shuddering, he sank slowly into the chair, and resting his arms upon the table, buried his face in his hands.

"Yes," he muttered in bitter despair. "I've staked everything, and lost, through my cursed ill-luck. If I exiled myself it would be running away from my creditors, as if I feared them. No, by God! I—I won't do that; I'll choose the other alternative."

With a firm, resolute expression upon his grave features he rose, strode quickly across the room, and, unlocking a Japanese cabinet, took therefrom a tiny phial of colourless liquid.

Holding it up to the light, he gazed upon it with a curious smile of gratification at having the poison in his possession. Strange that a man should laugh when about to take his own life; yet such is frequently the case. What is the motive that prompts him to smile when the grave is before him? What, perhaps, but the fascination of suicide. There are some men who at first feel like jumping from a high elevation into the void below. The feeling grows if at all indulged. There is a strange and, indeed, wonderful fascination in high precipices. The very fact that life can be taken is fascinating often to fatality. The majority of cases of suicide by pistol or by poison would not have occurred if the weapon or potion had been absent. Their very presence keeps the temptation to use them before the would-be suicide with more or less power.

In this case it was the same as many others. Hugh Trethowen's lucidity of mind, granting that there was mental aberration, could not have been fully absent. The fascination of rest, of a possible life beyond, of dramatic sensationalism—all combined—may have been the chief motive-power.

Nevertheless, he stood looking at it calmly. He was bent upon his purpose.

Lifting the glass of brandy and soda, he poured the contents of the phial into it, afterwards tossing the bottle into the grate. His hand trembled a little, but by setting his feet firmly he overcame this sudden nervousness, and looked around him for the last time calmly and seriously.

"Well, here's health to my creditors, and long life to the men who, posing as my friends, have ruined me!" he said bitterly, with a harsh laugh.

Heaving one long sigh, he raised the glass to his lips. He was preparing to drink it at one gulp.

At that moment there came Jacob's well-known tap at the door, and he entered, bearing a letter upon a salver.

Trethowen started, and quickly replaced the glass upon the table. He was confused, and felt ashamed of being caught in the act of self-destruction, although the old man could not have been aware of what the glass contained.

Without a word he took the letter, and Jacob retired.

Tearing it open impatiently, he eagerly read its contents. It was a purely formal communication from Messrs Graham and Ratcliff, an eminently respectable legal firm, who, some years before, had transacted his late father's business, and who now expressed a desire that he should call at their offices in Devereux Court, Temple, at noon on the following day, as they wished to have an interview with him on a most important and pressing matter.

He re-read the letter several times; then, without a word escaping his lips, flung the contents of the glass upon the fire.

The letter puzzled him sorely. He resolved to call at the address given and ascertain the nature of the mysterious business.

It had saved him.

Chapter Five
Under St. Clement Danes

The office was small, dingy, and undusted, with a threadbare carpet that had once been green, long rows of pigeon-holes filled with faded legal papers, and windows so dirt-begrimed that they only admitted a yellow light, which added to the characteristic gloom.

Before a large writing-table sat Mr Bernard Graham, solicitor and commissioner for oaths, interestedly reading some documents which had apparently been taken from a black tin box that was standing open near him. He was a clean-shaven, wizened man of sixty, with scanty white hair, a forehead denoting considerable self-esteem, a pair of small, cold grey eyes, and an aquiline nose, surmounted by pince-nez with tortoiseshell frames. Attired in broadcloth of an antiquated cut, he looked exactly what his clients believed him to be—a respectable family solicitor, the surviving partner of the once popular firm of Graham and Ratcliff.

"Hum! the dates correspond," he was murmuring aloud, as he jotted down some memoranda, after glancing through an affidavit yellow with age. "There can be no doubt that my surmise is correct; yet the whole affair is the most extraordinary within my experience. I wonder whether there are any minor points that will require clearing up?"

Selecting another document, somewhat larger than the former, he opened it, and readjusting his glasses, read it through slowly and carefully, breaking off several times to make notes of dates and names therein set forth.

"No," he exclaimed at last, as he laid the paper aside; "we must first establish the identity, then everything will be straightforward. It all seems remarkably clear."

Leaning back in his writing chair, his features relaxed into a self-satisfied smile.

"Some one must benefit," he observed aloud, his face again assuming a thoughtful look. "There is such a thing as murder through revenge. Now, I wonder how I should fare if—"

The door suddenly opened, and a clerk appeared bearing a card.

"Show him in," commanded the solicitor, after glancing at it.

A moment later Hugh Trethowen entered.

Dressed fashionably, with a flower in his coat, he looked spruce and gay. The settled look of despair had given place to a pleasant smile, and as he advanced with elastic tread and greeted the old gentleman in his usual easy, familiar manner, it would have been hard to believe that twelve hours ago he had been on the point of taking his life.

"Well, Graham," he began, as he put down his hat, and took the chair opposite the solicitor; "now, what is it you want with me? I've been breathing an atmosphere of debts and duns lately, so, if any of my creditors have been so misguided as to put their claim into your hands, I may as well give you the tip at once that I'm not worth sixpence."

"Creditors are out of the question, Mr Hugh," the old solicitor replied, smiling, and leaning back in his chair.

"I wish they were," said Hugh fervently. "Give me a recipe to get rid of them, and I'll try the experiment at all hazards."

"You have no need, my dear sir,—no need whatever."

"No need!" repeated the younger man in astonishment, for the words seemed like an insinuation that he knew the secret means by which he intended to evade his difficulties. "Why, what do you mean?" he asked seriously. "I tell you, it is pay or smash with me."

"I regret to hear that, but you will adopt the former course," Graham replied mysteriously.

Hugh laughed sarcastically.

"That's very likely, when I have no money. But, look here, what do you want with me?"

"To impart some news."

"News!" exclaimed Trethowen, suddenly interested. "Good or bad?"

"Both."

"What is it? Tell me quickly," he demanded, with an impatient gesture.

"Simply this. I wish to congratulate you upon your inheritance."

"What inheritance?"

"Well, the information it is my pleasure to communicate will undoubtedly cause you mingled pain and satisfaction. Briefly, your brother, Douglas Trethowen, is dead, and—"

"What!" cried Hugh, starting to his feet in amazement. "You're humbugging me!"

"I repeat, your brother is dead," resumed the old solicitor calmly, looking intently into the face of the man before him. "In consequence of that event you inherit the whole of the estate."

"Good heavens, is this true, Graham?" he asked breathlessly.

"It is. Therefore I don't think you need trouble yourself over creditors any longer. You can now pay, and wipe them out."

The old man laughed at the effect his words had produced, for Hugh Trethowen was standing in mute astonishment.

"But how do you know Douglas is dead?" he asked.

"There is little doubt of it," answered Mr Graham coolly. "Read this," and he handed him a newspaper cutting.

Hugh scanned it eagerly, with an expression of abject amazement. The statement was to the effect that it had just transpired that the man found murdered in an omnibus at Charing Cross had been identified as Mr Douglas Trethowen, of Coombe Hall, Cornwall. Upon the body some cards and letters had been found, which, for some unaccountable reason, had at first been kept secret by the police.

"I can scarcely believe it," Hugh ejaculated at length. "Besides, after all, it is not absolutely certain that it is he."

"Not at all," admitted Graham, with a puzzled look. "Of course, you, as his brother, must identify him."

"Yes," said the other, very thoughtfully; for it had suddenly occurred to him that he had not recognised the features when he saw the body taken from the omnibus.

"No time must be lost," observed the solicitor. "The identity must be established at once. The inquest will, I believe, be held to-morrow."

Hugh hesitated, and for some moments remained silent.

"You see, I've not met my brother for six years, therefore I might be unable to recognise him. He has been abroad during the greater part of that period, and his appearance may have altered considerably."

"Nonsense, my dear sir,—nonsense. You would surely know your own brother, even if a dozen years had elapsed," he answered decisively.

"And suppose he really is Douglas?"

"The will is explicit enough," the elder man said, pointing to an open document before him. "This is a copy of it, and no codicil has been added. In the same manner as your late respected father, Mr Douglas left the whole of his affairs in my hands. Fortunately for you, he never married, and the property is yours."

He felt bewildered. Such agreeable news was sufficient to animate with immoderate joy a ruined man who, a few hours previously, had contemplated suicide.

"Now, speaking candidly, Graham, have you any doubt that it is Douglas?"

"None."

"Why?"

"Well—for the simple reason that I believe he is dead."

"That's an evasive answer. Tell me the reason."

"Unfortunately, I cannot divulge secrets entrusted to me, Mr Hugh. You may, however, at once rest assured that I am absolutely ignorant both of the motive of the terrible crime and the existence of any one likely to commit it. If I possessed any such knowledge, of course, I should communicate with the police without delay," the old gentleman said calmly.

"Then you refuse to state your reasons?" exclaimed Trethowen, a trifle annoyed.

"I do, most decidedly. All I can tell you is that I knew your brother had returned from abroad; and, as a matter of fact, he wrote making an appointment to meet me yesterday, but did not keep it."

"From that you conclude he is dead?"

"Combined with various other circumstances."

"Well, Graham, it's hardly satisfactory, you'll admit," observed Hugh. And then he added: "Of course, if you refuse to tell me anything else, I can do nothing."

"Excuse me, Mr Hugh," answered the solicitor blandly. "You can go to the mortuary at once and identify the body."

"If I fail, what then?"

"I don't think you will fail," replied Graham, with a meaning smile.

"You'll come and assist me?"

"I shall be very pleased to accompany you, but must claim your indulgence for a few moments while I put away these papers;" and he commenced gathering up the scattered documents and replacing them in the box.

When he had finished he locked it carefully, and then, struggling into his overcoat, and putting on his hat, he followed Hugh Trethowen out.

An hour later they returned and reseated themselves. "The whole affair is so enshrouded in mystery that I doubt very much whether the murderer will ever be discovered," Graham remarked, taking up some letters that had been placed upon his table during his absence.

"I agree with you. It's a most remarkable crime."

"But, after all, what's the use of puzzling one's brain?" the solicitor asked. "You inherit the estate, with an income that should keep you in luxury for the remainder of your days, therefore why trouble about it?"

"That is so; but supposing Douglas is still alive—I only say supposing— now what would be the result?" Graham shrugged his shoulders, and his visage elongated.

"It's no use apprehending such a *dénouement*. You are absolutely certain that the body is his, are you not?" he asked.

"I'm positive of it. The curious deformity of the ear I remember quite distinctly."

"Then you will swear before the coroner to-morrow that he is your brother?" he observed, regarding the young man keenly.

"I shall."

"In that case no more need be said. We shall immediately proceed to prove the will, and you will be master of Coombe."

"Indeed," exclaimed Hugh, with a light laugh, as he rose to depart. "I'm in luck's way to-day. A few hours ago I little thought myself so near being a wealthy man."

"No; it must be a very pleasant surprise," the old gentleman said, rising and grasping his new client's hand. "I heartily congratulate you on your good fortune, Mr Hugh. I shall call upon you at noon to-morrow, and we will attend the inquest together. Your interests will be safe in my hands, so for the present good-bye."

"Good-day, Graham. I'll expect you to-morrow," Hugh replied, and, lighting a cigar, he went out.

Chapter Six
Valérie Dedieu

"Look! there she goes! Isn't she lovely? By Jove, she's the most charming woman I've ever met!"

"The less of her sort there are about, the better for society at large, old fellow."

"What? You know her?"

"Yes. Unfortunately."

"Oh, of course. Some frivolous tale; but I'll not hear a word of it. Some people are never satisfied unless they are polluting a fair name, or washing their neighbour's dirty linen."

"That's meant to be personal, I suppose?"

"As you please."

"And where did you make her acquaintance, pray?"

"Quite casually; a week ago."

"And you've taken her for three drives, and walked on the promenade with her?"

"If I have, what crime have I committed beyond arousing your jealousy?"

"I'm not jealous in the least, I assure you, old chap," replied Jack Egerton, smiling. "But the fact is, Hugh, I've always considered you a man, and never believed that you could develop into a brainless, lovesick swain. Yet it appears you have. We've known each other long enough to speak plainly, and if you take my advice you'll steer clear of her."

"Why do you give me this mysterious warning, old chap?"

"She's bewitching, I admit: but a pretty face is not all that is desirable in a woman. If you're on the lookout for a suitable partner—and it seems you are—I advise you not to make her your wife, or you'll repent it. Besides, a rich man like yourself can choose from among the younger and possibly better-looking bargains offered by anxious but impecunious mothers."

"Oh yes; I know all about that," replied Hugh impatiently. "I shall never take any advice upon matrimony, so you are only wasting breath. The man who frowns at coquetry is often willing enough to wink at the coquette. I'm master of my own actions, and were we not old friends, Jack, I should consider this abominable impertinence on your part."

"But, my dear fellow, it is in your own interests that—"

"Bother my interests! Have another cigar and shut up!"

"Very well, as you please."

The two men, who were thus discussing the merits of a female form which had just passed, were seated at an open window at the Queen's Hotel, at Eastbourne. It was an August morning, warm, with scarcely a breath of wind. The cerulean sky reflected upon the clear sea, glassy and calm in the sunlight, while the white sails of the yachts and the distant outlines of larger vessels relieved the monotonous expanse of blue, and added effect and harmony to the scene.

A fashionable crowd of loungers were passing and reusing the window, keeping under the shadow of the uses: for the fair ones who frequent seaside resorts, presumably for health, never desire their faces tanned. Now that the legal formalities had been accomplished, and Hugh Trethowen found himself with a comfortable competence, he, no longer world-weary, had recommenced a life of enjoyment. It was a pleasant reflection to know that his creditors had been paid in full, that he had repaid the thousand pounds he had obtained dishonourably, that he was no longer likely to be troubled by duns, and that his trusted servant Jacob had been reinstalled master of his chambers. He had spent a few weeks at Coombe, and formally taken possession of the home of his youth; then he returned and went to Eastbourne, having induced Egerton to put aside work and spend a short holiday with him.

After this discussion regarding the lady, he sat back in his chair, with a cigar in his mouth, looking unutterably bored. Truth to tell, he was a little out of temper; the weather was oppressive, and he hated discussions, as he always argued that life was too short, and breath too precious, to waste on trying to convince any one against his will.

As he sat there he gazed out upon the expanse of blue, and lapsed into silent contemplation.

The object of his admiration, who had just passed their window, was dressed with elegance and taste in a dainty pearl-grey creation of Worth's, a hat of the latest French mode, the whole being surmounted by a cool-looking lace sunshade, the tint of which served to enhance her extraordinary beauty.

She was one of those women frequently met with in Society, whose past is enveloped in a mist of uncertainty, yet they cannot be termed adventuresses, for their adventures, as far as known, are nothing extraordinary, and *les conveyances* have always been respected and rigorously preserved. Men liked her because her foreign accent and gesture added a vivacious piquancy to her manner, and women tolerated her because she was affable, fashionable, and *chic*. Scandalous tongues had certainly done their utmost to injure her reputation, but had failed. She numbered many smart people among her friends, but not even her enemies could accuse her of vulgarity or indiscretion. All that was known was that she possessed ample means, moved in a good set, and was a conspicuous figure wherever the *haut monde* poured forth her children—at Trouville, Royat, Brighton, on the *plage* at Arcachon, or the Promenade des Anglais at Nice, according to the season and fashion.

"Let's go for a stroll, old fellow," suggested Hugh, rising, and tossing his cigar out of the window.

"I've some letters to write."

"Oh, let them wait. Come along."

Egerton's features were clouded by a frown of displeasure. He yawned wearily, but rose and accompanied his friend.

They strolled along the parade, and back, and then out to the end of the pier. Trethowen's eager eyes soon descried the object of his admiration, seated alone under the shadow of the pavilion, apparently engrossed in a novel. She looked up in surprise at their approach, and after mutual greetings they seated themselves beside her.

Valérie Dedieu, whose features were flushed—for she had been startled by their sudden appearance—was certainly remarkably pretty. She was gentle and winning, with a well-formed head, and a tall, graceful figure that any woman might have envied. Her large, expressive dark eyes, protected by their fringe of long lashes, had that look, at once stubborn and gentle, provocative and modest, wanton and ardent, of the Frenchwoman. The expression of her face was ever changing; now her eyes, cast down demurely, seemed to indicate a coy modesty; now her pouting lip betrayed a slight annoyance, only to be succeeded by a charming smile which disclosed an even row of pearly teeth.

As Hugh gazed upon her he remembered his friend's mysterious warning, and asked himself what evil could lurk under so innocent a countenance.

"I had no idea you were acquainted with M'sieur Egerton," she exclaimed, suddenly turning to him.

"Oh yes; we are old friends," Hugh replied, smiling.

"Ah! what an age it is since we met," she said, addressing the artist, her words just tinged with an accent that added charm to her musical voice.

"It is, mademoiselle," he answered, somewhat sullenly; "I scarcely expected to come across you here."

She darted a sharp, inquiring glance at him, and frowned, almost imperceptibly. Next second she recovered her self-possession, and with a light laugh said: "Well, there seems some truth in the assertion that the world is very small after all."

"There does, and encounters are sometimes unpleasant for both parties," he remarked abruptly. "But you'll excuse me, won't you? I see a man over there that I know, and want to speak to him."

Valérie gracefully inclined her head, and Egerton, rising, lounged over to the man he had recognised.

The moment he was out of hearing, she turned to Trethowen, and said:

"Then you and Jack Egerton are friends?"

"Yes; I find him a very agreeable and good hearted fellow."

"That may be." She hesitated thoughtfully; then she added: "You do not know him as well as I do."

"And what is your objection to him?" asked he in surprise.

"Hugh, yesterday you told me you loved me," she said, looking seriously into his face.

"Yes, dearest, I did. I meant it."

"Then; as I explained to you, I have many enemies as well as friends. Jack Egerton is one of the former, and will do all in his power to part us when he finds out our affection is mutual. Now you understand my antipathy."

"Clearly," he replied, puzzled. "But I know Jack too well; he would not be guilty of an underhand action."

"Do not trust him, but promise me *one thing*."

"Of course, I'll promise you anything to make you happy. What is it?"

"That you will take no heed of any allegations he may make against me."

She was intensely in earnest, and gazed at him with eyes that were entirely human in their quick sympathy, their gentleness—in their appeal to the world for a favouring word.

"Rest assured, nothing he may say will ever turn me from you, Valérie."

She heaved a sigh of relief when he gave his answer.

"Somehow or other I am always being scandalised," she exclaimed bitterly. "I have done nothing of which I am ashamed, yet my select circle of enemies seem to conspire to cause the world to deride me. Because I am unmarried, and do not believe in burying myself, they endeavour to besmirch my fair name."

She spoke with a touch of emotion, which she ineffectually tried to hide.

Then, as Hugh addressed her in a tone in which respect melted into love, she quivered at the simple words in which he poured forth his whole soul:

"I love you. Why need you fear?"

He uttered these words with a slight pressure of the hand, and a look which sank deep into her heart.

Then they exchanged a few tremulous words—those treasured speeches which, monotonous as they seem, are as music in the ears of lovers. The artist and his friend were by this time out of sight, and they were left to themselves to enjoy those brief half-hours of happiness which seldom return, which combine the sadness of parting with the radiant hopes of a brighter day, and which we all of us grasp with sweet, trembling joy, as we stand on the threshold of a new life.

And Valérie—forgetting everything, absorbed in a dream which was now a tangible reality—sat silent, with moist and downcast eyes. Hugh continued to smile, and murmured again and again in her ear:

"I love you."

The pier was almost deserted, and, heedless of the rest of the world, they sat enraptured by love, lulled by the soft splashing of the sea, and bathed in the glorious golden sunshine.

Chapter Seven
Aut Tace, aut Pace

On the following afternoon there was held in the Floral Hall of the Devonshire Park one of those brilliant orchestral performances which always attract the fashionable portion of Eastbourne visitors. The concerts, held several times each week, are extensively patronised by the cultured, and even the crotchety, who hate music, and regard Mozart and Mendelssohn as inflictions, look upon them as a pleasant means of idling away an hour. This afternoon, however, was devoted to operatic selections, and the hall was filled with a gay throng.

Trethowen had gone over to Hastings to visit some friends, and Egerton, who found time hanging heavily upon his hands, strolled in to hear the music. As he entered, the first object which met his eye was Valérie, who, dressed with becoming taste and elegance, was sitting alone, casting furtive glances towards the door, as if expecting someone.

After a moment's hesitation he walked over to where she sat, and greeting her briefly with a pleasant smile, took a chair beside her.

"Where is your friend?" she asked abruptly.

"He went to Hastings this morning."

"When will he return?"

"I'm sure I don't know," replied the artist carelessly.

"I suppose the attraction of your fascinating self will not allow him to remain absent long. Am I to—er—congratulate you?"

Her dark eyes flashed angrily, as she exclaimed in a low, fierce tone:

"You've tricked me! You've told him!"

"And if I have, surely it is no reason why you should make an exhibition of your confounded bad temper in a public place. If you wish to talk, come into the grounds," he said in a tone of annoyance.

"Yes; let's go. I've something to say."

The conductor's baton was tapping the desk as they rose and passed out upon the pleasant lawn beyond. Walking a short distance, they seated themselves under the shadow of a tree, in a nook where there were no eavesdroppers.

"Well, Valérie, what have you to say to me? I'm all attention," said Egerton, assuming an amused air, and calmly lighting a cigarette.

"*Diable*! You try to hide the truth from me," she said, her accent being more pronounced with her anger. "You have warned Hugh; you have told him to beware of me—that my touch pollutes, and my kisses are venomous. Remember what you and I were once to each other—and you, of all men, try to ruin my reputation! Fortunately, I am well able to defend it."

"Your reputation—bah!"

"Yes, m'sieur, you may sneer; but I tell you, we are not so unequally matched as you imagine. If you have breathed one word to Hugh of my past, I can very easily prove to him that you have lied; and, further, you appear to forget that certain information that I could give would place you in a very ugly predicament."

"Oh! you threaten, do you?"

"Only in the event of your being such an imbecile as to reveal to Hugh the secret."

"Then, I may as well tell you that up to the present he knows nothing. Yet, remember, he and I are old friends, therefore it will be my endeavour to prevent him falling into your accursed toils, as others have!" he exclaimed angrily.

"Cursed toils, indeed!" she echoed, with a contemptuous toss of her pretty head. "The idea of a man like you setting himself up as Hugh Trethowen's protector! It's too absurd. I wonder whether you would still be friends were he to know the truth about you, eh?"

"It matters little," he answered sternly. "You'll keep your mouth closed for your own sake."

"What have I to fear, pray?" she asked impatiently. "It seems you think me a weak, impressionable schoolgirl, who will tremble under your menaces. Why, the worst accusation you can make, is that I have been guilty of that crime so terrible to the eyes of the hypocritical English—unconventionality. Don't you think I could easily disprove your statements, especially to a man who loves me?"

"Loves you!" repeated the artist, with a harsh, derisive laugh. "He wouldn't be guilty of such romantic folly."

"You are mistaken."

"Then I can quickly put an end to his fool's paradise."

"How?" she asked breathlessly.

"I will find the means. If nothing else avails, he shall be made acquainted with the history of La—"

"Hear me!" she interrupted fiercely. "We are both past masters in the art of lying, John Egerton; we have both led double lives, and graduated as deceivers. Breathe one word to him, and I swear that at any cost the world shall know your secret. You should know by this time how futile it is to trifle with me, especially when I hold the trump card. Hugh has been your friend, but now he is my lover; and, furthermore, I mean that he shall marry me."

The man was silent.

He admitted to himself that her bold, passionate words were true. He was powerless to give his friend an insight into her true character, fearing the consequences, and knowing too well how relentless she was, and that she would not spare him.

"If I carry out my intentions and tell him everything—"

"Then you will suffer, and in his eyes I shall remain immaculate," she exclaimed quickly, watching his face intently.

Calm indifference had been succeeded by a wearied, anxious expression, and in his eyes there was a look of unutterable hatred. She waited for him to answer, but he continued smoking thoughtfully.

"*Ne m'échauffez pas les oreilles,*" she urged in a less irritated tone. "You must admit, Jack, there are certain bonds between us that for our own sakes must not be broken. The folly of disclosing my past to Hugh is palpable, for it would mean speedy ruin to yourself, and be of no possible benefit. Therefore but one solution of the difficulty remains."

"What is it?"

"Well, I have already told you what form my revenge would take were you to expose me, and I think you acknowledge that to tell all I know would be most undesirable from your point of view."

He bowed in assent.

"I'm glad you admit the inefficacy of your attempt to bounce me," she continued. "I can suggest but one thing, namely, that we resolve to preserve our compact of secrecy."

"At the cost of my friend's happiness?"

"At any risk. But let me first assure you that Hugh's happiness will not be jeopardised by the adoption of this course."

"There will be no—er—danger, I suppose?"

"What do you mean?"

"Men die sometimes."

"I don't understand your insinuation. I confess I love him, so it is scarcely probable that any harm will befall him if it is in my power to prevent it."

He thrust his hands deep into his pockets and frowned. Then he exclaimed decisively:

"Your words have no effect upon me. I am determined he shall judge you in your true light."

She glanced at him in anxious surprise, for, truth to tell, she was unprepared for this bold reply. She hesitated whether she should change her tactics, as she was well acquainted with his obdurate nature, and in her heart feared to lose the man whose tender passion she half reciprocated. But her quick, impetuous character quickly asserted itself, and attained the mastery.

"You—you blighted my life!" she cried in a towering rage, her face blanched with passion. "And even now, when I have an opportunity, you debar me from atoning for the past, and becoming an honest woman! I am not such a blind fool, however, as to bow calmly to your tyranny. I have already sacrificed too much, so I give you but one chance to save yourself."

"To save myself. Bah! you are talking nonsense."

"No, believe me, I'm not," she declared, her dark eyes flashing with anger. "Either you give your promise of secrecy now, at once, or before the day is out I will give you up to the police."

Jack Egerton drew a long breath, and his countenance grew visibly paler. He was cornered, and saw no possible means of evading the dire alternative. If he divulged the secret, it would mean disgrace, ruin, even worse.

She smiled triumphantly at his bewilderment. It was true, as she assured him, she held the trump card, and was playing the dangerous game dexterously, as only a clever, scheming woman could.

"Which do you choose?" she asked in a cool, indifferent tone, as if putting forward some very commonplace plan.

"You're an idiot," he exclaimed in vehement disgust.

"I'm well aware of that fact, *mon ami*," replied she, with a supercilious curl of the lip. "Such a compliment is particularly appropriate. I was an idiot to allow you to have the freedom you now enjoy. Remember, however, I have yet a talisman that will sooner or later cause you to cringe at my feet."

"Never."

"Then you must put up with the consequences," she answered calmly, nervously twisting the ribbons of her sunshade. "But I warn you, that if we are to be enemies you will find me even more merciless than yourself. Your own folly alone will bring upon you the retribution you so richly deserve."

"Bah! what's the use of being dramatic? If it's a fight between us, your record is quite as black as mine."

"Ah! you would have to prove that; but in the meantime I should have the satisfaction of seeing you sent to penal servitude. You have been acquainted with me long enough to know that I do nothing by halves. I am determined that now, before we part, you shall swear to keep my secret, or I will put you in a convict's cell."

"But think of the injury you would—"

"Enough! Words are useless. You must choose now."

Her handsome face was perfectly impassive; a cruel, sarcastic smile played about her lips.

She had been watching his features narrowly, for the pallor and the nervous twitchings clearly showed the agitation her decisive alternative had produced. Passionate love for Hugh Trethowen had alone prompted her, for she saw that if this man gave him an insight into her past he would turn his back upon her in ineffable disgust. Hers was a Bohemian nature, and she had led a strangely adventurous life, though few were aware of it. Her early education in the Montmartre quarter of Paris had effectually eradicated any principles she might have originally possessed, and up to this time she had enjoyed the freedom of being absolute mistress of her actions. Yet, strangely enough, now she had met Hugh, her admiration of his character had quickly developed into that intense affection which is frequently characteristic of women of her temperament, and she discovered that his love was indispensable to her existence. There was but one barrier to her happiness. Egerton knew more of the unpleasant incidents of her life than was desirable, and for the protection of her own interests she was compelled to silence him.

From the expression on his face she felt she had gained her point, and rose with a feeling of absolute triumph.

"Now," she demanded impatiently, "what is your decision?"

"Your secret shall be kept on one condition only," he said, rising slowly, and standing beside her.

"What is that, pray?"

"That no harm shall befall Hugh," he replied earnestly. "You understand my meaning, Valérie?"

"It isn't very likely that I should allow anything of that sort to occur. You seem to forget I love him."

The artist was convinced that her affection for his friend was unfeigned. She was but a woman after all, he argued, and probably her life had changed since they last met. Her answer decided him.

"Well, which will you do?" she again asked, with an anxious look.

"I will tell Hugh nothing of the past," he said briefly.

"Ah! I thought you would come to your senses at last," she exclaimed, with a short, hysterical laugh. "Then it is a compact between us. You take an oath of silence."

"I swear I will divulge nothing," he stammered.

Then Valérie breathed again, and it was impossible for her to hide the satisfaction with which she regarded his words.

"Divulge nothing," she repeated, quite cheerfully. "Undoubtedly it will be the best course, especially as we both have hideous secrets which, if exposed, would bring inevitable ruin upon us both. Was it not Marmontel who said 'La fortune, soit bonne ou mauvaise, soit passagère ou constante, ne peut rien sur l'âme du sage?'"

They chatted for a few moments, then moved away together in the direction of the Floral Hall—not, however, before she exclaimed—

"If you break your oath you will bitterly repent."

Chapter Eight
Under Seal

Surrounded by a thickly-wooded park, where the deer abound in ferny coombes and hollows, stood the home of the Trethowens.

The house, to which a long elm avenue formed the principal approach, was an imposing pile, and dated for the most part from the reign of Queen Anne. Standing out prominently, its grey walls were almost wholly ivy covered, and from its grey slate roofs rose stacks of tall chimneys backed by thick masses of foliage. Striking as was its exterior, within the arrangements were antiquated and behind the times; for comfort had not been sacrificed to modern improvement, and vandalism had never been a distinctive quality of any of its masters.

In the great old entrance-hall, with its wide hearth and firedogs, were paintings by Fuseli and carvings by Gibbon, in which the motto of the Trethowens, *Sit sine labe fines*, was conspicuous, while the rooms, furnished with that elegant taste in vogue when the house was built, contained many unique specimens of Guercino, Chari, and Kneller.

Indeed, Coombe Hall was one of the finest mansions in North Cornwall.

During Douglas Trethowen's absence the place had been left with only a gardener and his wife as caretakers. The park had been neglected, grass had grown in the gravelled carriage-drive, and the fine old gardens had been allowed to become choked with weeds. Though the whole place had a potency to set men thinking, perhaps the most quaint, old-world spot was the flower garden, with its spreading cedars and shady elms, its lichen-covered walls overrun with tea-roses, jasmine, and honeysuckle, with black yew hedges forming pleasant shades to the pretty zigzag walks. Here, long ago, dainty high-born dames in patches, powdered wigs, and satin sacques fed the peacocks and gathered the roses, or, clad as Watteau shepherdesses, danced minuets with pink-coated shepherds with crooks in their hands. Here, the scene of many a brilliant *fête champêtre*, syllabubs were sipped, and gorgeous *beaux* uttered pretty phrases, and, perchance, words that were the reverse of delicate, and were punished by being lightly tapped by fans.

Amid these unprofaned, old-world surroundings, Hugh Trethowen found himself, having been called thither by urgent business, for a portion of the house was in process of renovation, and the architect required his instructions.

Familiar as was the home of his childhood, yet he had not been there a week before his habitual *blasé* restlessness returned. Only a few days ago he had bade farewell to the woman he loved, but already he was longing to be again at her side, and had decided to return to her on the morrow.

He had been inspecting the progress of the work of putting the garden in order, and the various other improvements, but time hung heavily upon his hands, and it was merely for the purpose of whiling away an hour or two that he resolved to ascertain the nature of the private papers left by his dead brother.

Thus it was that he was sitting in the fine old library, cigar in mouth, lazily scanning some letters and documents scattered before him. He found little of interest, however; but as his chair was comfortable, and as the golden sunset streaming in through the diamond panes illumined the room with a warm light, he experienced a languid satisfaction in making himself acquainted with his brother's secrets.

One by one he took the letters and digested their contents. Many were Cupid's missives, couched in extravagant language, and still emitting an odour of stale perfume. Some were tied together in bundles from various fair correspondents, others were flung indiscriminately among a heterogeneous accumulation of bills, receipts, and other papers similarly uninteresting.

At last, when he had finished the whole of those before him, he sat back, and for a long time smoked in meditative silence.

"By Jove," he exclaimed at last, aloud, "Douglas must have had a variety of lady friends of whose existence nobody knew. And they all loved him, poor little dears. No doubt his money attracted them more than his precious self, yet he was too wide awake to allow himself to become enmeshed in the matrimonial net." And he laughed amusedly. "Their pretty sentiments, kisses indicated by crosses, and mouldy scents, were all to no purpose," he continued, taking up one of the letters, and contemplating the address. "What a disappointment it must have been when he went abroad, and left the whole of the artless damsels to pine—or rather to seek some other fellow likely to prove a prize. And their presents! Good heavens! he might have set up a bazaar with the jewellery, slippers, smoking caps, cigarette cases, match-boxes, and other such trash mentioned in their dainty notes. I suppose I shall find the whole collection bundled into a cupboard somewhere, for they must have been forgotten as soon as received. What strange beings women are, to be sure!"

Having finished his cigar, he stretched himself lazily, yawned, and exclaimed:

"Now I wonder whether there's anything else worth looking at? Such letters are quite as amusing as the comic papers."

He glanced at them carelessly, with an uninterested listlessness, for he felt half inclined to burn them, as at best they were only rubbish. It was a pity, he thought, that such a fine old piece of furniture as the Chippendale bureau should be used for no better purpose than to store these forgotten and useless communications. Again, why should he harbour the evidences of his dead brother's flirtations.

As these and similar thoughts were passing through his mind, he suddenly gave vent to an exclamation of intense surprise. Withdrawing his hand quickly from the bureau, he rushed across to the window in order to examine more closely the object which had evoked his astonishment.

It was a coloured cabinet photograph.

He gazed upon it in dumb amazement, for the light revealed the pictured face of Valérie Dedieu!

Evidently it had been taken several years ago, as the hair was dressed in a style that was now out of date; still there was no doubt as to the identity of the original. With the exact contour of the features he was too well acquainted to regard it as a striking resemblance heightened by imagination. He examined every detail with eager eyes, and was convinced that the photograph was hers. The colouring, so far from altering the expression of the features, added a lifelike look, enhancing the beauty of the picture. The lips were parted, disclosing even rows of small white teeth; the counterfeit presentment seemed to smile mockingly at him.

"Valérie's photograph!" he ejaculated, running his fingers through his hair, and gazing around in blank bewilderment. "How could it have come into Douglas's possession? Strange that I should find it here, unless—unless she, too, loved him."

"No," he added savagely, a moment afterwards. "Why should I think that? I'll not believe it until I have proof. And then, after all, they may not have been acquainted; the photograph may have come into his possession in some roundabout way. By the way," he continued, as a sudden thought occurred to him, "I might possibly discover something further."

Again he returned to the bureau, still holding the photograph in his hand, and after a few moments' eager search drew forth a small packet of letters tied with pink tape and sealed with red wax.

They had evidently been carefully preserved, for he discovered the packet concealed at the back of one of the small drawers in the interior.

With hands trembling with feverish excitement he took them to the window. Hastily he broke the seals, drew off the tape, and found there were three letters.

He felt a sudden throb at his heart, a touch of suspense that was painful, as he opened the first anxiously.

"Her handwriting!" he ejaculated excitedly, at the same time taking from his pocket a letter he had received that morning from Valérie, and placing them side by side.

The peculiarities of the fine angular calligraphy were exactly similar.

He read the letter. It was disappointing.

Merely a plain, curt note, commencing: "Dear Douglas," making an appointment to meet at the Midland Hotel, St. Pancras, from which place it was dated and signed with the initial "V."

The discovery had wrought a great change in him. He was not the same man. A cloud overspread his countenance, and he remained buried in thought.

When he roused himself to glance at the second letter, he seemed yet more melancholy.

It certainly was an interesting and correspondingly mysterious communication.

Dated from 14 Rue d'Amsterdam, Paris, it commenced without any prefix, endearing or formal, and bore unmistakable signs of having been hastily written. It read as follows:

If you do not call before midday to-morrow I shall know that you refuse to entertain any conciliatory measure. Time does not admit of argument; I must act. At least, I must leave Paris to-morrow night, and even then all may be known. Fail to come, and I shall know you are my enemy. If I am unfortunate, rest assured I shall not suffer alone. Take my advice and seek me the moment you receive this, as it is imperative we should arrange matters before my departure. This course will be the best for you.

V.

"There was some secret between them!" Hugh said to himself in a strange half-whisper, as he finished the curious epistle. "I wonder what it was? It is clear she had a very strong motive in her desire to see him, and the letter, from its general tone, appears to relate to some transaction in which they were both implicated."

Suddenly the words of Jack Egerton, when he had pointed Valérie out at Eastbourne, recurred to him.

"The less of her sort the better," he mused, gazing out of the window abstractedly. "I never asked Jack what he meant by that mysterious allusion. Perhaps, however, he didn't mean it seriously, and only said it in chaff."

He remained silent for some moments.

"Why," he suddenly exclaimed, "why should I believe malignant stories, when there is nothing to prove them? These letters are certainly strange, yet, after all, they may relate to some purely matter-of-fact affair."

Truth to tell, he felt half inclined to believe there had been a deeper meaning in the artist's words than he imagined, and was stupefied in the agony of mental struggle. He stood rigid and confounded, gazing in turn at the letters and photograph, utterly unable to account for the curious and secret correspondence that had evidently taken place between his late brother and the woman who had promised to become his wife.

At last he opened the remaining letter, and was astonished to find it merely a blank sheet of notepaper, inside which was carefully preserved a scrap of half-burned paper about two inches square. Apparently it was a portion of a letter which, after being torn across, had been thrown into the fire. By some means the edges had been burned, the remainder being severely scorched.

It was written on one side of the paper, and the words, which were in French, and in a disguised hand, revealed a fact which added interest to the discovery. Necessarily few, they were very pointed, and translated they read:

Our agreement... dies I will... meet in London... of that sum on June 13th... Montabello to his rooms on the Boulevard... defy detection by...

He read and re-read these words, but could glean little from them. The small piece of blackened paper had presumably formed part of a note, but it was clear that the writer was illiterate, or intentionally ignorant, for in two instances the orthography was faulty.

Try how he would, Hugh was unable to disguise the fact that it was a promise to pay a certain sum, and the mention of the word "dies" seemed as if it had connection with some dark deed. Perhaps it alluded to the secret referred to by Valérie in the former letter! With tantalising contrariety, any names that had been mentioned had been consumed, and nothing but the few words already given remained as indication of what the communication originally contained.

Nevertheless, thought Hugh, it must have been regarded as of considerable importance by his brother, or it would not have been so carefully preserved and concealed. So crisp was it in its half-consumed condition, that he was compelled to handle it tenderly, otherwise it would have crumbled.

Having satisfied himself that nothing further could be gathered from the almost obliterated words, he replaced it carefully inside the sheet of notepaper, and proceeded to make a thorough search of the bureau.

In vain he took out the remaining letters and scanned them eagerly, hoping to find something which would throw a further light upon the extraordinary missives. None, however, contained any reference to Valérie, or to Paris. When he had finished, he summoned old Jacob, and ordered him to make a fire and burn all except about half a dozen, which appeared of a business character.

Placing the photograph and the three letters in his pocket, he stood thoughtfully watching the old man as he piled the bills and the billets-doux upon the wide-open hearth and ignited them.

The mysterious correspondence sorely puzzled him, and he was determined to find out its meaning. Undoubtedly, Douglas and Valérie were intimately acquainted, and from the tone in which she wrote, it appeared as if from some reason she was afraid of him, and, further, that she was leaving Paris by compulsion.

His thoughts were embittered by a vague feeling of jealousy and hatred towards his brother, yet he felt himself on the verge of a discovery which might possibly lead to strange disclosures.

Curiously enough, our sins find us out very rapidly. We cannot tamper with what is right and for the best in order to secure what is temporarily convenient without invoking Nemesis; and sometimes she comes with a rapid tread that is a little disconcerting.

Though he experienced a strange apprehensive feeling, Hugh Trethowen little dreamed of the significance of the communications which, by a strange vagary of Fate, had been placed under his hand.

Chapter Nine
Denizens of Soho

A dirty, frowsy room, with furniture old and rickety, a ceiling blackened, and a faded carpet full of holes.

Its two occupants, dark, sallow-looking foreigners in shabby-genteel attire, sat conversing seriously in French, between frequent whiffs of *caporal* cigarettes of the most rank description.

Bateman's Buildings, Soho—where, on the second floor of one of the houses, this apartment was situated—is a thoroughfare but little known, even to dwellers in the immediate vicinity. The wandering Londoner, whose peregrinations take him into the foreign quarter, might pass a dozen times between Frith and Greek Streets without discovering its existence. Indeed, his search will not be rewarded until he pauses halfway down Bateman Street and turns up a narrow and exceedingly uninviting passage between a marine-store dealer's and the shop of a small vendor of vegetables and coals. He will then find himself at Bateman's Buildings, a short, paved court, lined on each side by grimy, squalid-looking houses, the court itself forming the playground of a hundred or so spirited juveniles of the unwashed class.

It is altogether a very undesirable place of abode. The houses, in comparison with those of some neighbouring thoroughfares, certainly put forward a sorry pretence towards respectability; for a century ago some well-to-do people resided there; and the buildings, even in their present state of dilapidation and decay, have still a solid, substantial air about them. Now, however, they are let out in tenements, and the inhabitants are almost wholly foreigners.

Soho has always been the abode of the French immigrant. But Time, combined with a squabbling County Council, has affected even cosmopolitan London; and Shaftesbury Avenue and Charing Cross Road have now opened up the more inaccessible haunts, rendering them more conventional, if less interesting. Notwithstanding this, it is still the French quarter. French laundresses abound in great variety, with cheap French cafés where one can obtain absinthe, groseille, or grenadine, and where Jacques Bonhomme can dine with *potage* and three *plats* for less than a shilling, while French bakers are a feature at every turn.

Within a small radius of Bateman's Buildings several thousand strangers struggle for the bare necessaries of life—deluded Germans, Belgians, and Frenchmen, who thought the English Metropolis a second El Dorado, and have found it nothing beyond a focus for squalid poverty, hunger, and crime.

The two men who were seated together in this upper room were no exception. Although not immigrants in search of employment, yet they were disappointed that the business which brought them over had not resulted profitably, and, moreover, they were considerably dejected by reason of their funds being almost exhausted.

They sat opposite one another at the table, with an evil-smelling paraffin lamp between them.

The silence was broken by the elder man.

"You must admit, Pierre," he exclaimed in French, contracting his dark bushy eyebrows slightly, "it is no use sitting down and giving vent to empty lamentations. We must act."

Pierre Rouillier, the young man addressed, was tall and lean, with jet black hair, a well-trimmed moustache, and a thin face, the rather melancholy expression of which did not detract from the elements of good looks which his features possessed.

"Why can't we remain here quietly in hiding for a time?" he suggested. "If we wait, something good may turn up."

"Remain and do nothing!" echoed Victor Bérard. "Are you an imbecile? While we rest, the chance may slip from us."

"There's no fear of that," Pierre replied confidently. "My opinion is that we can remain here for a month or two longer with much advantage to ourselves."

"Bah!" ejaculated his companion, a short and rather stout man, about ten years his senior, whose brilliant dark eyes gleamed with anger and disgust.

"Well, speaking candidly," continued Pierre, "do you really think it advisable to do anything just now?"

"I see nothing to prevent it; but, of course, it would be impossible to carry out our primary intention just at present. In fact, until the business is more developed any attempt would be mere folly."

"Exactly. That's just my reason for remaining idle."

"The fact is, you're afraid," exclaimed Bérard, regarding him contemptuously.

"Afraid of what?"

"Of making a false move," he replied; and then he added: "Look here, Pierre, leave everything to me. Hitherto we have transacted our various affairs satisfactorily, and there's no reason why we should not be successful in this. It only requires tact and caution—qualities with which both of us are fortunately well endowed. When it is complete we shall leave this wretched country."

"As for myself, I shouldn't be sorry if we were going to-morrow," remarked the younger man morosely. "I'm sick of the whole business."

"Oh, are you?" exclaimed Bérard fiercely. "What in the name of the devil is the matter with you, you impudent coward? We entered upon this affair together; our course is quite plain, and now, just when we are within an ace of success, you want to back out of it. You're mad!"

"Perhaps I am," replied Pierre warmly. "But you are too enthusiastic, and I have a presentiment that the whole affair will end in disaster."

"Disaster! You talk like a woman," Bérard exclaimed. "How is it that other delicate matters you and I have negotiated have not ended in a *contretemps*, eh?"

"*Nom d'un chien!* And what have we gained by them? Why, simply nothing. You have been clever, it's true; but in this, if we don't wait until a more favourable opportunity occurs, we shall bungle. And if we do, you know the consequences."

"But while we are waiting we must have money from somewhere."

"We must wait," declared Pierre. "We ought to out of this wretched rabbit-warren, and dress a bit more respectably. Do you think we're likely to (unreadable). *Je n'ai pas un rond*," he added in the argot of the criminal circles of Montmartre.

Bérard shrugged his shoulders, and pulled a wry face.

"We can but try," he observed, selecting a fresh cigarette and lighting it.

At that moment the stairs outside creaked, and a light footstep was heard upon them.

"Hark!" exclaimed the younger man. "She has arrived! She promised she would come to-night."

The words were scarcely uttered before the door was flung open unceremoniously, and Valérie Dedieu entered.

Her most intimate friends would scarcely have recognised her had they met her in the street in broad daylight. A common and shabby tweed ulster enveloped her figure, and upon her head was a wide-brimmed, dark-blue hat, battered and faded.

Her disguise was complete.

"Well, you see I'm here as requested," she exclaimed, as she burst into the room, and, taking off her hat, flung it carelessly upon the ragged old leather sofa.

"Ah, *ma petite lapin*, we're glad you've come," Bérard replied, with a smile. "If Mahomet can't go to the mountain because he has no decent clothes, then the mountain must come to Mahomet."

"That's so," she observed, with a light laugh, seating herself on a chair at the table. "I look nice in this get-up, don't I? Pierre, give me a cigarette. You've apparently forgotten your manners towards a lady," she added reproachfully.

The trio laughed. The younger man did as he was commanded, and gallantly struck the match, igniting the cigarette for her.

"Now, how have you been getting on?" she inquired.

"Deuced badly," Bérard replied. "We're hard up and must have money."

"Money! *C'est du réchauffé!* Valérie cried in dismay. *Mon Dieu!* I've none. I'm almost penniless, and must have some from you."

"What?" cried Rouillier. "You can't give us any?"

"No, not a sou," she replied. "An appearance such as I'm bound to keep up requires a small fortune, and I tell you just now my expenses are something enormous."

"Then how do you expect we can live?" asked Bérard, with an injured expression and violent gesticulation.

"I'm sure I cannot tell you, my dear Victor. You know better how to obtain funds than I. Live as you've lived for the past five years. You both have enjoyed luxury during that time, and I suppose you will continue to do so somehow or other."

"This handsome *salon* looks like luxury, doesn't it?" remarked Pierre, smiling contemptuously, as he cast his eyes around.

"Well, certainly there's nothing gorgeous about it," she admitted, laughing, although she shuddered as she realised its discomforts.

Bérard shook his head impatiently. He did not care to be reminded of days of past splendour, and he hardly knew whether to be pleased or not at her visit.

"Look here," he said, gazing up at her suddenly. "It's no use chattering like an insane magpie. What's to be done?"

"I don't know, and I care very little," she replied candidly. "I want money, and if I don't get it the whole affair will collapse."

And she blew a cloud of smoke from between her dainty lips with apparent unconcern.

"But how are we to get it? No one will lend it to us."

"Don't talk absurdly. I have no desire to be acquainted with the means by which you obtain it. I want a thousand pounds. And," she added coolly, "I tell you I *must* have it."

The two men were silent. They knew Valérie of old, and were fully convinced that argument was useless.

Leaning her elbows upon the table, she puffed at her rank cigarette with all the gusto of an inveterate smoker, and watched their puzzled, thoughtful faces.

"Would that sum suffice until—?" Bérard asked mysteriously, giving her a keen glance, and not completing the sentence.

Although her face was naturally pallid, it was easy to discern that the agitation of the last few moments had rendered it even more pale than usual, and her hand was twitching impatiently.

"Yes," she answered abruptly.

"Couldn't you make shift with five hundred?" he suggested hesitatingly.

"No," she said decisively; "it would be absolutely useless. I must have a thousand to settle my present debts; then I can go on for six, perhaps twelve months, longer."

"And after that?" inquired Pierre.

She arched her eyebrows, and, giving her shoulders a tiny shrug, replied—

"Well—I suppose I shall have the misfortune to marry some day or another."

All three smiled grimly.

"How are matters progressing in that direction?" Victor asked, with a curious expression.

"As favourably as can be expected," replied Valérie in an indifferent tone. "If a woman is *chic* and decorous at the same time, and manages to get in with a good set, she need not go far for suitors."

"Have you seen the Sky Pilot?" inquired Victor, with a thoughtful frown.

"Yes, I met Hubert Holt a few days ago at Eastbourne. He asked after you."

"Shall I find him at the usual place?"

"Yes; but it would not be safe to go there."

"Then I'll write. I must see him to-morrow."

"Why?"

"You want *le pognon*?" he asked snappishly.

"I do."

"Then, if we are to get it, he must give us his aid," he said ominously.

"Ah!" she exclaimed, evidently comprehending his meaning. "But you are not very hospitable," she added. "Have you got anything to drink?"

"Not a drop."

"*Malheureux*! you've fallen on evil times, my dears," she said, laughing uneasily.

Taking out her small, silver-mounted purse, she emptied its contents upon the table. This consisted of two sovereigns and some silver. The former she handed to Victor, saying,—

"That's all I can give you just now."

He put them into his pocket without a word of thanks, while she sat back in her chair whistling a few bars of a popular *chansonette eccentrique*.

"Pierre," Bérard said sullenly, at the same time vigorously apostrophising the "*diable*," "we're in a difficulty, and the only way we can obtain the money is by another—er—disappearance."

"What, again?" cried Valérie. "Why, poor Pierre is vanishing fast enough already. He's almost a skeleton now," and she pointed at his lean figure derisively.

"I don't get enough to eat nowadays," declared he, pulling a wry face.

"Do stop your chatter, Valérie," Victor said angrily, "I'm talking business."

"Oh, pardon, m'sieur?" and she pouted like a spoiled child.

"It's generally a safe trick. How much would it bring in?" asked the younger man of his companion.

"Two thousand sterling."

"Just the sum," interrupted mademoiselle, striking the table in her enthusiasm. "We'll divide it. When can I have my half?"

"As soon as possible, but don't be impatient, as hurried action means certain failure."

"All right," she replied boldly, removing the cigarette from her lips, and contemplating it. "You can keep your fatherly advice for somebody else," she added, grinning across the table at Rouillier.

Tossing the cigarette into the grate, she rose.

"What, are you going so soon?" asked the younger *homme de faciende*.

"Yes, it's late; and, besides, I can't go straight home in such a get-up as this."

Cramming on her battered hat, she pulled it over her forehead, and then struck an attitude so comic that neither of the men could refrain from laughing. When they grew serious again, she said—

"Now, one word; shall I have the money? I think we understand one another sufficiently to agree that it is imperative, don't we?"

Victor Bérard nodded an affirmative. He had decided. "You will promise me?"

"Yes, you shall have it, notwithstanding the risks," he replied. "Of course, the latter are very great, but I think if we carry out our plans boldly, it will be all right."

"*Bien*," she said in a satisfied tone. "And now you can both come out with me, and have the pleasure of regaling me with a glass of wine; for," she added, with a little mock curtsey, "I feel faint after all this exertion."

"Very well," said Pierre, as both men rose and put on their hats.

"We'll drink to another successful disappearance," Valérie said, patting him playfully on the cheek. "The dear boy will prove our salvation from misery, provided he doesn't blunder."

"Not much fear of that," answered the young man she caressed. "It isn't the first time, so trust me to bring it off properly. I know my work too well to take an incautious step," he remarked in a low whisper, as the strange trio descended the creaking stairs.

"That's all very well," muttered Bérard, "but we can't afford to act rashly, for it'll be a complicated and extremely ugly bit of business at best."

Chapter Ten
Deadly Pair

A month had elapsed.

In the exquisite little drawing-room of a first-floor flat in Victoria Street, Westminster, where tender lights filtered through the golden shadows of silken hangings, sat Valérie. Her attitude was one of repose—deep, unruffled. From the crown of her handsome head to the tip of her dainty shoe she was perfect. With her eyes fixed seriously upon the ceiling, she sat crouching in her chair with all the abandon of a dozing tigress. The room, a glowing blaze of colour, and carpeted with rich skins, was a fitting jungle. With all a woman's cunning she had chosen a tea-gown of pale heliotrope silk, which, falling in artistic folds, gave sculptural relief to her almost angular outline, and diffused a faint breath of violets about her.

She gave a stifled yawn and drew a heavy breath, as one does when encountering some obstacle that must be overcome.

"I wonder whether he will come?" she exclaimed, aloud.

As she uttered these words the door opened, and Nanette, her discreet French maid, entered.

"M'sieur Trethowen," she announced.

He followed quickly on the girl's heels, with a fond, glad smile.

"I must really apologise, my dear Valérie. Have I kept you waiting?" he cried breathlessly, at the same time bending and kissing her lightly.

She gave her shapely shoulders a slight shrug, but watched him with contemplative eyes as he rushed on.

"I thought I should be unable to take you out to-day, as I was detained in the City upon business. However, I've brought the dog-cart round. The drive will do you good, for the weather is superb."

"Indeed," she said languidly. Putting out a lazy, bejewelled hand, she drew back the curtain that hid the window, and gazed out upon the bright afternoon. "Yes, it is lovely," she assented. "But you must excuse me to-day, Hugh. I am not feeling well."

"Why, what's the matter?" he asked in alarm, noticing for the first time that there was a restless, haggard expression about her eyes.

"Oh, it's nothing," she replied with a smile; "really nothing. A mere headache. I shall be better to-morrow."

"Can I do anything for you?"

"No, thanks," she answered, motioning him to a seat beside her.

"No, no, at your feet; Valérie—always at your feet," the young man replied gayly, throwing himself down before her, and flinging his head back in order to gaze more intently into the dark, brilliant eyes above him.

Keeping time with a heavy finger, he sang, in a not unmusical baritone, two lines of an old French love song:

> "Non, ma jeunesse n'est pas morte,
> Il n'est pas mort ton souvenir."

But his fair companion was almost oblivious to the importance of the burden of his melody. With her little pointed chin against the rose of her palm, she sat lost in a world of reverie.

"Do you ever see Jack Egerton now?" she asked suddenly.

He smiled, accustomed to her wilful wanderings.

"Yes, frequently," he said in turn. "We have known one another so long, that I look upon him as my best friend."

"Your best friend!" she echoed. "Ah! that is to be regretted. Then you could not have known him when he was a student in Paris."

"No; tell me about him," Hugh asked anxiously.

"Although I knew him, I shall say nothing beyond the fact that his was an unenviable reputation."

His lips were parted in surprise as he looked at her.

"My darling," he said, a trifle coldly, "you can't expect me to judge my friend without being aware of his offence."

"His offence?" she exclaimed, with a start. "What—what do you mean? What do you know of his offence?"

He was astonished at her sudden and intense interest.

"Nothing beyond what you have just told me," he replied calmly, although her strange agitation had not escaped him.

It seemed as if she had unintentionally referred to something she wished to hide. Drawing a long breath, she quickly recovered herself.

"Ah, I understand," she said; "I thought you were referring to—other things."

The mention of Paris had brought vividly to his memory the strange letters and the photograph he had discovered among his dead brother's papers. A dozen times he had resolved upon approaching the subject, in an endeavour to find out how they came into his possession, but each time he had refrained from doing so because he feared causing her annoyance.

Piqued by the uncomplimentary terms in which she had spoken of Egerton, he uttered a question which the moment after the words fell from his lips he regretted.

"Valérie," he said, grasping her hand, and gazing earnestly into her eyes, "I have a curious desire to know whether you ever were acquainted with my brother?"

The light died out of her face instantly. She turned pale as death, her delicate nostrils dilated, and her lips quivered strangely.

"What do you mean?" she gasped.

"I simply asked whether you were ever acquainted with my brother Douglas, who was murdered, poor fellow."

"Murdered!" she cried hoarsely. "Was Douglas Trethowen murdered?"

"Yes; I thought you were aware of that painful incident."

"*Dieu!*" she ejaculated, with a shudder. "I knew he was dead, but I was told he died of fever," she said in a harsh, low voice.

"Then you knew him?"

"No—I—we were not acquainted," she replied, endeavouring to remain calm, at the same time passing her slim hand across her blanched face.

Her breast heaved convulsively, and her limbs trembled. But it was only for a moment.

"Strange that you did not know him," Hugh said in a tone of distrust.

"What caused you to think that he and I were friends?" she asked, rather haughtily, bracing herself up with an effort.

He hesitated. He was on the point of telling her of his discovery and demanding an explanation, but he decided that such a course might be indiscreet.

"Well," he replied, "I had reason for believing so."

"What was your reason?" she inquired, breathless with anxiety, as if half fearing his reply.

He had determined not to tell her the truth.

"Oh, a very foolish one," replied he, with a laugh. "It was a mere fancy."

"Only a fancy," she said dreamily. "Are you sure it was nothing more?"

"Why are you so anxious to know?" he demanded, raising her hand to his lips.

"It's feminine curiosity, I suppose," she said, smiling.

"Well, then, I assure you it was only an absurd notion that somehow took possession of me."

"An absurd notion," she echoed absently. "Why, of course it is! How could I have known your brother when I have been so little in England?"

"You might have met him in society."

"No; believe me, to my knowledge I have never seen him. If I had, what difference could it make?"

"If you entertained any affection for him—"

"What nonsense you are talking to-day, Hugh," she interrupted, with a little derisive laugh. "I really believe you are jealous."

"Perhaps I am," he admitted; "but, you see, I love so well that any such shortcoming you really must excuse."

He laughed inwardly at the glibness of his invention.

But her manner had suddenly changed.

"You will love me always, will you not, Hugh?" she whispered earnestly.

"Yes, dearest; of course I shall," he replied tenderly. "I have spoken unkindly—forgive me."

Bravely smothering a storm of rising sobs, she held him with both her small hands until she had sufficiently controlled herself to speak.

"I thought a few moments ago that—that you no longer cared for me," she said, with an effort, watching the effect of her words with wide-open, earnest eyes.

"No, Valérie, you were mistaken," he replied in a low, intense tone. "I love you, and nothing shall ever part us."

They had risen, and were standing together before the fireplace.

For a moment she stared vacantly before her. Then she threw herself into his arms, and, clinging to him convulsively, hid her face upon his shoulder.

"I love you, Hugh; I love you more than I have loved any man," she murmured.

He strained her to his heart—a heart remorseful, even miserable and unhappy. Not even her declaration of love brought him a ray of consolation, for the gnawing consciousness of some deep mystery connected with her past, and the danger of their love for one another, had crushed all happiness from his soul.

And although he was feigning love and endeavouring to console her, yet there was no help for it—they were inseparable, their beings were knit together, their hearts were one.

She possessed the fatal power of fascination. He was under her spell.

With an effort to shake off the gloom that was possessing him, he spoke to her words of comfort.

She tried to reply, but a great sob choked her utterance.

Presently she released herself gently but firmly, saying—

"You must go, Hugh; you have been here too long, and I am not well to-day. I want to be alone."

"Yes, you are right," replied he woefully. "I ought not to have caused you this pain. I am to blame."

Yet something of hope returned to him as he spoke, for she clasped her arms around his neck, and, clinging to him closely, fixed upon him a look of moving appeal.

Slowly she drew down his head towards her face, and then gave him a warm, passionate kiss.

"Good-bye, Hugh," she said in a broken pleading voice. "Remember you have one who loves you more dearly than life."

"I've been a fool. Forgive me for speaking as I did," he entreated.

"Yes," she replied, with a sigh; "if we love one another, why should there be any mistrust between us?"

Why? Had he not cause for apprehension? he asked himself.

But her arms were about his neck, her head pillowed upon his shoulder. The sweet perfume of violets intoxicated him. In a moment he became convinced that she was terribly in earnest, and was confident of her intense affection.

"I have no mistrust whatever, darling," he said reassuringly, stroking her hair with infinite tenderness.

"I—I am satisfied," she murmured. "But tell me, Hugh, once more, that I shall be your wife."

"Yes, indeed you shall, dearest; I care for no one else but you," said he, with a grave look.

Her labouring heart throbbed against his as their lips met in a long last caress. His anguished soul invoked the blessing on her that his quivering lips refused to utter, and he tore himself away.

He took one look back, and saw her totter a few steps after him with arms outstretched, then stop.

Gazing upon her with a loving glance, he waved his hand, and passed out.

When he had gone she stood motionless and silent for a few moments, looking wildly around, but mute under the leaden weight of her thoughts. Then she walked with slow, uneven steps to the ottoman by the fire, and sank upon it.

The fierce strain had been removed from her nerves, and her happiness found vent in hysterical sobs.

"I hate myself. It's horrible, and yet I am powerless," she cried passionately.

Then she lapsed into a silence broken only by long, deep sighs.

Chapter Eleven
The Fourth Passenger

"I think the trick is almost accomplished."

"So do I."

"Is everything ready?"

"Yes; but remember, we must keep very cool. A false step means ruin."

The man addressed laid his finger significantly upon his lips and replied—

"Of course. I quite understand."

This whispered conversation took place in the upper room at Bateman's Buildings, on the same evening that Hugh had visited Valérie, and the two men who stood aside talking in almost inaudible tones were Victor Bérard and the Rev. Hubert Holt. In every particular they were dissimilar. The former was well-dressed and wore several flash-looking rings, while the latter was in clerical attire of the most unassuming and orthodox cut. Both appeared earnest and anxious, glancing uneasily toward Pierre Rouillier and a companion, who were sitting at the table facing each other.

"Come," exclaimed Pierre, addressing the other in French, "fill your glass. Good stuff like this never hurts one."

His compatriot, who was evidently more than half intoxicated, raised his head, and stammered—

"You're—you're right, *mon ami*. Such cognac warms the blood this weather. Let's have another glass before we go."

He, like the others, was dressed in well-cut clothes, but it was curious that when the dim lamplight fell upon his face it disclosed features strangely resembling those of the man with whom he was drinking.

Adolphe Chavoix was about twenty-eight years of age, tall and dark, with closely-cropped jet black hair, and a sallow, rather sullen-looking face. The brandy had given an unnatural fire to his eyes, his cheeks were flushed, and as he grasped his glass his lean bony hand had the appearance of the talons of a bird of prey.

Bérard and his clerical companion continued their conversation in an undertone.

The Rev. Hubert Holt, upon whom the international gang of adventurers had long ago bestowed the sobriquet of "The Sky Pilot," certainly did not, amid such surroundings, present the appearance of a spiritual guide. True, he was the shining light of the church of St. Barnabas, Camberwell, where he held the office of curate, but as a clerical luminary he was by no means of the chalk-and-water type. On the contrary, he could wink wickedly at a pretty girl, drink a glass of "fizz," or handle a billiard cue in a style only acquired by long practice. Nevertheless, he was considered thoroughly devout by his aged and antiquated vicar, and not having joined the ranks of Benedicts, was consequently the principal attraction at mothers' meetings and other similar gatherings of the more enlightened parishioners of the mean and squalid parish of St. Barnabas. They, however, were in blissful ignorance of the character of his associates, otherwise it is more than probable that the pulpit and altar of the transpontine church would have been at once occupied by mother fledgling pastor.

"Suppose the whole business came to light? How should I fare?" asked the sable-coated ecclesiastic thoughtfully, after they had been in conversation some minutes.

"Bah! *Vous-vous moquez des gens*! Besides, you are always safe, surrounded as you are by a cloak of honesty. I tell you, the game can never be detected."

"Don't be too confident; it's a bad habit. Hugh Trethowen may suspect. *Il est dégourdi*, and if he should discover anything, depend upon it we should have the utmost difficulty in clearing ourselves. Somehow, I don't like the fellow; he knows too much."

"What nonsense you talk," replied the Frenchman impatiently. "He can never know the truth. He loves Valérie, and you ought to know her well enough to recognise her consummate tact and ingenuity."

"Exactly. But why are you so positive that strict secrecy will be observed?"

"Because—because the only person who knew the secret has been silenced."

"Who?" demanded Holt in a hoarse whisper.

"Egerton."

The curate thrust his hands into his pockets, and gazed upon the floor a few moments.

"Well, I tell you candidly I don't half like it," he remarked apprehensively.

"Content yourself; neither of us are such imbeciles as to run any risks. Have you not already assisted us and shared our profits?"

Holt bit his lip. It was an allusion to unpleasant reminiscences.

"That is so," he admitted, twirling the small gold cross suspended from his watch-chain. "And what is the extent of my remuneration this time?"

"One hundred pounds."

"The job is worth double."

"You'll not have a sou more, so think yourself lucky to get what I offer."

"If I refuse?"

"You dare not," interrupted Victor in a changed tone. "Think of what your future would be if Valérie uttered one word."

"Yes—yes," Holt replied, with a fierce frown. "I know I've linked myself with you. I'm your cat's-paw, however detestable your shady transactions are."

"You always receive money for your services."

"Yes," he muttered between his teeth. "Gold with a curse upon it."

Bérard shrugged his shoulders unconcernedly and said—

"I suppose we shall each owe an ornamental wax taper to St. Jean le Baptiste for to-night's manoeuvre." Turning away he went to a drawer, from which he took a card-case and some letters, placing them in his pocket.

"Now, Sky Pilot," he continued resolutely, as he walked up to where Holt stood, "are you ready?" The curate held his breath.

"Very well," he replied, after a brief pause, "I suppose I must do the bidding of my masters."

"It would be best—that is, if you respect your position as a holy man," the Frenchman replied, with a mocking laugh.

"Come, gentlemen," he exclaimed aloud, turning to the pair seated at the table. "It's time we started, or we shall not keep our appointment."

"There is no immediate hurry, is there?" asked Chavoix in a husky voice.

"Yes," Bérard replied, "we must be at West Brompton at eight."

"In that case I'm ready," said he, rising, at the same time casting a longing look at the unfinished bottle of cognac before him. With unsteady gait he stumbled across the room, and, with the assistance of Pierre, arrayed himself in his overcoat and hat—not, however, without some difficulty and much good-humoured banter.

The other men sought their outdoor garments, and descended the stairs together, Bérard remaining behind a moment to blow out the lamp and lock the door.

A few minutes later they were strolling across Soho Square, which, at that hour, was dismal and deserted. A four-wheeled cab stood on the opposite side of the square, and they hailed it. When they had entered the conveyance, Holt gave the coachman orders to drive to the underground station at Charing Cross with all possible speed.

While passing along the more unfrequented thoroughfares the interior of the vehicle was dark, and of this Pierre and Victor took advantage. As for Chavoix, he had arrived at the drowsy state of intoxication, and quickly sank into a corner, where the rocking of the rickety old vehicle soon lulled him into a heavy slumber.

Pierre, who was seated at his side, turned and grasped his hand. First satisfying himself of the man's unconsciousness, he slowly, and with deliberate caution, unbuttoned his overcoat. As he accomplished this without rousing him, Bérard withdrew from his pocket a card-case, a folded paper, and several other articles.

Not a word was uttered. With much dexterity Pierre also unbuttoned the black frock-coat Chavoix wore, and, diving his hand into the breast-pocket, abstracted an old morocco letter-case, with some loose cards and about half a dozen letters. Hastily glancing at these, he transferred them to his own pocket, while, at the same time, Bérard bent over and carefully substituted them for those he had just produced.

After feeling in both pockets of the sleeping man's vest, as if to reassure himself that nothing remained, Pierre commenced to rebutton the overcoat. While so engaged Chavoix stirred uneasily and uttered a grunt, but a moment afterwards he subsided again into the dull, heavy slumber of intoxication, thus allowing the expert pickpocket to accomplish his task.

As the cab rumbled down Villiers Street, Bérard grasped him roughly by the shoulder, exclaiming in French—

"Wake up, old fellow. Come; pull yourself together."

Starting, rubbing his eyes, and with a muttered and husky, "Pardon, messieurs," he commenced a profuse apology for sleeping in their company. This, however, was suddenly interrupted by the vehicle coming to a standstill before the station.

The four men alighted, and Holt, after a brief consultation with Bérard, took first-class tickets for West Brompton.

Pierre's arm afforded Chavoix a friendly aid as they descended to the platform; for, although the latter was not sufficiently inebriated to attract attention, yet his equilibrium was slightly disarranged.

When the train drew up they entered an empty first-class compartment, and continued their journey westward, a decidedly jovial quartette.

On leaving the next station, Westminster, Pierre remarked that he had developed a great thirst, and, curiously enough, Holt immediately produced a nickel travelling flask filled with brandy, which he held up triumphantly. Amid the laughter which followed an assertion of Chavoix's, to the effect that priests always appreciated good liquor, Pierre took the flask, and, unscrewing the top, placed the mouth to his lips.

Then he handed it to Adolphe.

"I'm so thirsty that I feel as if I could drink all that's in the flask," remarked the latter.

"You couldn't do it in your present state," argued Bérard incredulously.

"It's very strong," commented Pierre. "I doubt whether you could drain it at one draught. In fact, I'm open to bet you half a sovereign that you won't."

"Bah! it's just as easy as winking," replied the intoxicated man, regarding the flask with a complacent smile. "With m'sieur's permission I'll drink his health."

"By all means," replied Holt, with a laugh. "I'm really afraid, however, that we shall be compelled to see you home afterwards."

"Never fear; I'm safe enough in your hands," he answered, with a grin. "If there's one thing I'm more fond of than another, it's good cognac. See!"

He lifted the flask to his lips, and drained it at one pull.

Scarcely had he done so when he uttered a loud cry of pain, clutching convulsively at his throat.

"*Diable*! it's—it's stronger than I bargained for!" he gasped, with an effort to laugh. "I feel as if everything—why, it's all going round. *Mon dieu*! You have—"

He struggled to his feet, but reeled back upon the cushions, and in a few moments was unconscious.

By this time the train had left St. James's Park, and was travelling at a fair speed midway between that station and Victoria.

When it arrived at the latter place three men only were in the compartment, and they alighted. They did not speak, but hurried along the platform as if unknown to one another. Victor and the curate of St. Barnabas gained the street. The former jumped into a hansom, gave the driver an address, and drove rapidly away, while the latter man walked swiftly across the station yard towards the terminus of the Brighton and South Coast Railway.

Pierre Rouillier, however, acted in a manner that was even more strange. Without emerging into the street, he passed quickly along the subway leading to the Chatham and Dover station. Gaining the platform, he glanced up at the great clock. It was twenty-six minutes past eight. Without hesitation he went to the cloakroom, and, producing a ticket, was handed a large valise, a rug, and a thick long ulster of dark tweed. Divesting himself of the light coat he wore, he donned the garment, then, beckoning a porter to carry his bag, went to the booking-office and purchased a ticket for Brussels.

"Just in time for the Continental train, am I not?" he asked of the man.

"Yes, sir; she leaves at eight-thirty, sharp. This way, please."

They hurried together to where the train stood, and the man, after depositing the valise under the seat of an empty first-class compartment, received his tip and withdrew.

Pierre then entered, but before he had time to arrange his belongings and comfortably ensconce himself the guard slammed the door, and the train glided away on its journey to the sea.

Another had been added to the long list of London mysteries.

Chapter Twelve
"A Crooked Bit of Business"

Mr Bernard Graham was sitting in his gloomy office in Devereux Court one afternoon a few days later.

His elbows rested upon his littered writing-table, his pince-nez poised upon his thin nose, and he was absorbed in the technicalities of a document when his lad entered with a card.

"I'll see him in one moment," he exclaimed, glancing at the card, and the youth withdrew.

Leaning back in his chair his face assumed a heavy, thoughtful expression.

"It's a crooked bit of business at best," he said, aloud to himself, "but the money is bequeathed in legal form, duly signed and witnessed; therefore, as far as I can see, nobody can prove to the contrary. I was rather apprehensive of the results, but, there—I suppose it was merely an absurd fancy."

He touched the gong beside him, and almost immediately Victor Bérard, his face wreathed in smiles and wearing a gardenia in his coat, was ushered in.

"So the preliminaries have been carried out satisfactorily," exclaimed the solicitor, as he motioned his client to a seat opposite him.

"Yes—so far," he answered in excellent English.

"Ah! I read the account in the papers, and saw at once you had had a hand in the matter."

"Your shrewdness scarcely astonishes me, *mon copain*," replied Victor, with a laugh, "especially when you knew that our exchequer was almost at vanishing point, and that we had decided on repeating the little ruse that has proved so remunerative formerly. We have worked *à coup perdu*, and, of course, all in the interest of the grand scheme."

"On this occasion there was no hitch, I suppose?"

"None. There is not even a shadow of suspicion," he replied, dropping into a whisper. "The body, when discovered upon the rails half an hour after we had left the train, was scarcely recognisable. The post-mortem revealed that the dead man had been drinking heavily, and the intelligent jury have this morning returned a verdict of accidental death. Here's the *Globe*—just out. Read for yourself."

He spoke between the whiffs of a cigarette, which he held daintily between his fingers.

"Most satisfactory. His death is believed to have been due to a fall from the carriage. But the identification? You have not told me," asked Graham anxiously.

"He was identified by the papers upon him; therefore now the verdict has been given, you will wait, say, a week, so as not to appear in too great a hurry, then proceed to act as before."

The other nodded, and removed his eyeglasses. His face preserved its keen craftiness.

"Nothing will transpire later? I mean nothing to our detriment."

"Nothing can. It is absolutely impossible for the truth to be known unless you or I divulge it ourselves, and I think that is not probable," he replied, with a mysterious smile.

"Scarcely. It would be an ugly matter for both of us."

The Frenchman affected not to hear the reply. He twirled his carefully-waxed moustaches, and took a long, steady glance at his well-dressed figure in the dingy mirror over the mantelshelf.

"Well, Graham," he said, "you know how to carry the business through. Holt and myself are at your disposal any time you require us, but don't delay a day longer than necessary, for I tell you candidly we must have the money."

"I assure you, my dear Bérard, I shall get the matter completed as soon as possible, for despatch will be the best course for all parties concerned, eh? Besides, as a matter of fact—"

The sentence was interrupted by the entry of the clerk with a second card.

Mr Graham pushed the vestige of grey hair from his forehead. He looked puzzled and perplexed when he read the name of the person who desired an interview; but, quickly regaining his habitual coolness, he intimated to the lad that the request should be granted in a few minutes.

"Have you—er—anything more to say to me?" he asked, turning to Bérard. "I can do nothing in the matter for at least a week," he continued, "but if Mr Holt and yourself will attend here at noon the day after to-morrow we can transact the necessary formalities, and take the first step towards realising."

"That will suit admirably," Bérard replied, with satisfaction. "I will not detain you longer, for I know you are busy;" and, shaking hands with his legal adviser, he made his exit by the door communicating direct with the passage.

"My most fervent hope is that our usual good luck will not desert us," the old solicitor reflected, when the Frenchman had departed.

Having again touched the gong, the door opening into the clerk's office admitted another client—Hugh Trethowen.

"Well, Graham, how are you?" he exclaimed, gayly tossing his hat and stick upon the table, and flinging himself into the chair just vacated by Victor.

"Thanks, I'm very well, Mr Hugh. Full of business, you know—full of business. Now, what is it you wish to consult me upon?"

"A rather delicate matter."

The old man's face grew grave, and much of the hectic flush vanished from his cheek. Readjusting the inevitable pince-nez, he leaned back and looked sharply at his visitor.

"A delicate matter," the solicitor repeated slowly. "Any financial difficulty—eh?"

"No, not at all," he laughed. "It's with regard to a lady."

"Ah," ejaculated the solicitor, heaving an unmistakable sigh of relief.

"What I want to know, Graham, is whether you, as my late brother's adviser, were aware that he was acquainted with a French lady named Dedieu?"

So suddenly was the question put that it caused him to start slightly. Although it was a poser, Bernard Graham was not nonplussed.

"Dedieu?—Dedieu?" he repeated thoughtfully, at the same time nervously twirling a quill between his fingers. "The name is uncommon, and not at all familiar to me. I—I'm sure I don't remember ever hearing it before."

"You don't believe, then, that my brother ever knew such a person?" asked Hugh.

"Well, really, how is it possible that I should know?" asked Graham, with suavity. "It was scarcely likely he would make me acquainted with matters of that description."

Hugh plied him with several well-directed questions, but the old man's memory was peculiarly vacant at that moment. He shook his head, reiterating his statement that his mind was perfectly blank upon the subject, declaring emphatically that he never heard of such a young person as Mademoiselle Valérie, whoever she was.

Such an element of truth did this statement possess, and so blandly was it delivered, that Hugh felt perfectly satisfied. For some time past he had been very much perturbed by the curious discovery of the photograph and letters, but his misgivings were now set at rest by this reassurance.

"Well, if you really don't know her, I need not take up any more of your time," he remarked, rising.

"I assure you, Mr Hugh, as the trusted adviser of your family, it would give me the utmost pleasure to assist you if I could, but her existence is quite unknown to me," protested the old man. "Was she a friend of yours, may I ask?" he added, with a mischievous twinkle in his dim eye.

"Well, yes, Graham. I have the pleasure of the lady's acquaintance."

"Ah, I thought so. Young men are not so eager about a woman's antecedents unless they love her."

"Form your own conclusions, Graham. I've an appointment, so good-day."

Laughing gayly, he departed, the old man bowing him out obsequiously.

After he had gone, the occupant of the dingy chamber stood for a long time before the fire cleaning his pince-nez upon his silk handkerchief, thinking over the errands of his two clients—so strangely dissimilar, yet so closely allied.

Chapter Thirteen
Studio Secrets

"If you please, sir, a lady wants to see you very particularly."

"A lady, Jacob," exclaimed Hugh Trethowen, who was in the lazy enjoyment of a cigar and a novel in his sitting-room, at the close of a dull, wet January day. "Who is she?"

"I don't know, sir. She wouldn't give her card."

"Young?"

"Yes, sir."

"Pretty?"

"Well, I suppose I'm not much of a judge at my time of life, Master Hugh," protested the old servant.

"Get along with you," laughed his master. "You can yet distinguish a pretty girl from a fossilised hag, I'll be bound. Show her in, and let's have a look at her." Rising, he glanced at himself in the mirror, settled his tie, and smoothed his hair; for the appearance of a lady was an unusual phenomenon at his rooms.

When the door opened he walked towards it to welcome his visitor, but halted halfway in amazement.

"Why, Dolly, is it you?" he exclaimed, gripping her gloved hand.

"Yes, Mr Trethowen; I—I don't think I ought to have come here—to your chambers," she replied, glancing round the room rather timidly; "but I wanted to tell you something."

"Surely there's no harm in interviewing the lion in his den, is there?" he asked, laughing. "Come, let me help you off with your cloak."

At first she hesitated, declaring that she could only remain a few minutes, but eventually he persuaded her to allow him to remove the fur-lined garment—an Operation in which he displayed a rather excessive amount of care.

Then he drew up a cosy armchair to the fire, and as she seated herself in it she commenced a desultory conversation, evidently loth to touch upon the matter of importance that had brought her thither.

Men at Hugh Trethowen's age are impressionable. They love, hate, and forget all in one day. For a brief period one fair daughter of Eve is thought enchanting and divine, but in the majority of cases another, fairer still, whose charms are increasingly bewitching, steps in and usurps her place, and she, though tender and fair—she may go anywhere to hide her emotion from an unsympathetic world, and heal her broken heart.

If the truth were told, as she fixed her sweet, affectionate eyes upon him, he was reflecting whether he really loved her in preference to Valérie.

"Why do you desire so particularly to see me?" he asked, blowing a cloud of smoke from his lips, and regarding her with a happy and somewhat amused expression.

Blushing, and dropping her eyes to the floor, she began to pick at her skirt.

"I hope you'll not be angry with me, and also that you'll keep my visit a secret," she said at last, with a little demure droop in the corners of her mouth, and just a suspicion of *diablerie* in her eye. "I want to tell you of some one with whom you are acquainted."

"Who?"

"Mademoiselle Dedieu."

He smiled, contemplating the end of his cigar.

"Ah, I have heard all about your infatuation," she continued seriously; "but, I suppose I must not reproach you, inasmuch as I have no right to do so," and she sighed.

"You have always been one of my dearest friends, Dolly," he remarked warmly; "and I hope you will continue so, even though I have promised to marry Valérie Dedieu."

"You—you have promised to be her husband?" she gasped in dismay.

"Yes. Why, surely you, too, are not going to defame her?" he exclaimed in astonishment. "Come, tell me what you know concerning her."

"Personally, I know nothing," she answered in an earnest tone, "but as your friend—as one who has your interests at heart, I would urge you to heed the warning you have already received. Has not Mr Egerton told you that she is not a fit woman to be your wife?"

"He certainly did say something once, in a vague sort of way."

"Why then do you not take his advice?"

"You do not know us, Dolly," he replied, looking straight into her eyes. "In matters of love we men usually follow our own course, whether it leads us to happiness or to woe."

"That is exactly why I came here to-day," she said anxiously. "I wanted to tell you what Mr Egerton says of her."

"What does he say?"

"Promise not to repeat anything I tell you."

"Upon my honour, I will not," he declared.

"A few days ago we were speaking of her, and he told me of your admiration and love. He said that if you knew the truth you would hate her like poison—that she had brought a curse upon others, and she would bring unhappiness and ruin upon you."

Hugh gazed thoughtfully into the fire.

"And you have come to tell me that, little one?" he remarked reflectively.

"Yes, I want to save you," was the earnest, naïve reply.

"To save me," he echoed, with a smile. "Why, any one would think I was in danger of going by the express route across Styx."

"I mean," she faltered, a trifle embarrassed,—"I mean that Mr Egerton knows more of her past than you. I feel sure he does, for she came to see him the other day, and they talked very excitedly. I was not in the room, of course, but—"

"Valérie at the studio! Why did she go?" he inquired, astonished.

"I don't know, but I heard her say she would pay him another visit to-day and hear his answer, so I presume he has to decide upon some matter upon which she is pressing him."

"To-day! She may be there now!" he cried, jumping to his feet with sudden impulse.

"Yes, most probably. She came the other day about four o'clock."

"Then I will go and demand an explanation," said he briefly, and, opening the door, he shouted to Jacob to call a cab.

Rather unceremoniously he hurried on his fair companion's cloak, and, getting into his own overcoat, they both descended to the street.

In a few minutes they were driving in the direction of Fitzroy Square, leaving old Jacob standing on the kerb in astonishment at his master's sudden flight in company with the strange lady.

The pretty model's words had caused Hugh to become thoughtful and morose. His face wore a dark, resolute expression, and he scarcely uttered a word during the journey.

Dolly Vivian regarded him as her friend. She had accomplished her object and felt satisfied.

In Tottenham Court Road he stopped the cab, and she alighted, so that they should not both arrive at Fitzroy Square together.

A few minutes afterwards he got out and rang the bell.

Walking unceremoniously past Mrs O'Shea, the aged housekeeper, he entered the studio unannounced.

Jack and Valérie were seated upon a low divan before the fire. He was holding her slim hand in his, and was uttering some low, passionate words. As the door opened their *tête-à-tête* was abruptly terminated, for the artist jumped to his feet, while she turned to face the intruder.

"I—I really must apologise for coming in without knocking," Hugh exclaimed roughly. "I didn't know you were engaged, old fellow," he added sarcastically.

"You! Hugh!" she cried, with a blush suffusing her cheeks.

"What, Valérie!" said Trethowen, laughing dryly. "I really didn't recognise you in the shadow. I'm sorry if I interrupted what must have been a pleasant conversation."

"Not at all, old boy," Egerton answered airily. "Mademoiselle Valérie merely called to have a chat."

Hugh's brow darkened.

"I think, as my affianced wife, Valérie owes me a full explanation of this mysterious visit," he said angrily.

"There's little to explain," she replied. "I merely called to consult Mr Egerton, who is an old friend, with regard to a portrait I desire painted."

He endeavoured to preserve a calm disinterested demeanour, but the attempt was a sorry one. Prompted by feelings of jealousy, he gave vent to his wrath.

"Your position when I entered was peculiarly affectionate," he said hotly.

He glanced at her, and caught the agitated expression of her face as she stood erect before him. Her eyes had a perplexed look, with just a suspicion of tears in their brown depths.

"No affection exists between us, I assure you," she declared boldly. "If you doubt me, ask Mr Egerton. He and I are merely friends."

Turning to the artist, Hugh asked—

"What have you to say, Jack?"

"I decline to be cross-examined," was the abrupt reply.

"Speak, and satisfy him!" urged Valérie imploringly. "Tell him if there is any love between us." She frowned, and, unseen by Trethowen, darted a sharp, imperative glance at him.

He fully comprehended her meaning. Raising his head, he confronted his friend, saying—

"You need have no fear. Valérie and I have known one another for years, but only as acquaintances."

He uttered the words mechanically, in strained, harsh tones.

"I don't believe it," cried the other, his face crimson with anger. "You are both playing me false, and I have detected you."

"You are mistaken," Valérie said defiantly.

"No; I assert it as the truth. The whole affair is so unsatisfactory that I will not believe it. Friends do not meet clandestinely in this manner. You are lovers!"

"It's a lie," cried Valérie emphatically.

"I repeat what I've said."

"Then, if you accuse me of duplicity, Mr Trethowen, I will bid you adieu," she exclaimed severely, at the same time offering her hand.

He took it, and was mollified instantly.

Bending over it, he murmured—

"Farewell, mademoiselle, until—until you can prove that I was mistaken. We shall not meet till then." For a moment she gazed steadily at the artist, but he did not stir. He stood with his arms folded, his face impassive.

Slowly she turned, and with a stiff bow swept haughtily out of the studio.

"Now," commenced Hugh, when the door had closed, "what explanation have you to give of this strange conduct, pray?"

"None."

"That does not satisfy me."

"My dear old fellow," exclaimed Jack, stretching out his hand, "you— you understand; I cannot—I'm unable to give any."

"Why?"

"Because it is impossible."

"Do you love her?" asked Hugh fiercely.

"Love her!" the other echoed, with a short laugh. "I swear to you, upon my oath, I hate her! Have I not already long ago expressed my opinion?"

"Is that still unchanged?"

"Quite—intensified rather than moderated."

"Well, perhaps I have been a trifle too hasty, Jack. It seems that you know much of her past. Tell me, what was the object of your interview?"

He was silent. Presently he said—

"Hugh, you are an old friend, and I wish I were at liberty to tell you, but I regret I am not. Request no explanation, and rest assured that Valérie and myself are not lovers, and, further, that we never were."

"Are you aware that Valérie and my late brother were acquainted?" Trethowen asked suddenly.

"How did you discover that?" exclaimed the artist in astonishment.

"Then you appear to know that she was a friend of his," remarked Hugh dryly.

"No; I—it's the first I've heard of it. Who told you?"

"I want to know whether it's a fact or not," persisted his friend.

"I don't know," he replied sullenly.

"You mean, you positively refuse to tell me?"

"No; it is inability."

The two men continued their conversation for a short time longer, then Hugh left and returned to his chambers, not, however, before the warm friendship which had previously existed between them had been resumed.

That evening Jacob handed his master a telegram from Valérie. She had evidently made a sudden resolve, and had lost no time in carrying it into effect, for the message read—

"As you appear to doubt my explanation I have decided to leave England for the present. If you desire to write, a letter to 46, Avenue de la Toison d'Or, Brussels, will always find me."

With a prolonged whistle he sank into his chair, staring aimlessly at the indistinct words on the pink paper which he held between his fingers.

He was half inclined to believe he had misjudged her.

Chapter Fourteen
On Cornish Cliffs

"Let us return now, Mr Trethowen. The night is chilly, and, besides, if we are too long, Jack—I mean Mr Egerton—will suspect us of whispering sweet nothings."

"And if he does, surely there's no harm, Dolly? He's not jealous of you, he—I mean, it isn't as if you were engaged to him."

"No, that is so," she replied; "he is such a prosaic old bachelor. Why, I assure you that ever since I have known him he's never hinted at love. I am his model, his friend—that is all."

"Do you know," Trethowen said, after a few moments' reflection, "I've often wondered, Dolly, how it is you have not married him."

"Why should he marry me?" she asked in surprise. "I'm only an artist's model, a woman who is looked down upon by fastidious prudes as immodest—yet the same women admire the pictures when in the galleries, and—"

"But supposing he loved you?"

She shook her head.

"He does not," she answered. "We are both Bohemians, and have many tastes in common. We found our ideas were similar years ago, when he was struggling for an existence in an attic and I was almost starving. Since that time to the present we have, in a pecuniary sense, shared one another's lot. If I became his wife it is possible neither of us would be so happy as we are."

But he only laughed, and said—

"He'll ask you one day, and then perhaps you won't refuse."

"Don't be absurd," she protested, with a smile. "I am quite content as I am."

Nevertheless, she heaved a slight sigh, and it was evident it was scarcely the truth she spoke.

Dolly Vivian had walked with him from the Hall to the outskirts of Bude, and they were now resting beside an old railing which protected the footpath along the edge of the high cliff.

The night was perfect. The light of the April moon flooded the valleys, illuminated the hilltops, and trailed along the plains of Cornish grass land in uninterrupted streams. The pale grey sea and pale grey sky were tinged with a faint blue; a few stars shone dimly here and there; the whole horizon was wrapped in mist, which took a tint of saffron-pink under the moon's rim, and was slightly darkened where sea and sky converged. There was utter silence, a stillness that was complete and absolute, as if every one in the world had died, and even the waves lapping the beach below scarcely whispered.

They stood together, their faces turned towards the scattered glimmering lights of Bude.

A fortnight ago, Hugh, holding out prospects of good sketching, had prevailed upon Jack to visit him, and at the same time had invited Dolly. They had spent a pleasant couple of weeks together, and this was their last evening; for Egerton had an appointment with a lady, who had commissioned him to paint her portrait, and it was imperative that he should leave for London on the morrow. He had pleaded that his correspondence demanded attention, and thus it was that Dolly and Hugh had gone for a short ramble after dinner, leaving the artist writing in the library.

The pair had been silent for several minutes, entranced by the charm of the moonlit scene. Hugh had grown grave and thoughtful, for his companion's emphatic protest puzzled him.

"Ah, well," he exclaimed, at length, "I suppose sooner or later all of us will be married and settled, as the old ladies say."

"You are speaking of yourself," she remarked mischievously.

"No—I spoke collectively. Marriage or burial will be the lot of all of us—some sooner, some later."

"Ah," she exclaimed, as if suddenly recollecting, "you have not spoken of Mademoiselle Valérie. How is she? Do you often hear from her?"

"I had a letter a month ago. She was still in Brussels, and apparently in good health."

"She has been absent some time now. When do you intend seeing her?"

"Soon—in a few days perhaps."

"A few days," she repeated thoughtfully. "Is she returning to London?"

"No; I have decided to travel back with you to-morrow, and then go on to Belgium."

"You haven't forgotten her, then?" she said in a strained, reproachful tone.

"Forgotten her!" he exclaimed. "Why should I?"

"It would be best," was the brief reply.

The thought occurred to him that she loved him, and that jealousy had prompted her to utter that remark.

"Why?" he inquired, rather sharply.

"Mr Trethowen—Hugh, hear me," she said imploringly, laying her hand upon his arm. "My friendship is as sincere towards you as towards Mr Egerton, but I cannot help telling you frankly what I think."

"Well, and what are those fearful apprehensions of yours, Dolly?" he asked, regarding her with an amused expression.

"Forgive me for speaking so plainly, but I somehow feel confident that this foreign woman will bring you only sorrow and misery."

"That's cheering," he remarked in his usual light and airy manner.

"Think seriously, and you will find I have some cause for apprehension," she continued in earnest tones. "Remember Jack, your friend, has warned you. He has told you that she is not a fitting wife for you. Besides, are you not convinced that there is some strange secret tie between them?"

"You are right, Dolly. It is an enigma I cannot solve. Sometimes I have even thought that he is afraid of her," Hugh said gravely.

"I feel sure he is. When she visited him on the first occasion they had high words, and though I could not understand, because they spoke in French, yet I'm absolutely certain she was threatening him."

"It's very curious," he remarked, after a pause.

He was a trifle annoyed that she should have approached such a delicate matter so bluntly, although he was convinced more than ever that the woman who was speaking thus loved him.

"Why go to her? Why not remain here amid these lovely surroundings and try to forget her?" the girl suggested.

"Impossible! I love her, and will not hear her disparaged," he replied, with more impatience than politeness, as he took a cigarette from his case and lit it. "Don't speak again upon the subject, please; we shall never agree. Come, let's turn back."

Murmuring an apology, she drew herself up from her leaning position upon the low rail, and together they pursued their way in silence along the lonely path. As they walked, a cheerful freshness was in the air. The wind was hardly perceptible, because it blew off the shore and was lost in passing through the wood whose solemn shadows crowned the cliffside.

But while this exchange of confidence was in progress, Jack Egerton's actions, viewed by even a casual observer, would have appeared strange.

As soon as Dolly and his host had departed, he rose from the writing-table, and, flinging himself into a chair before the fire, abandoned himself to reflections that appeared particularly gloomy. He sat almost motionless for fully half an hour, when Jacob entered with a letter.

"Whom is it for?" asked the artist.

"For the master, sir," replied the old man, placing it upon the table, and retiring.

From where he sat, Egerton noticed a foreign stamp upon the envelope. He rose, and took it in his hand. A glance sufficed to tell it was from Valérie.

He turned it over and over, reading and re-reading the superscription.

"I wonder," he said aloud, "whether it contains anything of interest?"

Then he turned towards the fire. There was a small copper kettle upon it, which had been ordered by Hugh to be brought up so that they might brew warm whisky. From the spout steam was issuing.

"Am I such a low, mean spy that I should contemplate opening my friend's letters?" he asked himself at last. "Yet—yet it is not for my own benefit. Would Hugh ever forgive me if he knew all? If he knew my secret—ah! by heaven! it's too horrible, the very thought of the crime, of its punishment, unnerves me. Coward—yes, coward at heart; afraid of justice, and under the thrall of a daring unscrupulous gang. What can I do, how can I act? Surely there can be no great harm in opening this."

He stood several moments in silence.

"Yes!" he exclaimed suddenly, "I'll do it!"

Then he held the envelope in the stream of steam. In a few moments the gum had become loosened, and he was reading the missive.

When he had finished it his face grew hard and stern. Slowly he replaced the letter in its envelope and re-gummed the flap in its original position. Standing before the fire, his arms folded, his head bent deep in thought, he muttered to himself:

"So that is your plan, Valérie! As a masterpiece of ingenuity and chicanery, it does you great credit, and fully sustains your reputation. But the bird is scarcely in the net yet. You have me under your merciless hand, it is true, and you know well that I dare not expose you, for you could send me to a convict's cell, or worse. No, I am not such a fool as to run the risk. I know you and your brutal myrmidons too well for that. I cannot show you in your true colours, except vaguely, and therefore ineffectually; still we may be quits yet."

Taking the lamp from the table, he placed it upon the old bureau wherein Hugh had found the strange letters and photograph.

"You gave me this to use in your interests," he continued, taking a small key from his pocket. "I've searched for the missing letters. I've been a thief, because I'm compelled, like the cringing slave that I am. But how little you dream of what still remains! The most cleverly-arranged schemes are apt to fail sometimes."

Inserting the key, he unhesitatingly opened the bureau. On pressing one of the dark panels of the side it fell forward, revealing a secret cavity, the existence of which Hugh had never discovered. All it contained was a slip of paper, together with an old copy of the *Gaulois* newspaper.

"Yes," he said, aloud, "these will prove useful, perhaps, some day. They will be safer in my possession than here."

Replacing the panel, he closed and locked the bureau, and, turning to the table, first read the words upon the piece of paper, then spread out the newspaper, and became absorbed in a long report which had been marked round with coloured crayon.

"And after all," he reflected, when he had placed the papers in his pocket, "I may be only forging fetters for my own wear. Who knows?"

Then he sank back into his armchair, and, lighting his meerschaum, calmly smoked until the return of the pair who had been gossiping by the sea.

Chapter Fifteen
Queen of the Silent Kingdom

One of the most pleasant thoroughfares in Brussels is perhaps that broad boulevard, lying on the La Cambre side, between the Fontaine Debroeckère and the Porte de Hal. The Boulevard de Waterloo is scarcely as fashionable as the Bontanique or the Regent, but it certainly possesses another and greater charm, inasmuch as the trees are more abundant, and, being older than those in the other boulevards, their branches meet overhead, forming long avenues of dark foliage which in summer constitute a cool and pleasant promenade.

Hugh Trethowen, dressed with evident care, had strolled from his hotel in the Place Royale one afternoon, three days later, and, walking up the Rue de Namur, had turned into this leafy resort of idlers.

Under a clear blue sky the sun shone upon the fresh green of the spring foliage, lighting up the usually sombre pathways with a shimmering golden light, and presenting the boulevard at its best, with its crowds of *flaneurs* strolling under the old elms, or seated enjoying the exhilarating air.

But by Hugh the picturesqueness of the scene was unappreciated. He was too deeply absorbed in his own thoughts to notice the beauty or charms of his surroundings; he was only bent on finding the house Valérie had given as her address. Crossing the boulevard without scarcely giving it a glance, he found himself before a long row of tall houses which line the left side, and constitute the Avenue de la Toison d'Or. Their dead white fronts were the reverse of artistic, although their general character spoke of stability and wealth, for the majority were of almost stereotyped exactness, each with its wide *porte cochère*, its enormous door, its three tall drawing-room windows with white jalousies thrown back, and its four storeys above.

With little difficulty Hugh discovered that the house he was in search of was situated at the corner of the Place Louise, and that its façade was more imposing than that of its neighbours.

Meanwhile, seated on a low gypsy chair, in a small but elegant room, Valérie was deciphering a long letter which had been just handed to her by the man who sat near, Victor Bérard.

"Well, what do you think of it?" asked the latter, twirling the needle-like points of his moustache, as she folded the paper slowly and replaced it in the envelope.

"It only shows how very near he was to bungling—the idiot! If he had, well—the results would have been too dreadful to think of."

"Matters are progressing as well as can be wished, and the disappearance has been accomplished excellently, with the exception of that one hitch—"

"Which might have sent us both to a very unfashionable lodging," she interrupted.

Nodding acquiescence, he replied—

"*Sapristi!* that's all very well. But you have the money; you can't grumble. Again, why need we fear the failure? You have beauty—indeed, you're the best-looking woman in Brussels. As long as you retain that charm, we need not be apprehensive."

"You pay me a pretty compliment, Victor," she laughed. "Nevertheless, I must admit my face has always been my fortune."

"And other people's misfortune, eh?" observed her companion, smiling grimly.

"Well, that's certainly one way of putting it, but you—"

"M'sieur Trethowen desires to see mademoiselle," Nanette said, for she had opened the door unobserved.

"Trethowen!" gasped Victor, twisting his moustache nervously. "He must not find us together."

"No," exclaimed Valérie. "Go quickly through the garden, and out by the side door."

He had already put on his hat, and without further hesitation he waved his hand, and vanished through a door communicating with the conservatory.

"*Au revoir,*" he said. "You will know how to manage him, and I will return at six to take you to the Molière."

She went to a long mirror and hurriedly arranged her hair; then, turning to the maid, ordered her visitor to be shown in.

"I wonder what his object is in coming here," she muttered to herself, as she sank into her wicker chair, and commenced twisting her rings round her shapely fingers perplexedly. "Surely he cannot suspect! Yet the threats of that fool Egerton still ring in my ears," and she frowned thoughtfully.

When her visitor entered she rose, calm and pale, to meet him.

"So you have returned to me at last, Hugh," she said in a faltering voice, almost overcome with emotion.

"Yes, dearest," he replied, placing his arm around her waist, and drawing her closely to him. "I have come to beg forgiveness for being so rash."

"My forgiveness!" she exclaimed in a tone of surprise, looking up into his face. "Why, I have nothing really to forgive."

"I judged you too hastily, Valérie, and, now I have learned the error of my ways, I have come over here to receive your pardon."

"And I grant that freely," she said, with a happy smile, for she was unfeignedly delighted that he had returned.

"Do you know," he said, as he slowly released her, and sank into a chair beside her, "I've been unspeakably dull and miserable. By Jove! life hasn't been worth living lately."

"Why?" asked she naïvely.

"Because you have been absent."

"I should scarcely have thought it," observed mademoiselle mischievously. "You had Jack Egerton's model. Surely she did not object to a mild flirtation?"

"Dolly Vivian! I flirt with her!" he echoed in surprise. "No, indeed, I've never done so. She is my friend, it is true; but nothing more."

"Ah, don't tell me that, Hugh. You men are all alike. A pretty woman's face, a smile, a pair of merry eyes, and you are captivated."

"But I have not been, except by yourself," he declared, grasping her hand, and raising it reverently to his lips. "You do not know how blank and colourless my life has been without you—what an utterly miserable existence mine is when we are apart."

He spoke low and earnestly, for all the fervour of the old love had returned, and, heedless of the warnings of his friends, he was repeating assurances of affection to the woman who held him in her toils for life or death. She did not reply, but, gazing trustingly into his eyes, her breast heaved convulsively.

"Tell me, shall we be the same to one another as before? Forgive me, and we shall live as if nothing had happened to mar our happiness," he urged.

"Then, you really love me still, Hugh?" she asked, in a low, tremulous voice.

"Still love you? Yes; my heart and soul are yours. I care for no other woman save yourself."

"Was it to be near me that you came here? Are you certain it was for no other reason?"

"No," he replied, puzzled at her question. "Why do you ask?"

"Out of curiosity," she stammered evasively. "I—I thought other business might, perhaps, have brought you here."

Glancing round the apartment, and recognising the elegance with which it was furnished, he complimented her upon her taste.

"Yes," she answered languidly. "This place suits me admirably. It is my home, and although I'm of a wandering disposition, and travel a good deal, I return here now and then to enjoy rest and obtain those comforts that are appreciable after hotel life. I am, perhaps, too cosmopolitan. Well, it is my failing. Since I was a girl, I have been accustomed to travel for pleasure, and I do so now in order to get life and variety, without which I don't really believe I could exist."

"Not if you were married?"

"Ah! possibly that would be different," she said, with a rippling laugh. "I could then take some pleasure in my home, and my husband would be my companion, whereas at present I have only Nanette, my maid. You have little idea, Hugh, of the wearying monotony of the life of women who are alone in the world. We are utterly defenceless, and must either be prudes, and lead the existence of nuns, of, if we dare go about and enjoy ourselves, we are stigmatised as fast, and looked upon as undesirable and contaminating companions. I am unconventional; I care not a jot for the opinion of the world, good or bad; and, as a natural sequence, women— many of them notorious, though married—revile me unjustly."

She uttered the words in all seriousness, and he felt compassion for her, as he knew well what she said was the truth.

"I can quite understand that your position is somewhat unenviable, Valérie; nevertheless, I have come here to-day to repeat the promise I made some time ago."

"Your promise! Why—"

"I love you dearly and will marry you, providing you will consent," he added, interrupting her.

Her head sank upon his shoulder, and she burst into tears of joy, while he kissed her fair face, and smoothed her hair tenderly.

"I promise you," he murmured, "if you become my wife you shall never regret. It is true, some say harsh things of you. I have heard gossip, but I've shut my ears to the lies of those who envy your good looks. In future, however, those who defame you shall answer to me."

She lifted her face, wet with tears, to his, and their lips met in an ardent caress.

"Yes, I love you dearly, Hugh," she declared, trying to subdue her emotion. "This day is one of the happiest of my life. If we are married, I swear I will be a true wife to you, notwithstanding the calumnies you have heard."

Thus, after months of estrangement, Hugh Trethowen again fell an easy prey to her fatal power of fascination; and he, blind and headstrong, saw her only as a beautiful woman, who was unhappy, and who loved him. Yet it has been the same through ages. Men, under the spell of a daughter of Eve, a temptress who is more than passing fair, become weak and impressionable as children, and are ruled absolutely by the woman they worship, be she good or evil.

Until the sunset streamed into the pretty room, and the silver bells of the dainty ormolu clock chimed six, they sat together undisturbed. Many were the pledges of undying affection they exchanged; then he left, promising to call next day.

When he had gone, Valérie reseated herself, and gave herself up to one of those debauches of melancholy in which she sometimes indulged; for, after all, she was not entirely devoid of sentiment.

Could Hugh have overheard the conversation between Victor and the woman who was his affianced wife an hour later, he would, however, scarcely have congratulated himself upon the result of the interview.

Victor Bérard and Valérie were together in a hired brougham on their way to the Theatre Molière, where they had previously secured a box.

"So you are friends again, eh?" Victor was saying, laughing. "Well, I must congratulate you upon your wonderful tact and diplomacy. The manner in which you have acted in leaving him to follow you here has allayed suspicion, and as long as you can exercise your power over him, we have nothing to fear as to the ultimate success of our plan."

"It was as good as a comedy," declared she, laughing heartily. "I told him how lonely I was, and did the emotional dodge—squeezed a tear or two, just to add to the realism—and it brought him to the point at once. You should have been there; you would have been highly amused, for he's such a believing idiot, that I can do just as I like with him."

"You're a clever girl, Valérie. With all your airs and graces, I believe you'd deceive the Evil One himself, if it was to your own interest to do so."

"I don't know whether to regard that as a compliment or not," she remarked merrily, as she drew her opera cloak more closely around her shoulders, and leaned back in the carriage listlessly. "I suppose, however, from our point of view, the amount of deceit and craftiness I display in dealing with him will secure the more or less successful issue of our scheme."

"If he knew everything, our position would not be a very enviable one, would it?"

"Scarcely. But, you see, my dear Victor, he doesn't know all, and will not, unless Egerton peaches, which he dare not do on account of his own neck. Therefore, we are quite safe, and can negotiate the little affair without interruption."

"I believe that you really care for the fellow a little—just a little," her companion said, with a sarcastic laugh.

"And supposing that I did? I am my own mistress and can act as I please," returned she, a trifle annoyed.

"*Bien!* you know best how to manage him, for you've had experience. I only urge you to be careful, and avoid any sentimental humbug."

"Bah! I want none of your advice," was all she replied, and a long silence ensued, which was not broken until the carriage drew up at the door of the theatre.

Chapter Sixteen
Dolly's Indiscretion

In London, evening was gradually creeping on. The mellow light that had penetrated into the studio in Fitzroy Square was fast fading, still Jack Egerton worked on in silence, glancing constantly across at the woman who sat motionless before him, straining her eyes over a novel she held in her hand.

Frequently he paused, and, stepping back a few paces, examined the effect of his work with a critical eye, comparing it with the original. Then he returned and retouched the picture again and again, until at last, after much perseverance, he apparently obtained the exact effect he desired. The picture was certainly attractive, and, although incomplete, yet fully sustained the artist's reputation for faithful delineation of the female form. It was a representation of Dolly Vivian reclining on a silken divan, attired in the flimsy gauzes, with rows of sequins across her forehead, heavy bangles upon her wrists and ankles, and her light brown hair, unbound, falling negligently about her shoulders. One tiny crimson slipper had fallen off, revealing a well-shaped naked foot, the other being bent under her as she lay with one bare arm flung over her head.

Her attitude of languor and repose among her cushions added to the Oriental character of the picture, and the richness of the silk with which the couch was covered, enhanced her beauty.

He had christened the picture, "The Sultan's Favourite."

While he worked she always preserved perfect silence. It was their rule. For hours she would sit scarcely moving a muscle, her attention engaged by a newspaper, a novel, or some fancy needlework, unless, perhaps, he addressed her, asking an opinion or advice. Then she would usually reply briefly and to the point, and resume her reading without disturbing her pose in the smallest degree.

Beside her, on a little inlaid pearl table, stood the cup of tea Mrs O'Shea had brought her an hour before, but which had been left almost untasted, so absorbed was she in her book. She did not notice that the artist had laid aside his palette, and was cleaning his brushes, until he exclaimed, —

"That will do for to-day, Dolly. You must be awfully tired and cramped, for we've had an unusually long spell."

His voice recalled her to consciousness. Stretching both arms above her head, she gave a stifled yawn, and slowly rose from her couch with a languid grace. Slipping her foot into the shoe, she stepped down to where he was standing.

"Why, what's the time?" she asked, noticing it was growing dusk.

"Half-past six," he replied. "I've an engagement to dine at the Vagabond Club at the Holborn at seven, therefore I haven't much time to lose. By Jove!" he added admiringly, "you look absolutely bewitching, my little *houri*. If Hugh could only see you now, 'pon my honour he'd go down on his knees and propose straight away."

"You think so, do you?" she asked artlessly, laughing and glancing down at her gauzy dress, a fair, bright-eyed odalisque. Then she grew serious, and examined the picture. "You've certainly made very good progress this afternoon with everything except the hand. The high light is scarcely perfect," she added, fixing her gaze upon the canvas, and moving across the studio to study the effect from the opposite direction.

"I must finish that to-morrow," the artist said, as he carefully wiped a small brush, and placed it aside. "The light has not been good for the last hour or more."

"The fingers, too, want retouching. They look just a trifle too stiff," she continued, with the air of a critic.

"Yes, I have noticed that. But I must now go and make myself presentable, for I haven't a moment to lose. Run and dress yourself, there's a good girl."

Already she was plaiting her hair, and coiling it deftly upon her head.

"Very well," she said, and tripped lightly away; but, losing a slipper in her walk, she was compelled to stop and recover it.

Then she disappeared into the small room adjacent, sacred to her use for purposes of dressing, and sometimes of resting after the fatigue of posing for prolonged periods.

Egerton, who laughed over the refractory slipper, and chaffed her good-humouredly, declaring that she let it slip off in order to attract his attention to the smallness of her foot, cleaned his palette, knocked the ashes from his pipe, and also left the studio.

When alone in her room, Dolly drew from her pocket a letter in a firm, masculine hand, which she had received at her home before leaving that morning.

"An evening at the Empire will perhaps brighten me up. At all events, it will be a change," she thought, after she had glanced over the note. "Besides, what harm is there? I don't care two pins for the fellow, but—nobody cares for me," she added, with a little disconsolate sigh.

Replacing the note in its envelope, she quickly divested herself of her transparent garments, and assumed a more unromantic and conventional attire. Having finished, she went to Mrs O'Shea's room to have her usual chat before returning home.

To-night, however, she did not remain long, for almost as soon as Jack Egerton had left the house she also followed.

The clocks were striking half-past seven as she entered Victoria Station, and was joined by a tall, dark man in evening dress, who raised his hat, smiled, and grasped her hand warmly. She had met him for the first time a fortnight before. While travelling in a train between Clapham and Waterloo he had spoken to her, and she being nothing loth to a mild flirtation, an acquaintance soon sprang up between them. Already they had spent several evenings together, and she had found him a very pleasant companion. Dolly Vivian was essentially a *fin de siècle* girl. Although admitting in her own mind that to dine and visit music halls with a man about whom she knew almost nothing was scarcely proper, yet the cause of her sudden longing for pleasure was not far to seek.

Since Hugh's departure for Brussels she had been gloomy and despondent, for it had been proved to her beyond doubt that he cared nothing for her, but was madly in love with the voluble foreign woman, who seemed to exercise a power over him that was incomprehensible. She had bidden farewell to the man she loved with every fibre of her being, and was now growing world-weary and careless. Her sister had died a year before, and she now found life in a mean, gloomy lodging, with her aged mother, very lonely and dull. In this spirit she met Henry Mansell, her new acquaintance, and discovered that the pleasures of variety entertainments drove away her sad thoughts. Her Bohemian nature longed to penetrate into phases of society hitherto forbidden to her, and she looked upon this as an opportunity for gratifying it. Egerton, who admired both her beauty and her many sterling qualities, frequently took her to concerts and theatres, but as their friendship was purely platonic, and, as during the years of their acquaintance he had never hinted at affection, his companionship at places of entertainment had become monotonous. Mansell, who flattered her, indulged her whims, and paid her those delicate attentions that women love, was more to her taste in her present state of mind. He spent his money freely upon her, and appeared infatuated with her beauty, while she, neither inexperienced nor *gauche*, was content that he should entertain her. Briefly, she was but a London girl of to-day, a single example of thousands of others who have a *penchant* for fast life, and who gratify it without overstepping the bounds—who rub shoulders with the *demi-monde*, but who are not of it. True they copy the "creature" in her clothes, her appearance, and even her manners, but the imitation is due to the fact that to be considered a trifle "fast" is alas! nowadays considered good form.

Dolly's movements that evening were scarcely those of the modest retiring girl she really was, and would have caused the artist much surprise had he been watching her.

From Victoria they drove to a café in Regent Street, where they dined together, walking thence along Coventry Street to the Empire Theatre. After half an hour in the stalls they went upstairs to the circle promenade, that recognised resort of the *jeunesse dorée*, and strolled up and down among the gay crowd. The brilliant light, the dreamy music of the ballet, and the ever-shifting figures around, combined, perhaps, with the wine she had taken, exhilarated her.

Among the crowd of men who passed up and down, there was one who watched them closely, but unobserved. A dozen times he sauntered past, cigar in mouth and hands in pocket, as if merely killing time like the others. Yet, had Dolly glanced up at the opportune moment, she would have seen meaning glances exchanged between her companion and the man who was keeping observation upon them so mysteriously.

But the pretty model was unsuspecting, and the man, after shadowing them for nearly an hour, went to the bar, and stood drinking, but in a position whereby he could observe their movements through the glass partition.

Presently Dolly and her companion returned to their seats, and sat for some time watching the performance.

"I must really be going now," Dolly said to her companion, as, an hour afterwards, they sat opposite each other in a private room at a neighbouring restaurant finishing their meal. "I've enjoyed myself very much indeed; I'm sure it's awfully kind of you to be so good to me."

"Not at all. I'm pleased you haven't been bored," he replied gallantly. "And I hope you'll honour me with your company on another occasion. Shall we arrange for one night early next week?"

"As you like," she answered, smiling.

"Very well; I'll write making an appointment, and we'll spend an hour or two at some other hall—the Alhambra, or the Palace."

"I left my cape outside in the passage. I'll fetch it, and commence to get ready," she said, and rising suddenly, left the room in search of her outdoor attire.

The moment he was alone her admirer reached over the table quickly, and took up her emptied wineglass. From his vest pocket he produced a tiny phial, the contents of which he poured into the glass, then, taking up the champagne, filled both his own glass and hers, replacing the latter in the position where it had originally been. It was accomplished in a few seconds, for scarcely had he put down the bottle before she reappeared.

When she had assumed her cape, and tied her veil by the aid of the dingy mirror over the mantelshelf, she noticed her glass had been refilled.

"I really don't think I ought to drink any more," she exclaimed. "I'm not used to so much, and it might affect me."

"Oh, I assure you it won't," declared Mansell, laughing. "It's a good brand, and I can recommend it. Besides the night is chilly."

He was watching her face narrowly, but he assumed a well-feigned air of unconcern. His argument, however, convinced her that another glass would do her no harm, thereupon she raised it to her lips and drank it. Being in a hurry to return home, she noticed no peculiar taste about it, and the man smiled faintly with self-satisfaction.

"I have to go to King's Cross, so I'll drive you home if you'll allow me," he suggested, as they descended to the street, and to this proposal she gladly acquiesced.

Outside they entered a brougham that was apparently awaiting them—and which Mansell incidentally remarked was his own—and were quickly driven along Shaftesbury Avenue, on their way to King's Cross.

Scarcely had they been in the carriage five minutes when she was seized with a sudden giddiness and faintness. At first she struggled against it, trying to rouse herself, for she attributed it to the wine she had consumed, combined with the heated atmosphere. Recognising the disgrace which would fall upon her should she return to her mother intoxicated, she determined that her companion should notice no difference in her manner. In the shifting lights that flashed into the carriage she felt confident that he would be unable to detect any change in her. It was by her voice alone that he could discover her intoxication, and, therefore, she continued the conversation in what she believed was the same tone as before.

Yet, as they drove along, the strange, sickening sensation increased, her eyes burned, and an acute pain on the top of her head caused a feeling as if her brain were a leaden weight. With alarm she became aware that it was gradually taking possession of her senses, and that to bear up against it was unavailing. Confused noises sounded in her ears, her breath became short, and she fancied she was falling from a great height. Then all the objects and lights in the street seemed to dance about her, and, with a suppressed groan, she sank back into the corner of the carriage inert and insensible.

The man by her side watched her gradually lapsing into unconsciousness with evident satisfaction, and, having taken both her arms and worked them up and down violently to assure himself of her total insensibility, he shouted to the coachman that he would go to another address—one which necessitated the brougham being driven back towards the place whence they had started.

Two hours afterwards a strange scene was presented in a house that stood by itself in the centre of a market garden, in a lonely position surrounded by fields midway between Twickenham and Isleworth.

In a small, bare attic, carpetless and almost devoid of furniture, the inanimate form of Dolly Vivian lay crouched in a rickety armchair. The feeble light of a guttering candle revealed the closed eyes and deathlike pallor of the features, while her breathing was almost imperceptible, so completely had the drug accomplished its work.

Near her stood Mansell and the man who had dogged their movements during the evening.

The wind had risen and was moaning mournfully around the house, causing the windows to rattle, and creating weird noises in the stillness of the night.

Suddenly a door creaked below. Both men started, and looked at one another.

"Listen! What's that?" asked Mansell in an awed voice.

"Nothing; merely the wind," the other replied sharply.

Mansell tried to smile, and said—

"I suppose you're right, but I feel as nervous as a cat."

His companion, who had driven the carriage, and who had taken Dolly's purse, handkerchief, and a letter from her pocket, and was scrutinising them carefully, uttered an exclamation of disgust and annoyance. The house being empty and untenanted, the wind, which had now increased to almost a hurricane, howled and sighed dismally.

"If anyone should find the brougham outside it would strike them as strange, wouldn't it?" suggested Mansell.

"Never fear; we're perfectly safe. It's a by-road, and not a soul comes this way. Besides, whom do you expect would walk about this lonely part at such an hour?"

Mansell crossed to where the girl lay, and, taking up the candle, gazed into her face.

"It's a pity to sacrifice her life," he remarked sympathetically. "She has done us no harm."

"Fool!" replied the other, with an impatient gesture, looking at him with threatening eyes. "Can't you see that if she lives she can frustrate all our plans? Even now I believe she knows our secret."

"She does?" gasped the other breathlessly.

"Yes."

"But are there no other means of silencing her?"

"No. She must die!"

The man, whose sinister face wore a heavy, determined expression, had drawn a long-bladed knife from its sheath, and it flashed in the light as he held it in his hand. Mansell noticed it, and shuddered.

"I cannot stay and see her murdered," he cried in horror.

"Very well; if you're so chicken-hearted, wait outside," the other replied roughly.

He saw it was useless to intercede for the life of the girl whose beauty he had admired, so obeyed the injunction. Pale and agitated, he waited upon the landing in the darkness.

The seconds seemed hours, but presently his companion emerged from the room carrying the candle, which, however had been blown out. As he struck a match, Mansell saw blood upon his hand.

Neither spoke, but both quietly descended the stairs. Then they again blew out the candle and left the house, locking the door after them.

A short distance away the brougham was standing without any one to look after it, the horse grazing quietly at the roadside.

Mansell entered, while his companion mounted the box, driving along the private road, and turning into the highway towards Twickenham.

Chapter Seventeen
Laroche

Upon a veranda overlooking the clear, rippling Ourthe, and protected from the hot sun by a striped awning, Valérie and Pierre were laughing and sipping kümmel. Lounging lazily in a loose-fitting cotton dress she looked cool and piquante, while he, attired in a suit of light tweed, with a soft felt hat set jauntily on his head, sat on the edge of the table, smoking a cigarette with an air of insouciance.

In the whole of rural Belgium it would probably be difficult to find scenery more picturesque than that surrounding the small town of Laroche. Ten miles distant from the Liège-Marloye Railway, it lies in the very heart of the Ardennes, nestling beside the gurgling Ourthe at the junction of five beautiful valleys. Above, rise bold, bare crags and high hills covered with sombre pines, while from a dark, rugged height frown the ivy-clad ruins of an ancient château.

The little place is charming, although to the gregarious, who find pleasure amid the summer turmoil of the Rhine, with its crowd of cheap-trippers and overflowing hotels, it presents the aspect of a veritable village of the dead. Its inhabitants have not yet become demoralised by the advance of progress; for, although a few rusticating Belgians from Brussels and Liège and one or two English families visit it during the summer, still its beauties are comparatively unknown. The streets are crooked and narrow, the houses quaint and old-fashioned, and pervading the whole town is an old-world air that is distinct and delightful. Kindly, genial, and honest, the people are an average specimen of the simple, rustic dwellers in the Walloon country, who look askance at the increasing number of tourists who intrude upon their solitude and alight at their unpretentious hotels. Modern improvement is almost unknown in this Arcadia. True, there is a steam tramway to Malreux, forming the link which connects the Larochois with the outside world, but the place itself is still, quiet, even lethargic; in fact, it is very much the same to-day as it was a century ago. The dusty, lumbering old diligences, with bells upon the horses, rumble through the streets at frequent intervals, always stopping at the Bureau de Poste; and it is so antiquated as to possess a guardian of the town in the person of a *garde du nuit*, who blows every hour upon his tin *trompette* from eleven o'clock at night until five in the morning—truly a relic of an age bygone.

It was a month since Hugh had left London, and the weeks that passed in Brussels after the reunion had been pleasant ones. He saw her daily, and was only content when in her company, driving in the Bois de la Cambre, shopping in the Montagne de la Cour, or taking her to the theatre. During this time he had been introduced to one of her relatives—the first he had known. When he called upon her as usual one evening, he found a man some ten years her senior seated in the drawing-room. His bearing was that of a gentleman. He was well-dressed, wearing in his coat the crimson button of the French Legion of Honour, and was introduced by Valérie as the Comte Chaulin-Servinière, her cousin.

The men shook hands, and quickly became friends. At first Hugh was inclined to regard him with suspicion and distrust, but on closer acquaintance found him a genial, reckless man of the world, who was possessed of plenty of money, and whose tastes were similar to his own. Being apparently a prominent figure in Brussels society, he introduced Hugh to various people worth knowing, and soon became his constant companion.

Had he known that the Comte Lucien Chaulin-Servinière was the same person as one Victor Bérard whose name was inscribed upon a rather bulky file preserved in the archives of the Préfecture of Police in Paris, it is probable that he would have shunned his companionship, and many evil consequences would thereby have been avoided.

Blissfully ignorant, however, and confident of Valérie's love and devotion, Hugh was perfectly happy as the weeks glided by, until one day she announced that she was compelled to depart at once for Namur to visit an aunt who was ill, and not expected to recover.

It was thereupon arranged that she should travel to Namur by herself, visit her relative, and that the Comte and Hugh should meet her three days later at Laroche. The suggestion was the Comte's, for he declared she was looking worn, and that a sojourn of a week or two in the invigorating and health-promoting Ardennes would do her good.

Valérie left on the following morning, but the dying aunt was a pure invention, and instead of remaining at Namur, she proceeded at once to Malreux, and thence to Laroche, where she arrived after spending the greater part of the day in performing the journey. At the Hôtel Royal she found Pierre Rouillier awaiting her, for the meeting had been prearranged, and it was for a more important and beneficial purpose than exploring the beauties of the neighbourhood that Mademoiselle Dedieu had journeyed so far.

Like everything else in the little town, the arrangements of the hotel were of Walloon simplicity, and scarcely suited to patrician taste, although there was a decided touch of novelty in dining at midday with only the "beer of the country" as beverage, and suppers at seven consisting of fresh eggs, the fare throughout being of a genuinely homely character.

They were sitting on the veranda on the second morning after her arrival. Having finished their liqueurs, Pierre suggested that, as he desired to talk confidentially, they should take a stroll in order to avoid the possibility of eavesdroppers. To this Valérie readily acquiesced, and, having obtained her sunshade, the pair started off up a by-path for a ramble up the steep hillside.

"You know your way about this place very well, I suppose?" she remarked, as they walked together.

"Yes, considering I have buried myself here for several months, and have no other occupation beyond strolling about or killing time in deserted *estaminets*. The winter here was most abominably dull; in fact, were it not for your sake—"

"You mean for the sake of your own neck," interrupted mademoiselle, smiling.

"Well, I admit it is not for your sake alone that I'm in hiding, but personating a dead man has its drawbacks. Within twenty-four hours of leaving London I arrived at this sleepy hole, and my name has since been Adolphe Chavoix, gentleman, living on his means. From the time I first set foot in the place I've never been five miles from it, and I expect I shall be compelled to remain here for months, perhaps for a year longer," he said dismally.

"Is it a safe retreat?"

"Safe! I should think it is! Why, I'm as well-known as the *doyen* himself. The rustics fancy I'm a decent sort of fellow, and I'm on visiting terms with almost everybody, from the imbecile old Burgomaster downwards. Why, the police commissary of the district is one of my closest friends. Bless you, I'm as safe here as if I lay in my coffin. But, tell me, what progress are you making?"

"As much as can be expected," she replied, taking his arm and leaning upon him in the stiff ascent. "I explained to you yesterday the plan we propose; but, of course, it is highly dangerous."

"For boldness and impudence I've never heard its equal," declared Pierre candidly.

"*Bien*, then you recognise how imperative it is that our arrangements should be elaborated before the *coup* is made. There were many obstacles in our path, but one by one these are being removed. When the course is quite open we shall act."

"He still loves you?"

"Yes," she replied with a grim smile.

"It will prove an expensive pastime for him," exclaimed her companion, laughing.

"But profitable to us. Think what it will mean if we succeed."

"We must succeed, sooner or later."

"Never draw hasty conclusions," remarked mademoiselle. "One awkward incident and the whole scheme might collapse. Even now I'm almost at a standstill for want of funds."

"Have you spent all the last?"

"Yes; and moreover, the man who furnished my place in Brussels two years ago threatens to take possession because I can't pay him, while I have heaps of other unpaid bills."

"Can't you sell your jewels?" suggested Pierre.

"They went long ago. All that I have now are only paste," she replied disconsolately.

"Wouldn't Trethowen lend you some if you told him some pitiful tale?"

"How could I ask him? You forget that he believes me to be rich, with the fabulously wealthy Comte Chaulin-Servinière as my cousin."

"Rather a new character for Victor," laughed the smart young man at her side.

"Oh, but he has assumed the part well, I assure you," she declared. "He looks after my welfare to just the right extent in the circumstances, and his bearing and appearance give him the stamp of the aristocrat, which is, of course, only due in some degree to the new suit he had for the occasion."

Pierre laughed heartily. He had never seen Hugh Trethowen, yet with the instinct of the adventurer who wages war against those possessed of money, it was a source of satisfaction to him to know that the victim was falling an easy prey.

By this time they had ascended the Chemin des Morts, and were pausing at the summit gazing upon the charming landscape outspread like a panorama at their feet. The spot itself was interesting, inasmuch as a quaint legend is connected with it. As they rested there he related it to her. It is alleged that once on a time a Seigneur of Harzé, who had died leaving behind him an unenviable reputation, was being carried to his last resting-place in the parish churchyard, when one of the bearers slipped, and the body fell over the cliff, and then from rock to rock, till it reached the river. The affrighted mourners saw in this terrible accident an unmistakable judgment of heaven, and did not dare to interfere.

When he had narrated the circumstance they continued their walk, passing through a small fir plantation until they came to a time-worn rustic cross. Near it, and overshadowed by some large bushes, was an old seat, upon which they sat continuing the discussion of Bérard's merits.

The shade was welcome after toiling up the hill, and Valérie, taking off her hat, allowed the soft breeze to fan her temples, while he lit a cigarette, handing her one also.

"I'm puzzled to know how we are to bring matters to a crisis without more money than we have at present," she said reflectively, after they had been talking some time.

"That's really a difficult problem," her companion replied quickly. "Don't you know anybody who would advance you a little?"

"No. Besides, it would be unsafe. We must now be exceedingly careful how to act."

"There is only one thing that I can suggest," said Pierre thoughtfully watching the smoke curling upward.

"How?" she inquired expectantly.

"Rook him at cards."

"*Ma foi!* An excellent suggestion!" she ejaculated enthusiastically.

"You could work it easily enough. Victor and he will be here to-morrow, therefore I should suggest that I start to-night for Spa. You three can follow after a day or two. There you can meet me, introduce me as a friend, and then I can proceed to pluck him of a few hundreds. I'm quicker with the paste-boards than Victor."

"He's a good player, I believe."

"That doesn't matter. If you can persuade him to play, I'll soon have some money."

"My dear Pierre," Valérie said, laughing, "he will do anything for me. I'm sure he would lose ten thousand francs without a murmur, if he thought he was pleasing me by tempting fortune. He does think such a lot of me that—that I sometimes feel inclined to love him genuinely. I'm almost sick of the base part I am playing."

Her face assumed a serious look, and she sighed. Pierre regarded her in astonishment.

"What? Giving way to sentiment, now we have gone so far!" he exclaimed. "It's all nonsense. To think of throwing up the game now would be sheer folly. Such a chance as the present does not always fall to our lot; therefore, it is only right, in our own interests, that we should take advantage of it. If you really love him—well, it will, perhaps, add to the realism of the incident, and won't do much harm to either of you. But then, you've loved others before—in fact, you loved me once—yet now I'm nothing in your eyes beyond a willing assistant in your various little affairs. No," he continued bitterly, "you have no real affection for any one. I am able to speak from personal experience. Yet you would bar our way and wreck our chance of making our fortunes, because you fancy you've fallen in love with this ass of an Englishman? You must be mad to think of such a thing."

"You misunderstand me," she said, her beauty heightened by the flush of anger that suffused her face. "Although I have neither intention nor desire to depart from the plan already laid down, I regret that it will be necessary to resort to the extreme measure in order to accomplish our purpose. That is all. As for your suggestion, it shall be carried out. You will go to Spa to-night, if you think there is no danger in the visit."

"Don't trouble yourself. I shall run no risk. You get him to play, then leave the rest to me. Within a week the money shall be yours. What do you think of the suggestion of making him defray the cost of his own misfortune, eh?" he asked, laughing.

"Decidedly ingenious, but it won't work!" shouted a voice in English, causing them to start.

There was a rustling among the thick bushes behind them, and next second Jack Egerton emerged into the path.

"Why are you here, spying upon us?" demanded Pierre, springing to his feet, and assuming a threatening attitude.

"Merely for my own information," replied the artist, with perfect *sang-froid*.

"Then, I hope you have obtained the knowledge you desire," Valérie said, her eyes flashing angrily.

"I have ascertained the depth of your vile scheme, if that is what you mean," he cried. "You little thought I should keep observation upon your movements. For a fortnight I've been watching you in Brussels as closely as a cat watches a mouse. The ingenious tricks I learned under your tuition stood me in good stead, and I have now seen your duplicity, and discovered the extent of your infamy. You are playing the old game, the—"

"My affairs do not concern you!" she cried, stamping her foot angrily.

"My friend's interests are my own."

"Your friend—bah!"

"Yes; I repeat it. I have overheard more than one of your interesting conversations, and am quite aware of your nefarious intention. You are using your beauty to lure him to his ruin."

"Quite heroic!" sneered Pierre. "This is indeed interesting."

"Before I have finished you'll probably find it more interesting, and to your cost," he replied fiercely. Then, turning to mademoiselle, he said: "You think I fear you, but you make a huge mistake. When we last met you threatened me with exposure if I dare tell him what I knew of your past."

"I did, and I mean it!" she screamed, with an imprecation in French. "Thwart me, and I'll show you no mercy."

"Then you will have an opportunity of exhibiting your vindictiveness," he observed calmly.

"What do you mean? If self-conceit did not furnish its own buoyancy, some men would never be able to carry their load."

"I mean that before to-morrow Hugh Trethowen will be upon his guard; he will understand the deep and complicated game you and your jail-birds of Montmartre are playing."

"You—you dare not breathe a word to him."

She spoke defiantly, her lips compressed, and her hands tightly clenched.

"Spare yourself," he replied, waving his hand deprecatingly. "Threats are utterly useless. I am determined to acquaint him with your cunning plot."

"The consequences will be upon your own head," said she, with affected indifference.

"I'm perfectly willing that they should," he answered, with a coolness that astounded her.

"When you stand in a criminal court you'll alter your tone," she declared, although unnerved at his willingness to face her vengeance.

"Possibly, when you accompany me there, you will do the same."

"Oh! How's that, pray?"

"Death is the penalty for murder," the artist exclaimed meaningly.

"Murder?" gasped Valérie wildly. "What—what do you mean? What do you infer?"

"Nothing, beyond the fact that if you give me up to the police, you yourself will also be deprived of liberty."

"Of what do you accuse me, pray?" she demanded haughtily.

"It is the business of the police to investigate crime, not mine."

In a moment Valérie vaguely conceived that the power she had exercised over him no longer existed. It was possible that he was in possession of some information which removed all fear he had of her. Apprehensive lest he should have learned her secret, she continued to question him, in order, if possible, to ascertain how much he knew.

But he was as wary as herself, replying to her sarcasm with pointed retorts that puzzled her.

Pierre in the meantime stood silent and thoughtful. He, too, saw plainly that their scheme might be checkmated, and that they were on the horns of a serious dilemma. If Egerton imparted the secret to Hugh, the whole of their plans would be frustrated, besides placing them in a very undesirable position. Moreover, the artist had desired to know the reason he had assumed the name of Chavoix instead of his own, and inquiries upon that point, if pressed, might result in extremely awkward revelations. He was therefore trying to devise some feasible means by which to avert a catastrophe that seemed imminent.

"Then, you really mean to carry your threat into execution?" asked mademoiselle, after they had exchanged several sharp passages of words.

Jack Egerton declared that he did.

The colour vanished from her face, and she clenched her fists in anger.

"Dare to do so, and you will rue the consequences till your dying day. You little think how completely you are in my power, or the character of the evidence I hold against you—evidence which is beyond dispute, since you yourself admit your guilt. Remember that at once I could, if I chose, demand your arrest. If you provoke me, I shall adopt that course—"

"And expose your own villainy," he remarked superciliously.

"I should adopt it as a measure of self-protection," she replied, with calmness. "I assure you, however, I have no desire to resort to such a measure, and I have, therefore, a proposal to make," she added.

"I have no desire to hear it."

"Listen, and I'll tell you," she continued determinedly. "You know that I have certain evidence in my possession, which it is most desirable that you should destroy—you know to what I refer. Were it ever placed in the hands of the police, you would spend the remainder of your days in a convict's cell. Well, my proposal is that it shall be placed in your hands on the day I marry Hugh Trethowen."

"You—marry him! You intend doing so?" he asked in abject astonishment, for he had not believed her desirous of an honourable union.

"Of course I do. And I repeat that, in consideration of your preserving silence regarding my past I am ready to do what I have told you. If not, there is but one alternative, as I have already explained—imprisonment and ruin. It is for you to decide."

This suggestion, the desperate device of a crafty woman, presented matters in a different light. It appeared to him that, after all, if she married Hugh she might reform and become an honest woman, while he himself would, by accepting her terms, render his own position secure. The proposal, he reflected, was one that required careful consideration, for he could not dispute the fact that he really feared her. He knew she could wreck his life.

"What is your answer?" she asked, watching his thoughtful face narrowly, and noticing with satisfaction his perplexity.

"I cannot give one now. I must think," he replied.

"Very well. Think well over the matter and its consequences before acting rashly. I fancy you will come to the same conclusion as myself—that a policy of silence is wisest." Turning to the young man beside her, she said, "Come, Pierre, we will return and leave him to his solitary reflection."

Rouillier laughed at the other's discomfiture, and turned upon his heel.

"*Bon jour, monsieur*," she said, addressing the artist, making a stiff curtsey, which he acknowledged with an impatient gesture.

Then she joined her companion, and they retraced their steps through the fir plantation towards the drowsy little town.

"Your nerve and ingenuity are really marvellous, Valérie," exclaimed Pierre enthusiastically, when they were out of hearing. "I should never have thought of such a scheme. We have got out of an ugly situation very neatly indeed."

"Yes," replied she confidently. "*Qu'il fasse ce qu'il lui plaira.* He's afraid to utter a word to Hugh."

And they both laughed gaily.

Chapter Eighteen
Lips Forsworn

The great ballroom of the Casino at Spa was filled with a cosmopolitan well-dressed crowd, who glided over its polished floor to the strain of a seductive waltz. The huge salon, with its white and gold decorations, its glittering chandeliers, its carved pilasters, and its enormous mirrors, was brightly lit, and presented a gay, dazzling appearance, the showy dresses of the women lending additional colour and animation to the scene of gay revelry.

Amid the ever-shifting crowd Valérie and Hugh, both excellent dancers, whirled lightly around, the smiling faces of both denoting perfect happiness.

Her evening gown, of pale pink filmy gauze, that bore the unmistakable stamp of the Rue de la Paix, suited her admirably, trimmed as it was in daring contrast, that upon a less handsome woman would have been voted hideous. Her diamond necklet sparkled and flashed under the glare of electricity, and this—although really only paste—was regarded with envious eyes by more than one woman in the room. As she leaned lightly upon the arm of the wealthy young Englishman, he thought he had never seen her beauty shown to greater advantage, and could not refrain from expressing his admiration in terms of flattery.

Although one of the most engaging little corners of Europe is assuredly the well-wooded, umbrageous dell in which nestles pleasantly the antique and old-fashioned watering-place, yet it cannot be denied that Spa itself has lost much of the gaiety and flaring splendour which characterised it in the wild gaming days of the past. In the Salle Levoz, where the gilding is faded and the hangings ragged, lords, dukes, and seigneurs of Louis XIV's time, junketed, gave their fêtes, and danced minuets; while in the disused Vauxhall the older glories of balls, ridottos, and gambling went on night after night during the last century. But nowadays Monte Carlo attracts the knight of industry and the systematic gambler. Nevertheless, Spa remains pleasant and pastoral, notwithstanding the existence of survivals that speak mutely of its departed grandeur.

It is essentially picturesque, with its miniature Place, its imposing Pouhon, or "pump room," its gay Casino, its luxurious *Etablissement*, its glaring Hôtel de Flandre, its "Orange," and other pleasant houses of entertainment. Close by are the charming promenades under thickly planted rows of trees, quaintly termed the "Seven-o'clock" and "Four-o'clock" walks. Here crowds of visitors languidly wander, sit under the trees, or halt in groups listening to the music from the bands in the kiosks.

Spa is still popular with all classes of visitors, from the English nobility to the shopkeeping element of Louvain, Brussels, and other contiguous towns; and the administration of the Casino appear untiring in their efforts to provide them with amusement in the form of fêtes, dramatic performances, concerts, balls, and other means of enjoyment and dissipation.

It was at one of the latter entertainments that Valérie and Hugh were amusing themselves, she having introduced him to Adolphe Chavoix.

When the dance concluded they strolled together through the wide corridor hung with pictures, crossed the reading-room, and walked out upon the balcony overlooking the Place Pierre-le-Grand, where they found the pseudo-Comte Chaulin-Servinière leaning upon the balustrade, smoking.

"Ah!" he exclaimed, as they advanced, "you, too, are tired of that close atmosphere. Faugh! I found it stifling."

"You don't dance, M'sieur le Comte, and therefore can't enjoy it," replied Valérie mischievously.

"Well, well, perhaps that's so," he replied. "But, by the way," he continued, turning to Hugh, "why don't you try your luck at the tables?"

"Oh yes, Hugh," said Valérie, as if suddenly struck by the excellence of the suggestion; "let's have a few games. It would be a pleasant change. Shall we?"

"I've no objection," Trethowen answered.

"I should scarcely think you had, considering how lucky you were when you played with me at the Cercle du Hainaut," remarked Victor, laughing.

"Fortune always favours the novice," Hugh declared.

"Then let's hope it will favour you again to-night. Come along," urged Valérie.

When the trio entered the *salle de jeu* a few minutes later, they found the tables crowded with players indulging in some innocent games of chance. Play is never high at Spa nowadays.

The room was neither large nor luxurious. A few busts stood upon pedestals around the mirrored walls, the card-tables were ranged down the side, and at the further end was a *chemin de fer*, which proved the chief source of attraction to the less venturesome. The incessant tick-tack of the tiny train and the jingling of money, mingled with the hum of voices, peals of exultant laughter, and staccato curses, produced an almost deafening din.

After wandering about the room for a few minutes, and watching the *chemin de fer*, they found a baccarat table in the opposite corner. Hugh seated himself upon the right hand of the banker, while Victor sat upon the left. Valérie "punting" right and left indifferently.

For about half an hour they played, staking small sums, which the bank almost invariably annexed, *tirage à cinq* cropped up, and discussions ensued upon it. This question always divides baccarat players into two camps. There are some who, when holding five as the total of pips on the cards in their hands, will ask for a third card, while others will not. This dispute, which is of constant occurrence, has exercised the mind of almost every one who has tempted fortune on the *tapis vert*. Yet, after all, it is a curious one, for if one considers the matter it will be seen that the chances of improving or reducing one's total by taking a third card are extremely doubtful. Gamblers, however, who believe in their good fortune, usually draw at five because they believe that one of the good chances will come in their way.

This was the course adopted by Hugh in one of the rounds. Up to that time he had been unlucky, and lost about two hundred francs; but, seeing that the count, who was an inveterate gambler, called for a third card, he did the same, with the result that he won back the sum he had lost, together with an additional hundred francs.

In several succeeding hands he adopted the same course, and although he was not successful every time, nevertheless he found he was not losing. As for his fair companion, she was apparently very unfortunate. Once or twice she won, but in the majority of cases she was compelled to pay. Victor played mechanically. He also lost, and the bank frequently raked in increasing piles of gold and limp, crumpled notes.

After they had played for an hour Valérie declared her inability to continue, owing to want of funds. Hugh offered to lend her a few louis, which she firmly declined to accept, and rose. He also got up, and, leaving Victor at the table, they descended to the large hall, where they seated themselves at one of the little tables, and ordered some wine. To Hugh the result of the play had not been unsatisfactory, inasmuch as he found on counting his winnings that they amounted to nearly two hundred francs.

"I'm passionately fond of baccarat," Valérie remarked, as they sat opposite one another, chatting and laughing. "It's so long since I played that I had almost forgotten the game. Had I had any more money in my purse to-night, I should most probably have staked it. Gambling, unfortunately, is one of my weaknesses."

"Why not accept some from me, and return? You might perhaps break the bank," he suggested, smiling.

"Ah no," she replied; "I don't care to play publicly. It is the same here as at Monte Carlo—the tables are patronised by *déclassé* women and half-tipsy men. Women who play in a place like this earn a bad name. I would rather play at the hotel. Adolphe will return presently,—he's an awfully nice fellow, the son of a silk manufacturer in Lyons,—and we could form a nice little quartette among ourselves. What do you say?"

"I'm quite agreeable," he replied. "You know, I alway obey your wishes."

She looked into his eyes affectionately, and uttered a few endearing words in a low tone that could not be overheard.

Presently they got up, went arm-in-arm up the grand staircase, and re-entered the *salle de jeu*. The count was no longer there, but they soon discovered him standing in his former position on the balcony, indulging in a smoke under the stars. He had lost, he said; his luck had forsaken him after Valérie had left the table.

Then they told him of the suggestion to play at the hotel—a proposition to which he immediately acquiesced.

Hugh Trethowen, truth to tell, cared very little about games of chance, but for the amusement of his idol he was prepared to make any sacrifice.

An hour before midnight the four assembled in a private sitting-room at the Hôtel de l'Europe. Pierre Rouillier—or Adolphe Chavoix, as he was now called by his fellow-adventurers—had procured a piece of billiard chalk, and marked the table at which they were to play. The heavy curtains of the windows overlooking the street were drawn, and over the gas lamp was a lace shade which caused a soft, subdued light to fall upon the table, while opposite the windows was a large mirror reaching from the wainscot to the ceiling.

"Who'll be banker?" asked Adolphe, as they seated themselves.

"Why, Hugh, of course," replied the count. "He's had all the luck to-night. Come, m'sieur, sit over there, and start the bank with your winnings," he added, addressing Hugh.

"Ah, my dear Count, I expect my luck will change," laughed Trethowen good-humouredly.

And, placing a chair for Valérie by his side, he took the seat indicated. He was not a practised card-player, neither did any apprehension of dishonest dealing cross his mind.

The game, he thought, was one of mere chance, and his opponents were just as liable to lose as himself. So he commenced by making a bank, and shuffling and dealing the cards.

The first few hands were uninteresting. Adolphe had arrived presumably from Paris only a few days previously, and had been introduced by Valérie as a friend of the family. As he entered heartily into every proposal for enjoyment, Hugh considered him a genial and pleasant companion. Overflowing with mirth and good spirits, he proved a much appreciated addition to the party.

At first the stakes were not high, and the fortune of the players were about equally divided. Hugh's pile of coin increased now and then, only to diminish again, but never falling short of its original size.

After a time the count increased his stake, twenty louis being put upon the game. Neither player, however, could make the fatal *abbattage*, and Hugh continued to hold winning hands, and rake the coins into the bank.

The game was growing interesting, and so intensely were the thoughts of the players riveted upon it that time passed unheeded. Two o'clock had struck, still the dealing and hazarding went on, while Nanette stood by quietly watching, and now and then replenishing the glasses of the men.

At length Hugh's good fortune forsook him, and a long run on the bank was made. For five hands his cards were useless, and each time he was compelled to pay, the result being that not a louis remained out of the pile of half an hour before.

Valérie expressed her regret at her lover's misfortune, and after some discussion it was decided to make a fresh bank, Hugh, as before, to be banker.

In order to obtain the necessary money he left the room, Valérie uttering some words of encouragement as he did so.

A few minutes later he returned with several crisp English notes in his hand. Having converted two of them into louis, play was resumed. Again the fates were against him. He was flushed with excitement, and played carelessly. A number of successive rounds he lost to Adolphe, whose pile of coin as rapidly increased as his diminished, while much good-humoured chaff was levelled at him by his companions.

Then, for the first time, he recognised the amount of his loss, and determined, if possible, to recoup himself.

Flinging his two remaining notes—each of the value of one hundred pounds—upon the table, he remarked rather bitterly—

"It seems I've been overtaken by a run of infernal bad luck. Will any one 'play' me for the bank?" .

"As you please," assented the count.

"*Ma foi*! you've played pluckily, although it's been a losing game."

"It's really too bad," declared Valérie pouting. "But I expect when Hugh has his revenge he will ruin us all."

"Scarcely," replied Trethowen, raising his glass to his lips.

"How much is in the bank?" asked Adolphe unconcernedly, as the cards were being dealt.

"Five thousand francs," replied Hugh, after a moment's calculation.

"Very well, I'll 'play' you," the young man said calmly.

The announcement caused each of the quartette the most intense excitement, for it meant that Pierre had backed that amount against the banker's stake upon the result of his tableau.

Every one was silent. Hugh scarcely breathed. He dealt the cards, and each snatched them up.

It was an exciting moment for all concerned, and there was a dead silence.

The adventuress exchanged glances with the count. Adolphe remained perfectly cool as he turned the faces of the cards upwards, a five and a four of diamonds, making a "natural" against which Hugh's cards were useless.

With a grim smile Hugh pushed the two notes and some gold over to his adversary, and, rising from the table, exclaimed—

"I think, after all, I'd better have remained a punter than aspired to be a banker."

"Never mind," said Valérie encouragingly, as she gathered up her winnings, "your good luck will return to-morrow."

"I shall ruin myself if I go on long at this rate," he replied. "I shall have to send to London to-morrow for a fresh supply, otherwise I shall be hard up."

"Not much fear of that," she said chaffingly. "But it's four o'clock, so we had better retire."

He took her hand and wished her *bon soir*, she afterwards leaving with Nanette, while the men also sought their respective rooms.

It was already daylight, and Hugh did not attempt to sleep, but, flinging himself upon a couch, indulged in calm reflections. His loss did not trouble him, for he could afford it, but the subject of his contemplation was a conversation he intended having on the morrow with the woman who had fascinated him.

Had he witnessed the scene at that moment in Valérie's sitting-room, the scales would have fallen from his eyes. *On n'est jamais si heureux, ni si malheureux qu'on se l'imagine.*

When the two men left him, they went straight to her.

"Well, how did I manage it?" asked Pierre, with a crafty twinkle in his eye, when the door had closed.

"Capitally!" she cried, with almost childish glee. "He doesn't suspect in the least."

Both men disgorged their winnings, and placed the money upon the table in the centre of the room.

It amounted to nearly eight thousand francs.

Selecting two four-hundred franc notes, she gave one to each of them as their share of the spoil, and, sweeping the remainder into a bag, locked it up.

"Pierre's idea was excellent," remarked Victor. "We wanted the money badly, and although the sum isn't very large, the manoeuvre is one that might be worth repeating, eh?"

"That's just it. The thing is so simple. I kept the winning hand concealed until the stake was large enough, then I played it."

"You're even smarter with the cards than I anticipated. Père Amiot didn't teach you to manipulate for nothing; you've been our salvation," observed Valérie.

"For your sake, mademoiselle, no task is too difficult," he said, with mock gallantry, bowing.

"A little of that sort of talk is quite sufficient," she answered, with a laugh.

The subject dropped, and for a few minutes they held a serious consultation, after which the two men wished her good-night, and departed stealthily along the corridor.

Nanette entered, and her mistress sank into a chair, reflecting silently, while she deftly arranged her hair for the night.

Chapter Nineteen
A Strange Compact

The morning was oppressive and sultry. Valérie, coming from her room, thrust open the window of the sitting-room, with an impatient exclamation, and sat with her elbows upon the window ledge inhaling what little air there was to be had. She lolled there, looking down upon the quaint street in an abstracted mood, for the men had gone for their matutinal walk after the glass or two of water at the Pouhon.

She was glad to be alone. To herself sometimes she appeared extraordinary and of an exceptional disposition, of the temperament of animals that are rendered faithful by brutal treatment. There were days on which she no longer knew herself, and on which she asked herself whether she were really the same woman. In reviewing all the baseness to which she had been bent, she could not believe that it was she who had undergone it all. She strove to imagine a degree of degradation to which her nature would refuse to descend.

As she sat, silent and thoughtful, the door opened softly, and a tall, dark, well-dressed man entered noiselessly. He was good-looking, with a carriage that was unmistakably military, and a carefully trained moustache. Glancing quickly round with eyes that had a rather fierce look in them, he walked over to where mademoiselle sat, and halted behind her chair.

"So I've found you at last, madame," he exclaimed harshly in English, placing a heavy hand upon her shoulder.

The unexpected voice startled her.

"*You!*" she gasped, jumping to her feet and turning pale.

"Yes," he replied, leaning against the edge of the table and thrusting his hands into his pockets with an easy, nonchalant air. "You scarcely expected this meeting,—did you, eh? Well, although it is a long time ago since you took it into your head to leave me, you see I haven't quite lost sight of you. And, after all, it is but natural that I should be solicitous of your welfare since you are my wife," he added grimly.

"Wretch! Why have you come here?" she asked in ill-concealed alarm.

"To see you, pretty one," he answered. "Three years is rather a long period to be absent from one's wife, you'll admit."

"Wife!" she cried in a tone of disgust. "Why not call me by my proper name? I was your slave, Captain Willoughby. You used me to decoy young men to your house so that you might fleece them at cards, and when I refused any longer to participate in your schemes you used brute force towards me. See!" she continued, unbuttoning the sleeve of her bodice, and exposing her bare arm—"see, I still bear a mark of your ill-treatment."

He smiled at her indignation.

"It's very pleasant to talk in this strain, no doubt," he observed, "but you have apparently overlooked one rather disagreeable fact—that when leaving Cannes, you took twenty thousand francs belonging to me."

"And what if I did, pray? I left you because of your cruelty, and I've not since applied to you for maintenance, nor even sought a divorce."

"That's true. But now you've had your fling, perhaps you won't object to return to your lawful husband."

"You must be an imbecile to think that I would."

"What! You will not?" he cried angrily.

"No, never. I hate and loathe you."

"That makes but little difference," said he coolly. "Nevertheless, as a wife would be of assistance to me just now, I mean that you shall return to me."

"But I tell you I will never do so," she declared emphatically.

"Then I shall simply compel you, that's all."

"You! *Sapristi!* Surely I'm my own mistress; therefore, do you think it probable that I should ever return to be the tool of a miserable cardsharper? No; I left you in the hope that I should never look upon your hateful face again, and if you think it possible that we could ever bury the past and become reconciled, I can at once disabuse your mind. If I were a sentimental schoolgirl it might be different, but I think you'll find me too clever for you this time," she said indignantly.

"Don't anticipate that I desire a reconciliation," he remarked in an indifferent tone. "Valérie Duvauchel—or whatever you now call yourself— is too well-known to be a desirable companion for long—"

"You need say no more," she cried in anger. "I understand. You want me again to entice men to their ruin. It is true that I am your wife. I curse the day when I took the idiotic step of marrying you, but I tell you once and for all that I'll never return to you."

"You shall," he cried, grasping her roughly by the wrist. "You shall—I'll compel you By heaven! I will!"

There was a look in his eyes that she did not like. She was cowed for a few moments, but her timidity was not of long duration.

"I defy you!" she screamed. "Do your worst. I'm perfectly able to defend myself."

"Then perhaps you'll defend yourself when you are arrested for the little affair at Carqueiranne. There's a warrant still out, and a reward offered for your apprehension—remember that."

In a moment she became confused, and her physiognomy, usually so lively, lost all its lightning glances. Her whole person seemed influenced by this unexpected and embarrassing announcement.

"Ah, I see!" she said in a husky voice. "Those are your tactics, are they? You would give me up to the police? Nevertheless, if you have no love for me, as you assert, why should you desire me to return to you?"

"I know my own business best," was the abrupt reply.

"That I don't doubt; yet you admit that it is best for us to be apart, although you are inclined to resort to the extremity of which you speak."

"Who are the men staying here?" he asked sharply. "Friends."

"Not very desirable ones, eh? I fancy I've met Victor Bérard somewhere before. If my memory doesn't fail me it was in Paris only shortly before the affair of the Boulevard—"

"Enough," she said hoarsely, for she understood that he knew of her alliance with the pair. "What does it matter to you who my associates are? We both have to seek our fortunes."

"True, but I like to look after my wife's welfare," declared he, with a sarcastic smile.

Captain Percy Willoughby was a jovial ne'er-do-weel who smiled at his lot, and gave himself up to it heedlessly. Weariness, anxiety, neediness took no hold upon him, and when a gloomy thought came to him, he would turn away his head, snap his fingers, and, raising his right arm towards heaven in caricature of a Spanish dancer, send his melancholy over his shoulder.

"I can do without your attentions, although I'm prepared to negotiate with you upon fair terms," she exclaimed, for she saw that it was only by skilful diplomacy that she could extricate herself from the ugly situation.

"What do you mean?" asked he in surprise.

"Business purely," she replied calmly. "It was unfortunate that I married you, still there is no reason why the world should know it; and, moreover, as there is no affection between us, I am willing to pay you to release me from my bond."

Willoughby knit his brows thoughtfully. He was not prepared for such a bold proposal.

"You have some scheme of your own in hand, I suppose?"

"That's my business."

"Well, how much are you willing to pay?" he asked, smiling at her suggestion.

"Twenty-five thousand francs—not a centime more. For that sum I require a written undertaking that you'll commence a suit for divorce against me forthwith. You understand?"

She recognised that if she failed to conciliate her husband's demands all her schemes would be irretrievably ruined, but her tact at such moments never deserted her, and she was determined that he should not levy blackmail upon her without strengthening her position thereby.

"You hesitate," she continued. "Why, the whole thing is simple enough. I will supply you with evidence and witnesses, and upon the day the decree is pronounced the money shall be yours."

"You must have some good fortune. Where will you get the money from?" asked he incredulously.

"What does that matter, as long as you have it? We shall then both be free."

"What guarantee shall I have that you will pay me after I have obtained the divorce?"

"I will give you a written one if you desire it, so that if I depart from my word you will still possess power over me," she explained, beating an impatient tattoo upon the carpet with her tiny slipper.

"Twenty-five thousand francs," he repeated. "You want me to sell you your liberty for that, do you?"

"Yes, if it pleases you to put it in that way." Then, with an air of unconcern, she added: "I merely suggest a bargain which you can either accept or reject. After all, it is, perhaps, immaterial."

"Your freedom must be worth a good deal to you if you are prepared to pay that price for it," her husband observed shrewdly.

"I desire to sever the tie, that's all."

"You enjoy perfect liberty," remarked the captain. "What more can you desire?"

"I cannot marry."

"Is that your intention?" he inquired, half convinced that this was the real cause of her conciliatory attitude.

"I really don't know," she answered unconcernedly. "Yet, even if I did, what would it matter if we were legally separated? You could marry also."

The captain was a polished rogue, and fully alive to the fertility of his wife's skilful devices. He knew she possessed an inexhaustible, imperturbable confidence, and was wondering what could be the character of the plan she was evidently bent upon carrying into effect. Twisting his moustache thoughtfully, he kept his keen eyes fixed upon her.

"I don't feel inclined to accept your remarkable suggestion," he observed at length. "You're a clever woman, Valérie, and you never forget to act in your own interests."

"Who but a fool does?" she laughed. His refusal was disappointing, nevertheless she preserved her calm demeanour, and, shrugging her shoulders indifferently, exclaimed: "Very well, I don't wish to press the matter. I shall merely refuse to return to you, whether you obtain the divorce or not. Surely twenty-five thousand francs and your law expenses would serve as a panacea to heal your broken heart. However, if you won't accept it, you'll be that much the poorer."

"Well, even supposing I desired to do it, I should be unable."

"Why?"

"Because I've no money with which to commence the suit."

"Oh, that obstacle is easily removed," she declared, diving into her pocket, and producing a well-filled purse, which bulged out with paper money she had won on the previous night.

Selecting three notes of 200 francs each she offered them to him, saying—

"These will be sufficient to start operations with. When that is exhausted telegraph for more, and you shall have it."

The gamester's impecuniosity caused him to regard the proffered notes with covetous eye. After all, he reflected, it would be an easy and profitable way of earning a good round sum. The prospect of being divorced from this beautiful yet heartless woman was not at all disagreeable. He might even make a rich marriage himself.

This latter reflection impressed itself upon his mind.

"Our marriage was a dismal failure—a miserable mistake. We hate one another heartily; therefore I'm willing to pay handsomely for the service you can render me. As we were married in London, you will have to return there and commence the suit," she said.

Willoughby was still undecided, but at length the temptation proved too great.

"Well, I suppose I must," he said, as he thrust the notes into his pocket after some further argument. "But won't you give me more? To you a divorce is worth double."

"No, not another sou. You can take it or leave it."

He saw that to endeavour to obtain more would be futile.

"It's agreed," he said, at last. "I'll sell you your liberty for twenty-five thousand francs."

"Ah! I thought you wouldn't refuse my munificent offer," she observed, with a light laugh.

Rising and walking to a side-table whereon were writing materials, she penned the following lines in French, in a fine angular hand:—

"I, Valérie Willoughby, agree to pay Percy Willoughby the sum of 25,000 francs upon the day a decree of divorce is pronounced absolute against me."

Blotting it hastily, she returned and handed it to him.

"That'll do," he said, folding it, and transferring it to his breast-pocket.

"But you will also give me an undertaking," she suggested, for she was astute, and determined that he should not have absolute power over her in the event of the collusion being discovered.

"As you please," replied her husband, after a moment's hesitation, and seating himself, he wrote an agreement promising to obtain the decree in consideration of the sum stated.

Once more Valérie had triumphed.

She had thought, on her husband's sudden appearance, that she had encountered that grain of sand which had before brought her to the ground, yet her audacity had conquered.

"Fool!" thought she, as his pen travelled over the paper. "He will be glad afterwards to buy back each drop of ink with his own blood. How dear a pen-stroke may cost one!"

Captain Willoughby, late of Her Majesty's 10th Hussars, had given way before a flood of adverse circumstances. Voluntarily, insolently, he flung away his pride and his past. He abandoned himself to that infernal thing, temptation; yet, after all, he had long ago sacrificed all that was sincere and grand in his nature. He cared nothing to what depth of dishonour he descended, as long as he obtained money.

"You will depart at once," she said imperatively, "and leave me to my own devices. You can write to me at Brussels, and I will see that witnesses are in attendance when the case is heard. Don't remain here any longer, for my friends may return at any moment, and must not discover you. Listen! There's some one coming along the corridor now. Quick!—go!" Snatching a card from a dainty mother-of-pearl case, she gave it to him, adding: "You'll find my address on this. Write to me. Next time we meet we shall not be man and wife."

"Good-bye, Valérie. May the future be more lucky than the past. Depend upon it, I shall call upon you for payment at a date not far distant," said the captain; and, taking up his hat and stick, hurriedly left the room, closing the door behind him.

His rapid exit was needless, as Hugh Trethowen and his companions had not yet returned.

When he had gone, Valérie's beautiful but pale face was illuminated by a smile of joy. She had proved the victor; she had, by sheer force of will, decreed and, as it were, realised the impossible. Was she not right to believe in audacity, in the absolute disdain of all law, since success was hers in this conflict in which the odds had been so terribly against her? She felt absolutely gay.

Leaning out of the window watching the passers-by, and gazing away over the superb valley—a peaceful sunlit, rejuvenescent prospect—she said aloud to herself—

"Who, I wonder, invented remorse? What is folly, remorse—the bugbear of man? It scares, but it doesn't bite. What foolery—conscience! I've my conscience and my heart like everybody else, but why should I reflect over what I've just done? After all, it is nothing—a mere commonplace transaction which will add considerably to my safety and well-being. Percy renders me a service, and I pay him dearly for it. Hurrah for life! What a magnificent morning!"

Chapter Twenty
Winged Hours

Sheltered from the blazing afternoon sun, Trethowen and Valérie were seated together under one of the ancient elms in the picturesque Promenade de Sept Heures. It was the hour when visitors lounge in the glade listening to the band and sip absinthe, while their children amuse themselves on the asphalte of the great covered promenade. The end of the long, shady avenue is quiet and secluded at this time of the day, as the exit is only a footpath ascending the steep hillside, and few persons come that way, the majority being attracted towards the music pavilion.

Valérie, always daintily attired, looked charming in a cool light dress of some soft material, which clung in graceful folds about her, and a large drooping hat composed entirely of flowers. She was serious, hesitating, and scraped the gravel aimlessly with the ferrule of her sunshade.

"Ah, you don't know, Hugh," she exclaimed, with a sigh, in reply to a question. "I—I've been horribly unhappy."

"Unhappy," he repeated in astonishment. "Why, what's the cause? You have life, gaiety, freedom—everything conducive to contentment."

"That's true," she answered. "But the past—I must strive to forget it. My whole life has been a series of dire misfortunes—an existence wasted because, until the present, I have never found one whom I could love."

"You really care for me, then?" he asked, looking earnestly into her fine eyes. "You will marry me at once, as you promised a moment ago?"

"Yes, dear," she said, her face relaxing into a glad smile. "I feel that, however unpropitious the past may have been, this is the turning-point in my life. Men I have hitherto known have all been hard-hearted and ready to hear me maligned, but you have sympathised with me in my unloved and defenceless position, and I cannot doubt that we shall be happy together."

"Why, of course we shall," he declared, drawing her closer to him, and kissing her through her flimsy veil. "I'm growing impatient to return to Coombe and settle down comfortably. The hollowness of life in a place like this palls upon one."

"Yes; I, too, am getting tired of it. I shall be pleased to go with you to your home. From the photographs it must be a lovely old place."

"Its antiqueness is its greatest charm," he replied. "But tell me why are you so unhappy?"

"Well, would you like to know the truth?" she asked, with a nervous little laugh.

"Of course I should."

"Then it was because I half-feared you did not care for me sufficiently to make me your wife," she said hesitatingly.

"And that caused you all this unhappiness? Well, now you know the truth," he added gayly, "there need be no more fear on that score. We will return to England and be married as soon as possible. Are you agreeable?"

Replying in the affirmative, she raised her face to his and kissed him affectionately, almost sadly.

As she withdrew her lips her teeth were firmly set, for, after all, she thought, was she not participating in a base plot and acting in a vile, despicable character? Yet, notwithstanding, she had caught herself actually imbued with genuine affection for this man she was pretending to love. She, a butterfly of fashion, who had been the evil genius of more than one man who had fallen victim to her charms, actually struggled with her conscience.

Drawing a deep breath between her teeth, she hesitated. Hugh attributed it to agitation; he little suspected that it was an effort to remain firm and carry out a nefarious scheme.

He was weak and captivated by her pretty face, she knew; still, after all, she could not deny that she, too, loved him, and for the moment she hated herself for practising such vile deception.

Although a cunning, crafty woman, recognising no law, either of God or man, all sense of honour had not yet been quite obliterated by the many clever plots and base schemes in which she had participated. All her youthful enthusiasm came to life again; the heart which she had thought dead, beat as it had never before done at the voice and smile of this strong, gentle, loyal-hearted man. Her love for him was silent but passionate; she adored him without telling herself that her right to love had long ago been forfeited.

Her beautiful oval face was calm and pale, faultless as that of an Italian Madonna, while her brilliant eyes received additional radiance from the lustre of her dark hair. She forgot her past; she felt as if she never had but one name upon her ruddy pouting lips—that of Hugh.

And he sat beside her, saying—

"I love you—I love you!"

On both sides it was a blind infatuation. Agony and torture she underwent as she put to herself the momentous question—Was she justified in accepting, when acceptance meant ruin? Was it just? Was it natural? Were the horrible passages of her life to haunt her, sleeping and waking, to madden her with their hideous vividness? Had her past deprived her of her right to live—of her right to love?

Hugh told himself that he had found his very ideal: his dreams, his faith, and love in all that is noble and upright in Valérie's mind, heart, eyes, and tone. She seemed to promise him the commencement of a new existence. With her he might again be happy; he would have some one to enter into his feelings, stand by him, and bestow on him that true affection that all men seek, but few, alas! find. He loved her with all the strength of his being.

Suddenly a thought flashed across Valérie's mind, and her resolution became concentrated on it. These were different manifestations of her dual nature. In a moment her lips were set firmly, and seemed silently to defy the feelings of affection that had just been stirred so strangely within her. She was contracting a debt to be paid for by a terrible penalty.

A glowing sunbeam, penetrating the thick foliage overhead, bathed the handsome Frenchwoman's light dress and olive cheeks with light, flecking the warm-tinted gravel on the walk. The distant band had paused. The deep silence of the avenue was broken only now and then by the low murmur of the trees. She revelled in the warm atmosphere, and felt lulled by the faint music of the rustling leaves. He, too, was lost in contemplation. In this green nook, with its gnarled trunks and fragments of blue sky revealed through the foliage, he felt far away from the world, as dreamy as if floating on a lake, as he abandoned himself to the enjoyment of the splendid afternoon.

"Then it is settled," he said, at last. "We will be married in London as soon as you can obtain your trousseau."

Had they not been so oblivious of their surroundings, it is probable they would have observed a man, half concealed behind a neighbouring tree, who had been keeping a close watch upon them. Creeping cautiously from his hiding-place, he drew himself up, and walked towards them with a pleasant smile on his face. It was Adolphe Chavoix.

"Ah," he exclaimed, as they looked up and recognised him, "I've been hunting for you everywhere. The Count wants us to drive to the Cascade. Come along, there's not a moment to lose, or we shan't be back in time for *table d'hôte*. Why, you've hidden yourselves all the afternoon."

"We plead guilty to the indictment, old fellow," Hugh replied, jumping to his feet enthusiastically. "The fact is, I've spent the afternoon very profitably, for I've won a wife."

"Oh!" he exclaimed in surprise, raising his eyebrows, and exchanging a quick glance with mademoiselle.

"Yes, Valérie has consented to marry me. We leave this place to-morrow, and shall be married in London within a month."

"Bravo! I congratulate you both," he said, grasping Trethowen's hand, and raising his hat politely to mademoiselle.

"Thanks, Adolphe," replied Hugh. "All I desire is that our future may be as bright and cloudless as to-day."

"What can mar it? Why, nothing! You and Valérie love one another—I suspected it from the first," he remarked, laughing. "You will marry, settle down in comfort and happiness, and grow old and grey, like—like the couple in your English song—Darby and Joan."

They laughed merrily in chorus.

"I don't much admire your prophecy. It's bad form to speak of a woman growing old," observed Valérie reprovingly. "Nevertheless, I'm confident we shall be as happy as the pair in the song. And when we're married, I'm sure Hugh will welcome you as one of our dearest friends."

"Of course," answered Trethowen. "Adolphe and the Count will always be welcome at Coombe. By Jove, when I get them down there I'll have my revenge at baccarat, too."

"Why, look, here's the Count coming after us," exclaimed Valérie, suddenly catching sight of a distant figure in a grey tweed suit and white waistcoat. "Come, let's go and meet him."

So the trio started off in that direction.

After meeting him they emerged from the avenue into the Place Royale, and Trethowen left them for a moment to purchase some cigars.

"I've had a visitor to-day," mademoiselle exclaimed, as she strolled on with Victor and Pierre; "some one you both know."

"Who?" asked the men eagerly.

"Willoughby."

"Willoughby!" gasped Bérard, halting in amazement. "Then he has tracked us! He must be silenced."

"Don't act rashly," remarked Valérie coolly. "You forget there's a bond between us that renders it extremely undesirable that he should divulge anything. For the present, at least, we are quite safe. I've effected a compromise with him which is just as binding on one side as on the other. After all, when everything is considered, our prospects have never been rosier than they are at this moment."

"But Willoughby. He can ruin us if he chooses. He knows of the affair at Carqueiranne."

"And what if he does? How could he prove who did it? If he knew, don't you think he would have had the reward long ago?" she argued.

"Has he seen Trethowen?"

"No; if he had, the circumstances might be different," she replied coolly.

"Keep them apart. They must not meet, for reasons you well understand," he said significantly; for, truth to tell, he feared the captain more than he did his Satanic Majesty himself.

"Of course, a recognition would be decidedly awkward," she admitted; "but they are not likely to see one another—at least, not yet. Up to the present my diplomacy has proved effectual. With regard to the ugly incidents which you mentioned, have I not coerced Jack Egerton into silence, and my husband, he is—"

"Here, by your side, dearest," a voice added, finishing the sentence.

Starting, she turned, to find to her dismay and embarrassment that Hugh had returned unnoticed, and was standing at her elbow.

"Why, you really frightened me," she said nervously, with a forced, harsh laugh. "I was explaining to the Count the reason I prefer living in England after our marriage. He says we cought to live in Paris."

"Oh," Hugh said indifferently, but made no further remark.

Mademoiselle and her companion were serious and apprehensive lest he had overheard their conversation.

Crossing the Place, they continued their walk in silence.

As they entered the hotel a letter from Egerton was handed to Hugh. When alone in his room he opened it, and found it was dated from London, and that it had been forwarded from Brussels.

"I suppose you are enjoying yourself thoroughly in the company of *la belle* Valérie," he wrote, after the usual greetings, and upbraidings for not answering a former note. "Well, you know my sentiments," he continued; "I need not repeat them. But, by the way, I have since thought that is perhaps because I once spoke harshly of her that you have been annoyed. I only had your welfare at heart, I assure you, and, as we are old friends, if I have said anything to vex you, pray forgive me."

"Bosh!" ejaculated Hugh savagely. "He tries to set me against her because he wants her himself. He gives no reason for his absurd warnings, but acts the sentimental fool."

He was about to toss the letter into the fire impatiently without reading further, when a name caught his eye.

The remainder of the letter was as follows:—

I am in sore trouble, and want your advice. Dolly has mysteriously disappeared. One night, three weeks ago, she left the studio and went home. After dressing she again went out, and since then nothing has been seen or heard of her. I have searched everywhere, and made strenuous efforts through the police and by advertisements to find some trace of her, but all seems futile. She has disappeared completely. Yet somehow I cannot think her silence is intentional, or that she has run away with some male companion, for she was not addicted to flirtation. You are one of her admirers, I know, so I want your advice as to the best course to pursue. I'm at my wits' ends, old fellow. Write and tell me what to do. I must find her; I shall never rest until I ascertain definitely what has become of her.

"Good heavens! What an extraordinary thing," ejaculated Trethowen, when he had concluded reading.

"Dolly missing! She might be dead for aught we know; yet such a fate cannot have befallen her. She cared for me a little, I know," he soliloquised. "Perhaps she had hoped that I should ask her to become my wife. Why," he gasped, as a thought suddenly occurred to him, "suppose she has committed suicide because I did not reciprocate the love she offered. Good God! if such were the case, I should never forgive myself—never."

Pausing, he gazed blankly at the paper in his hand.

"Yet—yet, after all," he continued thoughtfully, "I love Valérie, and shall marry no woman but her. There can be no reason why I should be miserable or bother my head over the mystery."

Chapter Twenty One
Purely Fin de Siècle

"Why are you so glum this morning, Jack? Hang it, you look as if you were going to attend my funeral instead of my wedding."

"Do I?" asked Egerton, yawning, and stretching himself out lazily in his chair. "I didn't know my facial expression was not in keeping with the joyousness of the occasion."

"Look here, old fellow," continued Hugh, walking over to his companion, and looking him earnestly in the face. "Now, before we start, tell me why you are so strangely indifferent. It seems as if you still entertain some curious antipathy towards Valérie." Egerton knit his brows, and, rising, assumed an air of utter unconcern.

"It's a matter I would rather not discuss, old chap," he said. "At your request I've consented to assist at your wedding, otherwise I should not have been here at all."

"Your very words betray you. Why should you have been absent, pray?"

"For certain reasons," the other replied briefly. Trethowen regarded his friend with surprise, not unmingled with annoyance.

"Ah!" he exclaimed, after a few moments' silence, "I see. You have not finished those mysterious warnings of yours. Why the deuce don't you speak right out and tell me what you mean?"

"I have no intention to malign the woman who is to be your wife, Hugh," the artist answered quietly. "I've given you certain hints already, and—"

"Enough of that," cried his companion, with some asperity. "Though you are an old friend, it gives you no right to interfere with my private affairs."

"That's true," Jack admitted hastily. "Don't for a moment think I desire to intrude unwarrantably. It's merely friendly advice I've given you."

"Friendly advice—bosh!" Trethowen said in disgust. "Whatever you know detrimental to Valérie, you'll oblige me by keeping in future to yourself."

The man addressed muttered something in an undertone, and, turning, gazed abstractedly out of the window.

They were in Hugh's sitting-room in St. James's on the morning fixed for the marriage. It was almost a month since Trethowen had left Spa, and the time had been pleasantly spent with Valérie at Brussels and Ostend. Now that they had returned to London, she had again taken up her abode in her little flat in Victoria Street, while the arrangements for the marriage were completed.

Jack Egerton, dressed more sprucely than usual, and wearing the orthodox lavender gloves and a flower in his coat, had called upon his friend half an hour before, and was waiting to accompany him to the church. His task he regarded with abhorrence. He would rather have done anything than assist at the ceremony, and see his friend bind himself to that dark-eyed Circe. Yet he, helpless and under the merciless thrall of the woman, was there by sheer compulsion. A fortnight ago he had received a letter from her. She did not ask or entreat, but commanded him to be present and act as Hugh's best man.

"I know," she wrote in French, "the task will be scarcely congenial, but your presence will inspire him with confidence. He has promised me he will ask you, and if you refuse, he will suspect that it is repugnant to you. Understand, he must know nothing of my affairs. When we last met at Laroche you threatened me, but I need hardly impress the necessity of silence upon you, having regard to the fact that the reward of your zealousness on your friend's behalf would be a life sentence. Accept his offer and attend the wedding, otherwise I shall know you are playing against me. If you do, beware! for I shall win. I have all the honours in my hand."

He was reflecting upon this last sentence as he stood staring aimlessly down into the street. She possessed the dark secret of his life, and held him in her power, so that he was compelled to do her bidding, to dance attendance upon her, and to witness her triumph at the expense of his dearest friend.

Grinding his teeth, he uttered an imprecation, as he realised how complete was her mastery, and perceived that his own ruin would be the only reward for saving Hugh.

The latter, who was watching him, misconstrued this outburst of impatience and went over and grasped his hand, saying:

"Forgive me, old fellow, for what I've just said. We ought not to quarrel, more especially to-day. I was rather hasty, but I love Valérie, and anything hinted against her excites my anger. Come, let's forget it." His companion succumbed to fate, having done all he could in the way of resistance. Laughing a trifle sadly, he replied—

"There's nothing whatever to forgive. I shall go with you to the church, and I hope—well, I hope your marriage will bring you nothing but happiness. Nevertheless, whatever is the result, remember I am still your friend."

Trethowen thanked him, although astonished at his friend's tone, and inwardly tried to account for his apparent sadness.

Could it be, that he entertained affection for Valérie himself? Or was it that their conversation that morning had brought back to his memory thoughts of the lost woman who, although his friend, assistant, and critic, was not his mistress? He had spoken very little of her, with the exception of describing the strange circumstances in which she disappeared. Still, any mention of her seemed to cause him sorrowful reflections.

Walking to a side-table whereon stood a bottle of champagne and some glasses, Hugh uncorked the wine, at the same time touching the gong.

In answer to the summons old Jacob appeared. He wore a large wedding-favour, and his scanty hair was parted and brushed with unusual care.

Having filled three glasses, his master turned to him, saying—

"Take a glass with us, Jacob, to celebrate the event. Come, Jack, here you are. It's no innovation to drink with a servant like my trusty old fossil here!"

The artist took the glass, and, as he did so, Hugh, holding up his own, gave the toast.

"Here's to the last hour of bachelorhood."

"Long life and prosperity to Hugh Trethowen!" Egerton exclaimed.

"And may they always lead happy lives!" added the old servant, in a weak broken voice.

"Hurrah! Let's hope so," remarked the bridegroom, and the trio tossed off their wine.

"And now we must be going," he added, a few minutes later. "You know my instructions, Jacob. You'll follow to Coombe at the end of the week. If any one calls, tell them—tell them I shan't be back in town for six months at least."

"Very well, Master Hugh," the feeble old man replied, smiling at his master's humour. "May God bless you both, sir!"

"Thank you, Jacob, thank you," Hugh replied heartily, as his man withdrew. "He can't make it out, I think," he remarked to Jack, with a laugh. "It'll be a fresh experience for him to have a mistress. But I feel sure she'll be kind to him."

Then they both finally examined themselves in a long mirror in the corner of the room, and, putting on their gloves, left the house.

An hour later the bell of the outer door of the chambers rang, and Jacob, still wearing his white satin rosette, answered.

On throwing open the door he was confronted by an unkempt wretchedly clad young woman, with tousled hair poking from under a battered crape bonnet, and a ragged shawl about her shoulders.

"Is Mr Trethowen in?" she inquired, in a voice that was refined, and certainly not in keeping with her habiliments.

"No, he's not," the old man replied sharply, for a woman of that class was not a desirable visitor.

"Where can I find him?" she asked anxiously. "I must see him, and at once."

"I tell you he's not here."

"Then where is he?"

Jacob, always a discreet and discriminating servant, did not like the look of this ill-attired stranger. He was particularly distrustful of females.

"I want to see him—to tell him something for his own advantage. It's imperative that I should see him immediately," she continued.

"Well," remarked Jacob, hesitating, and reflecting that it might possibly be to his master's advantage. "The fact is, he's gone to be married."

"To be married!" she echoed, staggering as if she had been dealt a blow.

"Yes; he and the French lady were to be married at twelve o'clock at St. James's. He's gone there to meet her."

"Where's the church? Quick, I must go there," she cried anxiously.

"In Piccadilly. Go to the top of the road here, turn to the right, and you'll come to it."

"Will he return here?"

"No; he goes to Cornwall to-night."

Turning suddenly, she ran hurriedly down the stairs. "Well, well," remarked the aged retainer aloud, as he closed the door and re-entered the sitting-room. "Now, I wonder what she wants? It's very strange—very; but, somehow, I believe I've seen a face something like hers before somewhere, only I can't recollect. Ah, well," he added, sighing, "I'm not so young as I was, and my memory fails me. After all, I suppose it's only fancy."

Then he helped himself to a glass of his master's old port in celebration of the happy occasion.

Meanwhile the slipshod female had turned from Piccadilly up the paved courtyard leading to St. James's church. She hurried, with wearied eyes and pale, anxious face, almost breathless.

At the door she was met by the pew-opener—a stout elderly female in rusty black—who, seeing her haste asked what she wanted.

"Is Mr Trethowen to be married here to-day?" she inquired.

"Trethowen! Yes. I think that's the gentleman's name. What do you want to know for?" she asked, regarding her suspiciously.

"I must see him. Is he inside?"

"No, he ain't. The party left a quarter of an hour ago."

"Gone!" she cried in dismay.

"Yes, they're married," remarked the woman. "Did you come to congratulate them?" she asked with a sneer.

"Married!" the other echoed, her face ashen pale. "Then, I'm too late! He's married her—and I cannot save him."

"You seem in rather a bad way over him," observed the woman, with an amused air.

"Where have they gone? Tell me quickly."

"How should I know? As long as the parties give me my fee, I don't ask no questions."

"Gone?" she repeated.

Reeling, she almost fell, but with an effort she recovered herself and shuffled with uneven steps down to the gateway, and in a few minutes was lost in the crowd in Piccadilly.

The woman who acted so strangely, and upon whom suspicions were cast as, with bowed head, she dragged her weary limbs slowly toward Hyde Park Corner, was Dolly Vivian.

Weak and ill, she was dazed by the bustle and noise surrounding her. Months of confinement, consequent upon a dangerous wound, had had their effect upon her, leaving her but the shadow of her former self. As she walked through the busy thoroughfare, it seemed to her an age since the night she had been decoyed and entrapped. Her experiences had been horrible, and she shuddered as she thought of them.

When she had recovered consciousness after being left by her allurer, she found an old and repulsive-looking woman bending over her holding a cup to her lips. Her mouth was fevered and parched, and she drank. Then, for the first time, she discovered that she had an ugly and painful wound in her neck. She had been stabbed, but not fatally, and the wound had been bandaged while she was insensible. Ignorant of where she was or how she had been brought there, she lay for weeks hovering between life and death. The lonely house, she found, was occupied by two persons—the woman who attended upon her and a rough-looking man. They treated her harshly, almost brutally, refusing to answer any questions, and never failing to lock the door of her room when they left.

The solitary confinement, added to the pain she suffered, both mental and physical, nearly deprived her of reason. Days, weeks, months passed; she led an idle, aimless existence, kept a close prisoner, and debarred from exercise that was essential to life. The window had been nailed up, and even if it would open it was too high from the ground to admit of escape. Each day she sat before it, gazing down into the orchard which surrounded the house and the wide stretch of market garden beyond.

One day, however, just as she was about to relinquish hope of assistance being forthcoming, and was sitting, as usual, at the window, she saw both of her janitors leave the house together, attired as if they meant to be absent several hours.

Her chance to escape had arrived. Rushing to the door, she tried it. Her heart gave a bound of joy as the handle turned and it opened. The woman had, by a most fortuitous circumstance, forgotten to lock it.

Nevertheless, there was still another point that required careful consideration. Her clothes had been taken from her, and the only garment she wore was a dirty, ragged flannel dressing-gown. Descending the stairs, for the first time since her abduction, she explored the place in an endeavour to find some clothes. In a bedroom on the ground floor she found an old dress, with a shawl, bonnet, and pair of worn-out boots—all of which had evidently belonged to the woman who had kept her prisoner. Attiring herself in them in almost breathless excitement, lest she should be discovered ere she could effect her escape, she opened the door and stole out.

Passing through the orchard, she followed a path down to a by-road, at the end of which she gained a broad highway, and presently came to a small town. On inquiry she found this was Twickenham. A lad told her the way to London, and she plodded onward, notwithstanding that lack of exercise caused her to quickly become exhausted. Through Richmond and Kew she passed, then along the straight broad road leading through Chiswick, Hammersmith, Kensington, and Hyde Park, until, in an almost fainting condition, she found herself at the corner of Jermyn Street, and sought out the house wherein Hugh Trethowen lived.

During her imprisonment she had made a strange discovery, but, alas! she had come too late, and now she turned away from the church disappointed and heartbroken. The mainspring of her life had snapped; nevertheless, she was determined to wait and obtain a revenge which she knew would be terrible and complete.

Chapter Twenty Two
The Pretty Artist's Model

"I've a good mind to burn them, and so put an end to all this confounded mystery; yet —"

Hugh Trethowen hesitated.

Standing pensively before the fire in his own den at Coombe a fortnight after his marriage, he was examining the photograph and partially destroyed letters, the unaccountable presence of which among his brother's possessions had caused him so much perturbation. As he held the photograph in his hand the pictured face of Valérie seemed to smile with tantalising seductiveness, and, with a fond husbands admiration, he told himself that in no way had her beauty deteriorated, but, on the contrary, she had grown handsomer.

Nevertheless, the fact that it had, together with the letters, been carefully concealed by his brother, was a problem which frequently caused him a good deal of uneasy speculation. The wording of the missives was strangely ominous, and there was no disguising the fact that they were in his wife's handwriting.

"I'm half inclined to tear them up and burn them. If I did, they certainly would worry me no longer," he argued, aloud. "I wish I could let her see them, and ask for an explanation. But I cannot; it would show mistrust."

He lifted his eyes from the photograph and gazed perplexedly around the apartment. More than once he had been sorely tempted to destroy the carefully-preserved documents; still the mystery surrounding them was fascinating, and he vaguely hoped that some day he might elucidate it.

Suddenly he turned and crossed the room resolutely, saying —

"No, I'll keep them; by Jove, I will! I must master these absurd apprehensions. What does it matter? The communications certainly relate to something which looks suspiciously like a mystery; nevertheless, it's probable that, after all, they only refer to some very commonplace affair."

Laughing sardonically, he paused for a moment to glance at the photograph under the stronger light shed by the lamp upon the table; then he opened the bureau and replaced them in a drawer.

"Bah! I'm a fool to think about them," he added, as he locked the flap and turned away. "Yet, why should they constantly recur in my thoughts, interfering with my happiness, and rendering me almost miserable? Even Jack's semi-prophetic utterances seem to convey some meaning when they are before me. Still, most people harbour a family skeleton in their cupboard, and I suppose this is mine. But there's no reason why I should bother my head over it; the solution will come some day, and until then I can wait."

He flung himself into a roomy armchair in a less thoughtful mood. That afternoon Valérie had driven to Bude to call upon the vicar's wife, whom she had met on several occasions in London, and, although nearly seven o'clock, she had not returned. The cold November wind howled dismally in the chimney as Hugh sat by the fireside already dressed, and awaiting dinner. For the first time since his marriage he found himself alone, with time hanging heavily upon his hands, and had recognised how utterly unbearable his life would be without her fair presence and kindly smile. His love for her was unbounded; she was, indeed, his idol.

While in this contemplative mood, a servant entered and handed him a letter on a salver. Taking it up, he glanced at the superscription. In was in a feminine hand which he did not recognise. Breaking open the envelope, he read and re-read the brief and almost incomprehensible message it contained. It ran as follows:—

Dear Mr Trethowen,—It is imperative that I should see you as soon as possible upon a matter of the utmost importance. To commit to paper the object of the interview I desire would not be policy, nevertheless it is of great moment to yourself. Can you make an appointment to meet me in London? Please keep this letter a strict secret from any one, even including Mrs Trethowen.—Yours very truly, Dorothy Vivian.

"I wonder what it can mean?" he reflected, with his eyes fixed upon the paper. "Evidently Dolly has turned up again, yet it's strange Jack has said nothing of her reappearance in his letters. Where can she have been, and why does she send me such a curious request? What can she know that concerns me?"

He re-read the letter silently, twisting his moustache in perplexity.

"I suspect that, if the truth were known, she's been on a holiday trip with some admirer. But I shouldn't have thought it of her, she was so quiet and steady-going. A matter of great moment to myself," he repeated. "It sounds mysterious, certainly."

Still holding her letter in his hand, he flung back his head on the cushion of his chair, and thought.

"After all, many men would feel flattered by such a note," he said aloud.

"Why, Hugh, dear, how long have you been sitting here all alone? What's that in your hand? A letter! In a girl's handwriting, too!"

The voice caused him to start from his chair and crush the letter hurriedly into his pocket. Valérie had opened the door noiselessly and crept up behind him mischievously, intending to startle him. She had been looking over his shoulder for several moments, vainly endeavouring to read the communication.

"You made me jump, darling," he said, laughing confusedly. "I've been waiting for you an hour."

"And been amusing yourself, it seems, by receiving a letter during my absence," she added cynically.

"I admit the letter came half an hour ago, but it contains nothing of which I am ashamed."

"Then I presume I may read it?" she suggested.

"Unfortunately, no," he replied, remembering Dolly's injunctions as to secrecy. "Its contents are of a strictly private nature."

"Unless it be compromising, I should scarcely have thought that any letter received by a husband who wishes to preserve a wife's confidence could contain secrets that she should not learn," Valérie remarked in a tone of annoyance.

"That is true, dearest," he said earnestly, taking her hand. "It is through no fault of my own that I am unable to show it to you."

"May I not know who the writer is?" she asked, standing erect, and looking handsome in the dinner-gown which she had assumed before coming in search of him.

Her husband shook his head gravely.

It was the first difference of opinion they had had since their marriage, and he could not view it but with regret. He hastened to assure her that she need have no fear that he was practising duplicity, that he loved her too well. For her part, she had long ago gauged the extent of his affection, and, truth to tell, had but little misgiving when she discovered the open letter in his hand. Nevertheless, she was curious to learn the identity of his lady correspondent, and, in consequence of being met with a decisive refusal, was somewhat piqued.

This, however, passed quickly. The unbecoming frown which clouded her brow soon gave way to an affectionate smile as she yielded herself to his embrace and returned his kiss.

A moment later a servant entered and announced that dinner was served. Then she linked her arm in his, and they strolled along to the dining-room, laughing lightly, and discussing the merits of the obese and highly respectable lady she had been visiting.

Valérie's nature was fantastic to a degree. She invariably sacrificed her interests to her caprices.

Thus the unpleasant episode passed, and in half an hour was entirely forgotten. Trethowen was as madly in love with his wife as on the first day his eyes fell upon her, and, surrounded by comfort and luxury, led a blissful, contented existence. Heedless of the future, and living only for the present, he adored her passionately, believing that the perfect felicity they now enjoyed would go on uninterruptedly and be of permanent duration.

How strange it is that all of us, however philosophic, at one period or other in our lives entertain a foolish conviction that we have found perfect and lasting contentment! We never reflect. If we did, we should recognise that there is no such thing as perpetual happiness, that joy is at best but temporary pleasure, productive of bitter reaction, and that so-called domestic bliss is a fallacy, always anticipated, often feigned, yet, waning and fading with the honeymoon.

On that day Dolly Vivian returned to Jack Egerton.

In the morning she had walked unexpectedly into his studio where he was busy at work, and, laughing at his surprise and consternation, proceeded to divest herself of her hat and jacket in apparently an unconcerned manner, as though she had never been absent. To his questions as to the cause of her disappearance and long silence she was perfectly indifferent, merely remarking in a severe tone that she was mistress of her own actions, and that she did not require intrusion upon affairs which were of a purely private nature. A suggestion of his that she had been on an escapade with a male escort she strongly resented; indeed, she became so angry at the insinuation that, fearing lest she should again absent herself, the artist was compelled to abandon his cross-examination and welcome her return with all the sincerity of an old friend.

"Then you won't tell me why you went away so suddenly and left no address?" he asked again, when they had been in conversation some time, and he had told her of his doings in her absence.

"No, Jack. Once for all, I refuse. My movements concern no one except myself."

"I, too, am an interested party," he argued, smiling gallantly.

"Well, yes. I suppose you haven't yet finished 'The Sultan's Favourite'?"

"No; there it is," he replied, pointing to a canvas placed with its face towards the wall. "I have not touched it since you left. It has been awaiting your return before I could finish it."

"Am I to continue my sittings, then?" she asked coquettishly.

"Why, of course," he replied, lolling against his easel and regarding her amusedly. "You know well enough what crude daubs my figures would be if I did not have your model. I owe the greater part of my success to you, and since your absence I've done absolutely nothing that has satisfied me."

She was well aware that the words he spoke were the truth. Through several years of desperate struggle against adversity she had been his adviser and assistant, watching with gratification his steady progress. Each picture he completed was more natural and more perfect. He could work from no other model, she knew, therefore it did not surprise her when he announced his intention to resume without further delay what promised to be his masterpiece, "The Sultan's Favourite."

In half an hour she had exchanged her dress for the filmy garments and velvet zouave of an Oriental beauty, and was lying half recumbent upon the silken divan in a careless, graceful attitude. When she had assumed exactly the same pose as before, with one naked foot dangling near the ground and the stray embroidered slipper beside her, she told him to commence.

During the morning the artist worked on in the best of spirits. Delighted at the return of his companion and *confidante*, whom he had despaired of seeing again, he chatted and laughed in a manner quite unusual to him, for he always preserved a rather morose silence when he had any difficult work in hand. One thing, however, was unaccountable, and caused him considerable surprise. When he had been painting about an hour he made a discovery. He was engaged in heightening the tone of the neck, and, finding her head cast rather too much shadow, asked her to turn a little more upon her side. She did so rather reluctantly, he thought—and then he noticed upon her neck, half-hidden by the heavy necklace of Turkish coins she wore, a long ugly scar.

"Why, Dolly!" he exclaimed in consternation, leaving his easel and walking up to examine her more closely, "what's the matter with your neck?"

"Nothing," she replied, somewhat embarrassed.

"But you've had a fearful wound. How did it occur?"

"It was a mere trifle. I—I fell down."

"Where?"

"In the street. I slipped and fell upon the kerb."

"A fall couldn't cause a cut like that," he exclaimed incredulously.

"It did. But don't bother about it," she replied, a trifle petulantly. "It has healed now, and I have no pain."

He looked at her steadily, and felt convinced that she was concealing the truth. Reassuming his former lightheartedness, however, he observed that the accident was most unfortunate, and, expressing a hope that she felt no evil effects from it, returned to his picture and continued to put in the lighter flesh tints.

About two o'clock he suddenly remembered that he had made an appointment to call upon a man at Holland Park with regard to a commission, and that it would be imperative for him to leave her for at least an hour. She raised no objection, therefore he changed his coat and took his departure, promising to return with all possible haste, as he wanted to finish the portion of the picture upon which he was engaged before the light failed.

When he had gone she rose languidly from her couch, and, shivering slightly, threw a wrap around her bare white shoulders, and seated herself by the fire. Soon Mrs O'Shea brought in her luncheon on a tray, and she ate with relish, chatting to the housekeeper meanwhile. After she had finished, and the old woman had retired, she rose and wandered round the studio in search of any fresh studies the artist might have made during her absence. She turned one which was hanging with its face to the wall, and discovered it was a likeness of the woman she hated—her rival, Valérie Dedieu. It was only a crayon drawing, but the features were lifelike, and the cruel, cold smile played upon the full red lips.

"I wonder," she said, aloud—"I wonder what secret tie there is between Jack and that woman? There is something, I feel certain, and I'll not rest until I solve the mystery. Yet—yet she is Hugh's wife—Hugh loves her!" she added bitterly.

With a sigh she replaced the sketch in the position she had found it.

"Yes, my precious mademoiselle," she continued menacingly, "you may well hide your face. Some day you will curse the chance which brought you and Hugh together. You little suspect the revenge that I am waiting for."

Pausing in thought, she ran her fingers through her dishevelled hair.

"And yet," she cried in dismay, as the sudden thought occurred to her, "by unmasking you, Hugh would suffer, for he adores you! The discovery of your villainy would break his heart. You are his wife—his wife—and for me—for me he cares nothing!"

A tear trickled down her cheek, but it was only for an instant; she brushed it away, and stood motionless for several minutes gazing disconsolately into the fire. Then she noticed that Jack's secretaire bookcase, which stood close beside her, was open. Feminine curiosity at once asserted itself, and the thought crossed her mind that it was possible she might discover some clue to the secret between the Frenchwoman and the artist.

At once she proceeded to search, at the same time listening attentively for any sign of the approach of Mrs O'Shea. Prying among the papers in the desk she could discover nothing which had any interest for her among the bills, letters, theatre programmes and memoranda it contained. Turning her attention to the small drawers above, her search was equally fruitless. One drawer she opened, however, contained nothing but an old newspaper folded small and lying along the bottom. A red mark upon it attracted her, and she took it out and unfolded it, but with disappointment she found herself unable to read it, as it was in French. Half a column on the front page had been marked round boldly with a red pencil, and was evidently some important report which had been carefully preserved. The heading was set in great capitals, and the type was larger than that in the body of the paper.

She glanced down the lines of print, but they were unintelligible to her. The heading, which was the only sentence she could make out, was "Le Mystère du Boulevard Haussmann," and the newspaper was the Paris *Gaulois*. Truth to tell, it was the paper which Egerton had abstracted from the bureau at Coombe when Dolly and he had visited Trethowen.

The "Sultan's Favourite" carefully scanned each line in an endeavour to discover some word that was familiar, but found none. She knew it contained details of some mystery or other, and that was sufficient incentive for her to try and translate it. Soon, however, she found that all her efforts were futile; so, refolding it, she was about to replace it in its former position when she suddenly reflected that if she copied out a portion of it she might get it translated by a governess who lodged in the same house as herself, and with whom she was on friendly terms.

Taking a seat at the desk, she spread out the paper before her, and carefully copied several sentences, taking heed to place the accents accurately, and scrupulously avoiding errors in orthography. Having covered two sheets of notepaper, she replaced the newspaper in the drawer, afterwards going into her dressing-room and putting her notes into the pocket of her dress.

Once or twice she felt inclined to laugh at herself for attaching so much importance to a mere newspaper report which seemed to contain nothing to connect it with the persons in whom she was interested, nevertheless she felt convinced that no clue was too small or insignificant for her to investigate. One discovery, amazing yet incomprehensible, she had already made, and it had whetted her desire to know the whole truth in order that her revenge might be more complete.

Egerton returned shortly afterwards. Handing her a bag of burnt almonds of a kind for which she had a particular weakness, he expressed a hope that she had not been dull, and quickly prepared to resume his work. With eyes sparkling like those of a spoiled child, she tasted the almonds, and gave him one, then, flinging aside her wrap, lay again upon the divan before him, laughing, and crunching her sweets.

The artist was in a mood even more joyful than before he went out, the cause being that he had been given commission for a portrait that was at once easy and lucrative, a fact which he triumphantly announced to his model, and upon which she congratulated him.

In November the light in London grows yellow early, and before four o'clock the artist had to lay down his palette for the day. Tea was brought in a few minutes later, and the pair sat *tête-à-tête* before the blazing fire, Dolly listening to the painter's technical description of the picture that he had been commissioned to execute.

Chapter Twenty Three
Without the Queen's Proctor

The last act of a matrimonial drama was being watched attentively by six rows of eager spectators.

Already the gas had been lit, for the dull yellow light of the wintry London moon was insufficient to illuminate the sombre Court. Upon the bench, at the rear of which hung a large square board covered with dark-blue cloth and bearing a golden anchor, the judge sat—grave, silent, almost statuesque. The public who filled the tiers of seats before him listened intently to every word of the story of a woman's faithlessness, which counsel was relating. It was an undefended, and therefore not an unusually interesting case. Nevertheless, the Divorce Court has an attraction for the curious, and is nearly always crowded, even when there are scarcely a dozen people in any of the Queen's Bench or Chancery Divisions. The very word divorce is sufficient to interest some, and for the novelty of the thing they desire to witness the procedure by which husband and wife are disunited.

Perhaps such curiosity is pardonable. It certainly is more excusable than the ignominious conduct of some *soi-disant* ladies, who consider it good form to attend a Criminal Court where a woman is indicted for murder, and there watch and comment audibly, and with heartless inhumanity, upon the agonies of their wretched sister who is being tried for her life. Such scenes at recent trials of unfortunate women have been a scandal to our civilisation.

In the Divorce Court, however, it is different. The surroundings are more refined. The *dénouement* of the marriage drama there enacted frequently develops into broad comedy before the curtain is rung down by the judicial decision. Even there, however, women gloat over the stories of the domestic woe of another woman, and ridicule the deceived husband with a cool indifference that is astounding; they are apparently quite unimpressed by the gravity of the question at issue.

The President had already disposed of half a dozen undefended suits, when the case of Willoughby *versus* Willoughby and Lapasque had been called on.

"Pardon me, Mr Grover. My attention was diverted for the moment, and I did not catch your opening sentences," the judge was saying to counsel for the petitioner.

"The facts of the case before you, m'lord, are briefly these," exclaimed the barrister, recommencing. "The petitioner, Captain Willoughby, late of the 10th Hussars, married the respondent, a French subject, at St. Mary Abbot's, Kensington, in June, 1884. The parties lived happily at Brighton, Leeds, Toulon, and other places until about a year had elapsed, when frequent quarrels arose. The petitioner discovered that his wife was carrying on an intrigue with a wealthy young man named Arthur Kingscote, with whom she had been acquainted before marriage. This led to an encounter between the two men at a Manchester hotel, with the result that my client was severely injured in the head, in consequence of which petitioner took proceedings against Kingscote, who was fined at the Manchester Police Court for the assault. This apparently incensed the respondent, and quarrels became of more frequent occurrence, until one day, while living at San Remo, Mrs Willoughby left her home unexpectedly, and never returned. Eventually, after a long series of inquiries, the petitioner found that his wife was living at Nice, and that she had formed a *liaison* with the co-respondent, Gustava Lapasque, who is one of the officials connected with the Casino at Monte Carlo. The evidence I shall call before you, m'lord, will prove the latter part of my statement; and as I understand there is no one present representing either respondent or co-respondent, I shall ask your lordship to pronounce the decree usual in such a case."

The captain having briefly borne out the statement of his counsel, the latter turned to the usher, saying—

"Call Giovanni Moretti, please."

In a few minutes a dapper and rather well-dressed Italian stepped into the witness-box.

"What are you, Signore Moretti?" asked Mr Grover, when the witness had been sworn and his name taken.

"Head waiter at the Hôtel Victoria, Nice," he replied in broken English.

"Do you recognise this lady?" counsel asked, handing up a cabinet photograph of Valérie.

"Yes," he said, taking a long glance at it. "The lady is Madame Lapasque."

"And this photograph?" continued Mr Grover, handing him another.

"Monsieur Lapasque. They both stayed at our hotel for nearly three months the summer before last. They came in July and left in October."

"During those months would you have many visitors at your hotel?"

"No; very few. It is not our season."

"In that case you would have plenty of facilities for observing them?"

"I saw them perhaps a dozen times each day. I superintended the waiting at *à déjeûner* and *table d'hôte*."

"You have no doubt that the lady was the original of that portrait?"

"Not the slightest," he replied, shrugging his shoulders.

"Have you seen the respondent, Mrs Willoughby, since?" the judge asked, in slow deliberate tones.

"Yes, I saw her here in London a few weeks ago. I was brought to England by Monsieur Willoughby to identify madame and give evidence."

"When you saw her, did you tell her that you recognised her as Madame Lapasque?"

"Of course I told her. She then grew angry, and ordered me from the room."

"Is that all the evidence you have, Mr Grover?" asked the judge, when he had concluded taking notes of the witness's cross-examination.

"No, my lord. I have further corroborative evidence," counsel replied.

The Italian walked from the box, and his place was taken by Nanette Rambert.

"What are you, Miss Rambert?" asked Mr Grover, glancing at his brief.

"Lady's maid."

"You identify these photographs, I believe?"

"Yes; the lady is Madame Lapasque, my late mistress, and the gentleman her husband."

"How long were you in the respondent's service?"

"About two years. At the time she engaged me at Cannes, monsieur was not with her, but about three months later he joined her, and we travelled first to San Remo, then to Rome, Homburg, and London."

"And you always believed Lapasque to be her husband?" asked Mr Grover.

"Of course, m'sieur. Madame always told me he was."

"How long ago did you leave her service?"

"About six months."

"Have you seen either since?"

"I have only seen madame. I was with M'sieur Willoughby, and we saw her come from a house in Victoria Street, Westminster."

"Did you identify her?"

"Yes, without the slightest difficulty. I did not, however, speak to her."

No other questions were asked the witness, and she left the box.

His lordship then recalled the petitioner, and questioned him at some length upon his wife's general conduct, to which the gallant captain replied with the sorrowful yet indignant air of the injured husband.

After counsel had delivered a brief and pointed address there was a pause. The judge was weighing the evidence. He read and re-read his notes, underlining words here and there with a pencil, while the Court silently awaited his decision.

Suddenly he looked up, coughed slightly, and, addressing Mr Grover, who at once rose, said—

"In this case I find that the wife has been guilty of misconduct, and I shall therefore grant a decree *nisi* with costs against the co-respondent."

Counsel, bowing, thanked his lordship, and, tying up his brief, left the Court, accompanied by the captain, while the onlookers stirred uneasily in their seats, whispered among each other, and then sat eager to be regaled with another story of domestic woe.

As the barrister and his client gained the large hall of the Courts, Nanette joined them. Mr Grover excused himself on the ground that he had an appointment at his chambers in the Temple, and, bidding them adieu, departed. The captain and the maid followed him down the steps, and, turning in the opposite direction, strolled leisurely past St. Clement's church and along the Strand.

Willoughby was elated. Not only had he freed himself from a tie that might some day prove detrimental, but—what was much more to the point—he was also entitled to claim twenty-five thousand francs, the price his wife had offered for her liberty. The matter had been rendered quite easy, the details, together with Lapasque's address, having been furnished by Valérie herself.

"You're a smart girl, Nanette," he exclaimed flatteringly, after expressing approbation at the manner in which she had given her evidence. "Your story had a ring of truth about it that was delightful, and in answering the questions you drew a long, serious face, and never once faltered."

Nodding her head knowingly and laughing, she replied—

"That's true, m'sieur. But, you see, I know the way to tell fibs as well as most people. I haven't been maid to mademoiselle without contriving to learn a few tricks. I was taught them when I first entered her service; now they come quite naturally."

"So it seems," he said, with an amused smile. "But, tell me, how do matters stand down at the country mansion? Is all serene?"

"Quite. Mademoiselle's new husband is such a mild-mannered young man, and has suspected absolutely nothing from the first. He's madly infatuated with her, and she can twist him round her little finger."

"Now, speaking candidly, Nanette," asked the captain, after a few moments' silence, "have you any idea what object she had in marrying him?"

"None; I'm as ignorant as yourself. It seems unaccountable, yet you may rest assured she had some very good reason for such a step."

"Of course, Trethowen has money, yet somehow I don't believe that her sole object was to become the wife of a rich man. It is a matter that has puzzled me ever since I heard of the match," observed the captain thoughtfully.

In truth, he was the reverse of sorry that his wife had entered into the alliance. Providing Hugh really loved Valérie, he saw there was a possibility of obtaining hush-money from him, as it was certain he would avoid the scandal which would inevitably result if his wife were prosecuted for bigamy.

Nanette, although unacquainted with many of her mistress's schemes, nevertheless knew so much that it would have been highly undesirable that any disagreement should occur between them. She was saucy and self-confident, yet discreet and—when occasion required—a model maid.

"You should be happy, m'sieur, now that you have obtained your divorce, and can live *en garçon* again," she remarked, her eyes sparkling with *diablerie*.

"So I am, Nanette," he replied with a smile. "Everything has come off just as I arranged that it should. In the judgment of a fool there are no wise men. To-night you must return to Coombe, and your mistress will pay you the money that was agreed. You might tell her that, the business being so far concluded, she may expect a visit from me in the course of a day or two, when I hope we shall be able to close the incident."

"Very well. I'll give her your message," replied the girl. "But you will not call upon her at Coombe? Surely that would be unwise," she suggested in concern.

"I haven't yet decided whether I shall go there or not. It all depends upon circumstances," he answered rather abruptly.

Then they turned into a restaurant for luncheon, and the captain celebrated the occasion with a bottle of Pommery, which Nanette assisted him to drink.

A week had passed.

Before a large fire in the private parlour of the Ship Hotel, at Bude, Percy Willoughby sat with legs stretched out and feet upon the fender. The ancient hostelry, which, although styled a hotel, was merely an inn, stood in a somewhat sheltered position under the rocks, and faced the sea. Fishermen were its chief customers, but on this particular night the smacks were out, and the place was comparatively quiet, with the exception of two loungers, who were holding a noisy argument in the bar. The room was low, with heavy oak beams across a ceiling blackened by the smoke of years, a sanded floor, a wide old-fashioned hearth, and straight-backed wooden chairs that had evidently done duty for a century. A tall, antiquated clock ticked solemnly in a corner, and the efforts at ornamentation were mostly in the form of shell-boxes and faded wool-flowers.

The wind moaned dismally in the chimney, and aroused the captain from his reverie.

"I suppose she'll come," he murmured aloud, as he rose, and, going to the window, drew back the curtain. The night was dark and cloudy. Nothing could be seen except the distant flashing light at sea, which glimmered for a moment like a star and disappeared. "The weather is certainly not very propitious, and I'm afraid if I went out alone in this confoundedly dark hole I should lose myself. But of course she'll come," he added reassuringly. "She dare not disappoint me." And he dashed the curtains together again and returned to his chair.

A few minutes afterwards Valérie entered. She wore a long fur-lined cloak, and a thick dark veil concealed her features.

"At last I'm here," she said glancing round, as if half fearful lest she should be recognised, and walking over to the fire, she warmed her benumbed hands. "It was by the merest chance that I was able to come. We've been dining with some people about a mile away, and I at last managed to slip out."

As she loosened her cloak he noticed that underneath she wore a charming toilet of pale blue silk.

"Well," he said, after they had greeted one another and seated themselves before the fire. "The affair we planned at Spa has proved successful, Valérie, and we're man and wife no longer."

"And an excellent thing, too," she remarked, ridiculing his sentimental tone.

"I entirely agree with you; we are much better apart. Nevertheless, although we are divorced, there surely is no reason why we should not remain friends, is there?" he asked, speaking in French.

"Oh, there's no harm in that, I suppose," she replied in the same language, laughing lightly. "I saw from the papers that you obtained the decree, and Nanette gave me a most graphic description of the hearing of the case. It must have been highly entertaining. I should so much liked to have been there."

"It certainly was a trifle diverting," the captain admitted; "but let's get to business. Have you brought the money?"

"No."

"What?—you haven't?" he cried in dismay. "Then why have you brought me down to this infernal hole?"

"For the benefit of your health," she replied with tantalising coquetry.

"I want the money," he declared angrily.

"If you'll be patient, and allow me to speak, I'll explain."

"I want none of your excuses; nothing but the money. In dealing with me, Mrs Trethowen, you'll have to play fair, or, by heaven! it will be the worse for you. Bear that in mind."

"Neither my intention nor desire is to deceive you," she replied haughtily; "but since you cannot talk without abuse, perhaps a week longer without your money will cause you to be more polite." And she rose and made a movement towards the door.

"Where do you think you're going?" he exclaimed roughly, rushing to the door and standing with his back against it. "I've come down here to be paid for the service I've rendered you at the risk of being prosecuted myself, and therefore you don't leave this room until I have the money."

His face was blanched with anger, and he spoke with determination. She had seen his countenance wear a similar look on more than one occasion, and knew that when in such a mood he was not to be trifled with.

"But you won't let me explain, Percy," she complained in a softened tone. "Do be reasonable."

"I am. I want the thousand pounds you promised."

"Hush," she said, holding up a finger. "We might be overheard!"

"Never mind. Do you intend to pay me?" he asked in a lower tone.

"Yes, but not all now. I'm really hard up, otherwise you should have every penny I promised."

"Oh, that's nonsense. You can get money from that confiding husband of yours, if you like—"

"But I don't like, so there's the difference," she interrupted. "I know my own business best."

"How much can you give me?"

"Two hundred pounds."

"Pooh! I'm not going to accept that," said he decisively. "What next? If you offered me five hundred as the first instalment, I might feel disposed to take it."

"Take it or leave it, you'll get no more just now."

"Look here," he cried fiercely, standing before her in a threatening attitude. "Do you think I'm going to be made sport of in this manner? If so, you've made a huge mistake. I want the money and I mean to have it. If you won't give it to me, then I shall be under the necessity of requesting a loan from your husband. That would queer your delightful little game, wouldn't it—eh?"

She drew a long breath, and for an instant the colour left her face. Nevertheless, it took more than a threat of that kind to disconcert her.

"You are at liberty to do even that," she answered, with a sardonic smile. "But you would be the sufferer, I'm thinking."

"I want none of your trickery. Pay me, and you'll never hear of me again."

"If I could believe that, it would relieve my mind very considerably," she observed with candour. "The facts are these: the whole of the money I have been able to scrape together only amounts to two hundred pounds. I admit it is but a small proportion of my debt, yet I think it should satisfy your present needs. Just now I cannot ask my husband for a large sum, as I can think of no excuse for wanting it."

"I should think it is the first time you were ever at a loss for a lie," he remarked sarcastically.

"It doesn't do to carry imposition too far. I flatter myself I know when and where to draw the line."

"I've some plans in hand, and must have five hundred pounds to carry them out. Not a penny less will be of any use to me."

"But I tell you I can't give it to you."

"Then I must get it from another source, that's all," he declared, selecting a cigarette from his case, and assuming an air of unconcern.

"Come, enough of this," she exclaimed petulantly; "I cannot stay here half the night arguing with you." Putting her hand into the breast of her dress she drew forth some bank-notes. There were four, each for fifty pounds. "Will you take these or not?" she asked, offering them to him.

"Don't I tell you they're no use? I must have twice as much."

"Then, I'm sorry I can't oblige you, and will wish you *bon soir*," she replied, with a mock curtsey.

"Why do you play with me like this?" he cried in anger, gripping her roughly by the arm. "I want five hundred pounds, and I'll have it before you leave this place."

"How is that possible when I do not possess it? Do talk sense."

"I'm talking sense. You have it; you can give it me if you choose."

"What do you mean?"

"The diamonds you are wearing. They're worth that, I suppose."

She hesitated, and holding her wrist to the dull lamplight revealed the diamond bangles which sparkled and flashed as she moved. His proposal was somewhat disconcerting, for the bracelets, as well as the necklet she was wearing, were a portion of Hugh's wedding gifts. She was puzzled to know how she should account for them if she yielded to the man's inexorable demands.

"I cannot. My husband would inquire what had become of them. What could I say? If I told him they were lost he would give information to the police, and you could not get rid of them without some ugly revelations resulting."

"It's no use arguing. I mean to have them."

He had taken the notes and thrust them carelessly into his vest pocket.

"No, my dear Percy, the thing's impossible."

"Nonsense," he cried fiercely, at the same time making a sudden snatch at the row of gleaming stones which encircled her white neck. When she saw his intention she put both hands up in an endeavour to prevent him, and gave vent to a slight scream.

But she was powerless. The clasp snapped, and the necklet was a moment later in his pocket.

"Return that at once," she cried, stamping her foot with rage. "If you don't I'll tell the police you've robbed me."

The captain stuck his hands into his pockets and laughed.

"Go and tell them, my dear," he said. "We should make an interesting pair before the magistrate."

"I never thought you were such a coward as to rob a woman," observed she, with indignant disgust, after demanding the return of her necklet several times, and being met with blank refusal.

"My dear Valérie," he replied coolly, "you needn't be surprised. When I want money, I'm ready to do anything in order to get it. But it's getting late," he continued, glancing at the clock. "Isn't it almost time you were at home?"

His bitter sarcasm maddened her. She did not speak for a few moments.

"I've had an illustration to-night of your fair dealing, Captain Willoughby," she said in a low, harsh voice, her face flushed with passion. "When I met you I meant to pay the amount I arranged, but now you've taken my jewellery from me by force, and acted as the scoundrel you are, not another farthing shall you have—"

"Oh, won't I? You'll pay up when I come to you next time."

"We shall see," she said meaningly; and, drawing her cloak around her, she pulled down her veil and left the room, banging the door after her.

She knew her way out, for it was evident that it was not the first time she had been there.

When alone, the captain reseated himself, and, taking the necklet from his pocket, examined it carefully with the eye of a connoisseur.

"Humph," he murmured to himself, "they seem well-matched stones. I shall ask old Vlieger two hundred and fifty for it, and he'll send it over to Amsterdam and get it out of the way in case any inquiries are made. You've had a very profitable evening, Percy, my boy—very profitable."

Chapter Twenty Four
Truth in Masquerade

Before Valérie had resided at Coombe six weeks she grew weary of the monotony of country life. In her discontented mood her surroundings were dull and uninteresting, while the local people she met lacked polish and *chic*, which, to her eyes, were the two necessary qualifications in acquaintances. Nothing was extraordinary in this, however. Women of the world meet in their life so many men and women—young, middle aged, and old—who commit all sorts of absurdities for or around them, that they end by entertaining a sovereign contempt for the whole human race, placing all persons in the same category. In each woman they see only an individual to impose upon and outvie in the matter of dress, and each fresh specimen of the genus man which is brought before them they regard only as a lamb destined for the sacrifice after being sufficiently shorn.

It was in consequence of an earnest wish she expressed that they had left Cornwall and travelled to Paris, taking up their abode at the Hôtel Continental.

Lounging in a capacious chair in the smoking-room, Hugh was scanning some letters he had just received. A few days had elapsed since their arrival, and this morning Valérie had gone out alone in order to visit her milliner in the Rue de la Paix. Left to his own resources, her husband had taken the letters that Jacob had forwarded to him, and, repairing to the smoking-room, endeavoured to amuse himself with their contents.

One which he had read and still held in his hand caused him to twirl his moustache thoughtfully and knit his brows.

Upon a half sheet of notepaper one sentence only was written, in a fine angular hand, and read:

"If you obtain a copy of the Paris newspaper, *Le Gaulois*, for 10th May, 1886, you will find in it something that will interest you."

It was dated from Chelsea, and signed by Dolly Vivian.

"Now, I wonder what on earth she means?" he exclaimed aloud, her strange request for an interview—to which he had not replied—recurring to him.

It was exceedingly curious, he thought, that she should write him these vague, puzzling letters, well knowing that he was married and could now be nothing more to her than a friend. There was a mystery about this last communication that had aroused his curiosity, and for some time he sat trying in vain to find an explanation of her strange conduct.

Suddenly he made a resolve. Gathering up his letters he thrust them into his pocket, and went to his room to get his overcoat.

"If your mistress returns, Nanette, tell her I've gone for a stroll, and shall return in an hour," he said to his wife's maid, who handed him his hat.

"Very well, m'sieur," the girl replied. Then, as Trethowen descended the stairs to leave the hotel, she watched him, and added to herself: "You will return in an hour, will you? Perhaps so; we shall see."

She laughed heartily, for something appeared to amuse her, and when he had disappeared she returned to her mistress's room and commenced packing a trunk.

As Trethowen walked along the Rue Castiglione, crossed the Place Vendôme, and went on towards the Boulevard des Capucines, a tall well-dressed man, with dark, pointed beard and curled moustaches, followed leisurely in his footsteps. This individual lounged aimlessly along, halting now and then to gaze into shop windows; nevertheless, from under the rather broad brim of his glossy silk hat a pair of keen grey eyes watched every movement of the man upon whom he was keeping observation. In the boulevard he was careful to cross to the opposite side of the way, in case the other should take a fancy to retrace his steps, for it appeared as if he did not desire an encounter. Sauntering along contemplating the engravings of the illustrated papers displayed in the kiosques, he loitered so naturally that to an ordinary observer he was but an honest citizen of the suburbs.

The morning was bright and frosty. Hugh, bent upon investigating the truth of Dolly's strange assertion, and unaware of the presence of the individual who had suddenly displayed such intense interest in his movements, walked down the Boulevard des Italiens, and, turning into the Rue Drouot, entered the offices of *Le Gaulois*.

Addressing one of the clerks at the counter, he said—

"I desire to search your file for May, 1886. Can I do so?"

"If m'sieur will have the kindness to fill up this form which we have for the purpose, I will see that the file is brought," replied the man politely, handing him a dip of paper and a pen.

Trethowen complied with this request, and waited rather impatiently, taking Dolly's letter from his pocket, and glancing at it to reassure himself that he had made no mistake in the date. There were many persons in the office, some transacting business and others reading that day's newspapers, which were spread open upon stands. Consequently he did not observe the entrance of three men, who, although coming in separately, met a short distance from where he stood, and held a hurried consultation in an undertone.

One of the men, apparently a respectable workman, took out an unmounted photograph from his wallet, glanced at it, and afterwards looked intently at Hugh who stood calmly unconscious of the scrutiny.

"It's our man, without a doubt," declared the workman emphatically. "I'd know him again amongst ten thousand."

"I wonder what his game is here?" asked the man who had dogged his footsteps from the hotel.

"Cannot you see? He's asked for the file of the month when the affair occurred," observed the third man. "Well, what of that?"

"The thing is quite plain. Out of morbid curiosity he wants to read what the paper said," replied his companion, who, turning to the workman, asked, "Have you any doubt that he is the same man?"

"None whatever."

"In that case we'll arrest him at once. He won't elude us this time."

The clerk had brought the formidable leather-bound volume and placed it upon a table, with the usual injunction that no extracts were allowed to be cut from it. Hugh was bending over it excitedly, and turning the pages to find the issue of 10th May, when he heard a voice behind him inquire—

"M'sieur Trethowen, I believe?"

Lifting his head in surprise, he faced his interrogator. "Yes," he replied in French, "that's my name, although I have not the pleasure of knowing yours, m'sieur."

"It scarcely will be a pleasure," the man replied, grinning sardonically. "I'm Paul Chémerault of the Detective Department, and I hold a warrant for your arrest," he added, producing a folded paper from his overcoat pocket.

"My arrest!" cried Trethowen incredulously. "What for, pray?"

He glanced in dismay at the two other men, who had now stepped up, and stood on either side of him.

"If m'sieur will come with us to the Bureau the charge will be explained. It is scarcely necessary to read it here and create a scene, is it?"

"I am an Englishman. By what right do you arrest me when I have committed no offence?" Hugh asked indignantly.

"That you are English we are aware, and also that you live at Coombe Hall, in the county of Cornwall. But as to your innocence—"

The man shrugged his shoulders significantly, and left his sentence unfinished.

"Of what offence am I guilty? Why, I've only been in Paris a few days."

"We know that. You arrived with madame, and have since stayed at the Hôtel Continental."

"Tell me what suspicions you have against me, and I shall be pleased to accompany you and make all necessary explanations."

Turning to the clerk the detective said, with a sarcastic smile—

"M'sieur will not require to use the volume now."

"Will you tell me of what I am accused?" asked Trethowen warmly.

"No; you will hear it read at the Bureau. Come, let us be going. We are attracting attention."

"I do not see why I should," argued Hugh angrily. "Take care, young fellow," said the detective, without getting at all excited; "you are spoiling your affair." This reply fell like cold water on Trethowen's anger. "We have a cab outside," continued the officer, "and we will drive to the Commissary's. You will calm yourself there. He'll soon settle the business, for he's a good-natured man. Come along."

Hugh made no reply to these exhortations. He saw that a cab was waiting outside, and that escape was impossible, therefore he accompanied the men and entered the vehicle. As they drove through the streets he remained in sullen silence, watching the festive aspect of the thoroughfares as they drove along. It was one of those dry winter mornings when the rich leave their chimney corners and walk towards the Champs Elysées to see if spring is coming, and to gain an appetite, while fashionable women, trip here and there, with their high heels beating an even tattoo on the dry sidewalks, and loiter before the milliners' windows—when the populace rejoice at breathing a balmy atmosphere and at not having to splash through mud. On such days as these there is joy in the air, and the panorama of the French capital, as seen from the quays, is truly a marvellous one.

Hugh Trethowen was amazed, puzzled to ascertain the meaning of this extraordinary arrest. Scarcely a word had been spoken since they started, but the detective, Chémerault, who sat opposite, very attentively examined the prisoner's features, as if trying to read the depths of his soul. Hugh noticed this inquisitorial look, and turned his head towards the window in the vehicle in a movement expressive of resentment.

They had covered the long line of quays at a slow, jogging pace, crossed the Pont Neuf, followed the Quai de l'Horloge, and turning off to the right, and passing a large gateway, stopped before a narrow passage.

"Here we are, m'sieur," said the chief detective, opening the door and springing out.

"You said that you would take me to the Commissary," exclaimed Trethowen, aroused from his reflections.

"It is all the same," replied the detective; "we are here, at the Préfecture of Police."

Hugh looked through the window, saw the two policemen on guard, the gloomy passage, the high frowning walls which enclosed the place, and threw himself back into the cab. He understood the truth. Instinctively he looked round for means of escape, but saw none.

One of the detectives graciously offered to assist him to alight, but, pushing the man aside impatiently, he got out. Bracing himself up against the emotion that at first overwhelmed him, he passed into the passage with his head erect and a gleam of assurance in his eyes. Chémerault and the man who had followed him from the hotel walked beside him. At the end of the corridor, flanked on both sides by the offices of inspectors and other officials, are the steps which lead to the office of the chief of the criminal investigation service.

"Which way shall I go?" asked Trethowen, pausing at the foot of the narrow, crooked flight, the stone of which is worn by the constant tread of detectives and criminals.

"Straight up; the door is before you on the first floor."

Hugh mounted the steps. He understood why his companions insisted on walking behind—that their politeness was merely prudence.

They entered a large bare room occupied by a couple of clerks, and meagrely furnished with a stool, a table, and a few rush-bottomed chairs. Chémerault offered a seat to his prisoner, who sat down without uttering a word. He was convinced that it was useless to struggle, and thought only of what crime could possibly be brought against him.

The clerks regarded the advent of the party with perfect indifference. They had seen many other well-dressed young men in a similar predicament, and after a casual glance at the prisoner continued their writing.

The detective asked them if the chief was in, and on their answering affirmatively, he went into an anteroom separating the outer one from the private office of the head of the department, and, after tapping at the door, entered.

Ten minutes later he emerged from the private room, and, after giving some instructions to the clerks, ordered the prisoner to accompany him into the presence of the chief.

During the brief interval which elapsed between the detective's exit and the prisoner's entry, the director of criminal investigations prepared himself for the interrogation. In the first examination, the advantage always lies with the examiner. The accused is unaware what mode of attack his interrogator is adopting, and cannot guess what points his replies are required to prove. The one is cool and calculating, the other confused, embarrassed, and dreading lest he should make any reply that may tell against him. The combat is by no means equal.

The chief, after reflection, looked steadily at the photograph which Chémerault had handed to him, then taking a bundle of blue papers from a pigeonhole at his elbow, untied the tape which bound them, and spread them out before him.

Just as he had done this the door opened and Hugh Trethowen advanced, conducted by the detectives.

"You may be seated, m'sieur," said the director of criminal investigations politely.

Hugh bowed stiffly, took the chair, and, striving to appear calm, waited to be questioned.

The chief did not commence at once. He always delayed his questions for a few moments in order to ascertain the sort of man with whom he had to deal. He looked at the prisoner and their eyes met. The doubts he had entertained with regard to the photograph were instantly removed. With that special memory for faces which an expert engaged in the investigation of crime acquires by long practice, he recognised the features of the accused, and in a moment decided how he should examine him and the principal points for confirmation.

Late that afternoon Monsieur Chémerault called at the bureau of the Hôtel Continental, and inquired for Madame Trethowen, saying that he had a note to deliver to her.

"Trethowen," repeated the clerk, looking through the book before him. "Ah, yes; Number 213. Left morning with her maid."

"Gone!"

"Yes. Madame's husband went out about eleven, she being already out. Almost as soon as he had gone, however, madame returned, paid the bill, and left, giving me this note for her husband when he came back."

"Perhaps it contains her address," remarked the detective, glancing at the superscription. "I'll see." Opening it, he found to his dismay that it contained only a blank sheet of paper.

"Oh," observed the detective to himself, "it seems she's playing a deeper game than I thought."

"Do you know whether she has left Paris?" he asked of the clerk, to whom he was known as a police agent.

"I really don't. The maid called the cab and I did not notice the number."

"You didn't hear the cabman receive any orders?" The clerk shook his head.

"Ah, that is unfortunate," observed the detective, perplexed. "Would not any one be likely to know where they went?"

"No; I was the only person in the courtyard when the cab drove out."

The detective, with an expression of disappointment replaced the paper in the envelope, and, announcing his intention of keeping it, placed it in his pocket. Then he left the hotel, and sauntered along to a small café in the Rue Auber, nearly opposite the Eden Theatre. That he had displayed a serious error of judgment in not acting with greater promptitude it was impossible to deny, and he was endeavouring to fix upon some plan whereby he could trace the woman who had left her husband so mysteriously and in such suspicious circumstances. Had he been wise, he told himself, he would have had an interview with Madame Trethowen as soon as her husband had been safely lodged inside the Préfecture. Now, however, he was baffled.

Evidently she feared a visit from the police, he argued, otherwise she would not have decamped, leaving only a piece of plain paper for her husband. Besides, the fact that she had left such a note was sufficient evidence to the detective that she was a clever woman, and, moreover, that she was desirous of hiding herself.

He remained at the café only long enough to swallow a glass of absinthe, then, hailing a cab, drove back to the Préfecture and consulted his chief.

From the central office inquiries were at once instituted, and within an hour it was ascertained that madame and her maid had driven from the hotel to the Gare du Nord, and left by the Brussels express, which started at 12:40. They had not booked to Brussels, but to Masnuy St. Pierre, a small Belgian town midway between Mons and Braine-le-Comte.

Monsieur Chémerault drove at once to the terminus, with the object of stopping them by telegraph before they left France. Almost breathless he alighted from his cab, and rushed upon the platform.

In a few moments he found the time-table of which he was in search. Running his finger down it, he saw that the train was timed to arrive at Quévy at half-past four, and at Mons at 5:02.

He glanced up at the large dock. It was a quarter past five.

"*Diable!* She's beaten us!" he cried with chagrin. "She's crossed the frontier and escaped!" At that moment one of his colleagues joined him. "We're too late," said Chémerault disappointedly. "She's got clear away. Somehow, I have a conviction that there is more in this case than we imagine. We must keep our eyes open, for if we arrest her, and she turns out to be the woman I believe she is, we shall find we have made a very important capture."

"Who is she?" asked his companion.

"Well, her name is Valérie—not an uncommon one, I admit; but if I was certain the surname she was once known by was Duvauchel, I would apply for her apprehension in Belgium, and extradition."

"Duvauchel! Why, that was in connection with the affair near St. Lazare, wasn't it—that celebrated case of yours?"

"Yes; I was unable to find a key to the mystery at the time, and now, after several years, the matter has come again into my hands quite unexpectedly," replied the detective. "To-morrow I shall recommence my inquiries, for the crime has always been particularly puzzling to me, and I should like nothing better than to be able to clear it up satisfactorily."

His companion expressed a hope that he would succeed, as both left the station, and directed their steps towards the Quai de l'Horloge.

Chapter Twenty Five
Shekels of Judas

Midnight in Brussels. Six months had passed since Valérie's hurried exit from Paris had baffled the most expert member of the Paris detective force.

The streets were quiet, almost deserted; the trees in the boulevards were stirred slightly by the soft wind, and the long lines of gas lamps flickered and cast an uncertain light as Pierre Rouillier, in evening dress, and with an Inverness cape about his shoulders, emerged from the Rue de Pépin, crossed the boulevard, and turned into the Chausée de Wavre. Whistling softly to himself, he continued his walk down the long, straight thoroughfare until within a few yards of the Rue Wiertz, where, before a large and rather gloomy-looking house, he halted. He gave two vigorous tugs at the bell, and Nanette opened the door.

"Ah!" the mud exclaimed, with familiarity, "it's a good thing you've come. Mademoiselle has been so anxious about you. Most of them are in a fine state."

"What! have they had supper, then?"

"Yes; and there are several fresh people—swells."

"Who are they?"

"You'll see."

"Who's there, Nanette?" asked a shrill, musical voice.

"M'sieur Rouillier, mademoiselle," replied the girl.

"Ah, Pierre!" said the voice; then it could be heard repeating in another direction: "Our young friend, Pierre, has arrived."

Immediately there was a chorus of approbation, and some one commenced singing the first verse of the *chansonette*, "Pierre, my long-lost love," as that distinguished personage walked into the room. Valérie was standing at the door, and whispered to him—

"There are some rich men here to-night. We can make a big *coup* if we are careful."

Then, turning to her guests, she exclaimed—

"Cease your chatter, please, just for one moment. Ladies and gentlemen, it is my pleasure to introduce to you—"

This was greeted with discordant cries—

"Enough! Everybody knows Pierre."

"Ladies, do please listen to me," implored Valérie. Continuing, Valérie again endeavoured to make herself heard.

"Gentlemen, I—"

At that moment somebody commenced to strum a waltz upon the piano, and, as if by magic, the twenty persons in the room rose to their feet and commenced to whirl madly round, while Valérie and Pierre stood at the door whispering and regarding the scene of Bacchanalian revelry with perfect satisfaction.

She liked to see her guests enjoy themselves.

"I want a few moments' private conversation with you," Pierre said, after they had been standing silent for a minute or two.

She acquiesced at once, and led the way to a small anteroom behind the drawing-room. It was furnished gaudily and cheaply, but quite in keeping with the rest of the house.

As he closed, the door, Pierre said—

"I've some good news."

"What is it?" she asked.

"Victor has fallen into the trap."

"Arrested?"

"Yes."

"Hurrah!" she cried, almost dancing for joy; "now we are safely rid of him we shall have nothing to fear. But, tell me, how did you manage to carry out the suggestion?"

"It was quite simple. We met in London three weeks ago, and I told him that he was running a great risk in remaining there, because the girl Vivian had discovered that it was he who gave her the little gash in the throat, and that she had placed the matter in the hands of the police. He asked my advice as to where he should go, and, of course, I suggested Paris. We arranged to go over separately, and meet at the old place a week later. He went, and as he stepped from the train at the St. Lazare he fell into the inviting arms of that vulture Chémerault."

"You had previously given information, I suppose?"

"Exactly."

"What was the charge?" she asked in a low tone.

"Complicity in the affair of the Englishman."

"Is he already sentenced?"

"Yes; to-day the Assize Court sent him to penal servitude for ten years. I had a telegram an hour ago. It will be in the papers to-morrow."

"Do you think that he'll peach upon us?" Valérie asked seriously.

"No, never fear that. He does not suspect that we put the police upon him; besides, he will live in the hope of escaping, and returning to you and your newly-acquired wealth."

"Yes, I suppose he will," she said, laughing. "But you've managed the affair very cleverly, and although it is hard to send such a boon companion to prison merely because you and I love one another, yet, after all, I suppose it's the best course."

"Undoubtedly, *ma chère*," he said. "Now both are safely in prison, we need fear nothing. Our manoeuvres have been successful in obtaining for us a fortune ample for our needs, and by keeping on this house, as well as yours in the Avenue de la Toison d'Or, we can continue to amuse ourselves profitably by getting our guests to stake their louis on the *tapis vert*. We have had many obstacles to face, but they are now all removed."

"Where is your wedding-ring—the one he gave you?" he asked.

She drew it from her purse, and handed it to him, wondering why he required it.

"This reminds you of him, I know," he said, as he turned and threw up the window. "See, I fling it away, for it's merely a worthless bond," and he tossed the ring as far as he could out into the road.

Valérie sighed. A tear stood in her eye. Even at that moment she was thinking of Hugh Trethowen. It was unusual for her to be troubled by recurring pangs of conscience, nevertheless his face had haunted her constantly during the past few months, and she could not get rid of the thought that some day a terrible Nemesis might fall and crush her.

"Why look so serious?"

"I was only thinking. It is one of woman's privileges," she said, laughing.

"Come, there is no cause for sadness surely. You have a handsome income. What more could you desire?"

Soon afterwards the unsuspecting guests departed, with aching heads and empty pockets. And Valérie was left alone.

Chapter Twenty Six
And You—A Clergyman

"Where is Mr Holt? I must see him at once."

"He's in the vestry, miss, talking to a gentleman. But he'll be disengaged in a moment," the verger replied.

"Very well. I'll wait."

The girl who had listened with disgust to the Sunday morning sermon preached by the Rev. Hubert Holt, and who had afterwards gone round to the vestry of the church of St. Barnabas, Camberwell, was Dolly Vivian.

A few days previously, while walking along Buckingham Palace Road, she unexpectedly passed the man who called himself Mansell. Attired as he was in the garb of a clergyman, she was not quite certain as to his identity with the man who had assisted in her abduction. Yet, with justifiable curiosity, she turned and set herself to watch him. For hours she dogged his footsteps, always at a respectable distance. First he went up Victoria Street, and along the Embankment to the City, then he crossed London Bridge and continued through the Borough and Walworth Road, ultimately entering one of a terrace of smoke-begrimed houses in Boyson Road, Camberwell. Once or twice while following him she contrived to obtain an uninterrupted view of his features, and each time felt more convinced that he was the man for whom she was in search.

When he had disappeared she returned, and noticed upon the railing outside the house was a small, tarnished brass plate bearing the name, "Rev. Hubert Holt." Carefully noting the number, she proceeded to make diligent inquiries, and was not long in discovering that Holt and Mansell was one and the same person, and that he was curate of St. Barnabas church, which was situated at the end of the road.

At first she was prompted to call upon him at once and denounce him; but on reflection she saw that such a course might not effect the object she had in view. She regarded him as a scoundrel, and in consequence carefully prepared a tableau by which she could obtain the information she sought, and if possible, compass his ruin. The vindictive nature latent in every woman was aroused in her when she discovered his hypocrisy, and she saw that if she met him face to face in the midst of his holy duties her revenge could be rendered more complete.

As she stood awaiting the interview her cheeks were flushed by excitement, and she nervously toyed with the buttons of her gloves. Her lips were compressed, her fair forehead was furrowed by an unbecoming frown of resolution, for she had resolved to meet him boldly, and show him no mercy.

"What name shall I tell Mr Holt, miss?" the verger asked, re-entering the small, bare anteroom a moment later.

"Never mind," she replied. "He—he doesn't know my name." Then the verger went out.

While she was uttering these words the curate's visitor—a tall, military-looking old gentleman—emerged from the vestry, leaving the door ajar.

Dolly pushed the door open and walked in, closing the door after her.

Holt was still in his surplice, standing beside the small writing-table.

He looked up as the intruder entered. The colour left his face, and he drew back in dismay when he recognised her.

"You!" he stammered. "I—I did not know you were here!"

"Yes," replied she sternly. "I'm not a welcome visitor, am I? Nevertheless, now I've found you, we have an account to settle."

He did not reply; but, the subject being distasteful to him, he walked quickly round the table and opened the door, which led into the church. She saw that his intention was to escape.

"Shut that door, if you don't wish our conversation to be overheard," she said, pale and determined. "Remember, you are in my hands, my reverend murderer!"

Starting at the word "murderer," he closed the door slowly, and stood with his back against it, and head bowed before her.

"Now," she said, advancing towards him, "first of all, I want to know what harm I have ever done you that you should drug me, and then attempt to kill me." The pointed question was asked in a tone that was the reverse of reassuring.

"I did not."

"To deny it is useless," she declared vehemently. "I have ample proof of your villainy; moreover, I intend that you shall be justly punished."

"Why, what do you mean to do?" he cried in alarm. He had been cleverly entrapped, and saw no means of escape from his irate victim.

"What I do depends entirely upon your attitude towards me," answered she in a calm tone. "Like a foolish girl, I trusted implicitly to your honour, and you—a clergyman—tried to kill me."

"I did not do it—indeed I did not."

"No; I am well aware that you were too cowardly to draw the knife across my throat. But you enticed me to dine with you: you put a narcotic into my wine and conveyed me to that house—for what purpose? Why, so that your cowardly accomplice might kill me." He was thoroughly alarmed. She evidently knew the whole circumstances, and it was useless, he thought, to conceal the truth.

"If—if I admit all this, may I not ask your pardon—your mercy?"

"Mercy!" she repeated. "What mercy did you show me when I was helpless in your hands? Only by a mere vagary of Fate I am not now in my grave. You thought you were safe—that your holy habiliments would prevent you being recognised as the man with whom I dined. But you made a great mistake, and I have found you."

"Will you not accept my apology?" he asked in a low voice.

"Upon one condition only."

"What is that?" he inquired eagerly.

"That you tell me the reasons which caused you to drug me, and the name of the scoundrel who assisted you," she replied calmly.

Their conversation was interrupted at this juncture by the reappearance of the verger, who inquired whether he would be wanted any more, as he had locked up the church, and was ready to go to his dinner. Holt replied in the negative, and the feeble old man departed, swinging his great bunch of jingling keys as he went.

When they were alone, the artist's model again referred to her stipulation, and pressed for an answer.

"No," he replied decisively, "I cannot tell you—I cannot."

"For what reason, pray?"

"The reason is best known to myself," he answered, endeavouring to assume an air of unconcern.

"You flatly refuse?"

"I do."

"In that case, then, I shall call the police, and have you arrested."

"No, my God! not that!" he cried; "anything but that."

"Ah, I can quite understand that police inquiries would be distasteful to you."

She paused, reflecting whether she should hazard a statement which she had overheard among other things in the conversation of her janitors at the lonely house near Twickenham.

At length she resolved to make an assertion, and watch its effect.

"If I'm not mistaken," she continued, regarding him closely, "the police are very desirous of interviewing you. They might like to hear some of your glib remarks about spiritual welfare, like those you made in the pulpit this morning."

"I don't understand you."

"If I speak plainer possibly you will. Some months ago a man was found dead on the railway. The affair is being investigated by the police, and—"

"God! You know of that!" he cried hoarsely, as he rushed towards her, and gripped her white throat with his hands in a frenzy of madness. "Speak lower—whisper—or—"

"No," urged Dolly, as coolly as she was able. "It would only add another crime to your list. Besides, if you comply with my stipulations, your secret will still be safe."

Her words had the desired effect. He released his hold, and, grasping her hand, pleaded forgiveness.

Flinging himself upon his knees before her, he pleaded for mercy, declaring that the injury he had done her was under sheer compulsion. He admitted he was a base, heartless villain, undeserving of pity or leniency; still he implored forgiveness on the ground that he had been sufficiently punished by a remorseful conscience.

But Dolly was inexorable to his appeals, and turned a deaf ear to his expressions of regret. She had come there for a fixed purpose, which she meant to accomplish at all hazards. It was evident he had some connection with the crime which she had heard discussed by the man and woman who had kept her prisoner, and it was likewise apparent that he was in deadly fear of the police. The effect of her remark about the murder had been almost magical, and she was at a loss how to account for it.

"Your entreaty is useless," she said coldly, after a few moments' reflection, stretching forth her hand and assisting him to his feet. She despised the cringing coward. "Before you need hope for leniency, I desire to know where Hugh Trethowen is to be found."

"I don't know him. How should I know?" he stammered confusedly.

By his agitation she was convinced he was not telling the truth.

"Oh, perhaps you will tell me next that you are unacquainted with Mr Egerton, the artist," she observed, with a curious smile.

"I've met him once, I think," replied the curate, with feigned reflection.

"And you declare solemnly that you know nothing of Hugh Trethowen?" she asked incredulously.

He shook his head.

"Then you are speaking falsely," she said angrily; "and the sooner we understand each other the better. You believe me to be a weak girl, easily cajoled, but you'll discover your mistake, sir, when it's too late—when you have fallen into the clutches of the police and your crime has been exposed."

"Do you think I'm going to allow you to give information!" he cried fiercely, shaking his fist threateningly before her face.

This outburst of passion did not intimidate her. Laughing, she said—

"I'm well aware that we are alone, and I'm completely in your power. If you are so anxious to murder me, you'd better set about it at once."

"Bah!" he exclaimed, turning from her with chagrin. "Why do you taunt me like this? Why did you come here and incite me to lay murderous hands upon you?"

"Merely because I desire some information—nothing more."

"Why do you seek it of me?"

"Because I know that with your assistance I can discover Hugh Trethowen. But we have parleyed long enough. I ask you now, for the last time, whether you wish me to show you mercy—whether you will answer my questions in confidence?"

He drew a deep breath, and stood motionless, perplexed and hesitating. They had emerged from the vestry, and were standing close to the altar. About her fair face shone a stream of richest life. This came from the painted window above—three bars of coloured sunlight, that bathed the hair in fire and left the dark body in deepest shadow.

"By betraying the secret I should run a great risk—how great you have little idea."

"Will not the risk be greater if you refuse to answer me?" she asked, looking at him steadily.

Her argument was conclusive. A few minutes, and he had apparently decided.

"Well, if you compel me, I suppose I must tell you," said he, dropping into a hoarse whisper. "If I do, you'll promise never to repeat it?"

"Yes," she replied eagerly.

"Swear to keep the secret. Indeed, it was through my efforts that your life was saved."

"I'll preserve silence," she promised. "Then, the truth is that you were the dangerous rival of a woman in the affections of a man whom she desired should marry her. The man merely admired her, but loved you. Having set her mind upon marrying him, she deliberately planned that you, the only obstacle, should be removed. The woman—"

"Whose name is Valérie Dedieu," interposed Dolly calmly.

"Why, how did you know?" he asked in surprise.

"I know more than you anticipate," replied she meaningly.

"Ah, it was a diabolical plot! The woman—I mean Valérie—planned it with Victor."

"Victor? Who is Victor?"

"Bérard—the man who attempted to take your life. But I was about to tell you how it was that I became complicated in the affair. The truth is, they compelled me. The Frenchwoman holds a certain power over me which causes me to be absolutely ruled by her caprices. In her hands I am helpless, for she can order me to perform any menial service, any crime, being fully aware that I could not—that I dare not—disobey her."

He spoke with heartfelt bitterness, as if the whole of the transactions were repugnant to him.

"And you—a clergyman!" Dolly incredulously observed.

"Yes. Unfortunately, our evil deeds pursue us. At times, when we least anticipate, the closed pages of one's life are reopened and revealed in all their hideousness."

"Yours is a bitter past, then?" she said in a tone of reproach. "Ah! now I understand. You are bound to mademoiselle with the same bond of guilt as Jack Egerton?"

"Who—who told you it was guilt?" he stammered.

"You and Mr Egerton are bound to Valérie Dedieu by a secret," she said.

An astounding thought had just crossed her mind. The Christian name Victor occurred frequently in the report in the *Gaulois*, which she had had translated, and which she had since treasured carefully, determined to use it as a final and unimpeachable document to bring Nemesis upon her enemy when occasion offered.

"I understand. Much is now plain to me," she continued in a firm, harsh voice. "Yet you have not answered my first question. Mademoiselle's husband left England some months ago, and has not since been heard of. Tell me, where is he?"

"I'm quite as ignorant of his whereabouts as yourself."

"Then, I'll put the question in another form. Why has Hugh Trethowen disappeared?"

"I don't know."

"I'm convinced that you know where he is."

"I do not. How should I?" he asked impatiently. "It is futile to prevaricate. If you are one of mademoiselle's myrmidons, as you admit, you surely can form some idea why he has disappeared so mysteriously. Are you not aware that he is no longer living with her, and that all efforts to discover him have been in vain?"

"I—I really know nothing, and care less, about your lover," he answered disdainfully. "Besides, why should you renew your friendship with him now he is married?"

His words maddened her. She had attacked her adversary with circumspection, but in her sudden ebullition of passionate indignation she gave vent to a flood of words, which, as soon as they were uttered, she regretted.

"I did not ask you to assist Hugh," she cried. "I know he—like myself—has fallen a victim to the machinations of your hired assassins. But you refuse to tell me where I can find him, and speak of him as my lover. Even if we do love one another, what does it concern you? Would you preach to me of morals?" This last remark caused him to start, and he scowled at her ominously. "I warn you," she said. "The day is not far distant when the whole mystery will be cleared up, and your villainy exposed."

"Perhaps so," he replied, with a forced laugh. "I'm sure I don't care."

"But you will, I fancy. You'll be glad enough, when the time arrives, to fall upon your knees, as you did just now, and beg for mercy."

"You're mad," he said in a tone of disgust.

She did not heed his remark, but continued—

"Perhaps," she cried, "you will deny that a celebrated case was recently investigated by the Assize Court of the Seine, and was popularly known as the Mystery of the Boulevard Haussmann. Perhaps you will deny that Valérie Dardignac and Mrs Trethowen are the same person; that she—"

"What are you saying?"

"The truth. Moreover, I tell you I intend having satisfaction from you who lured me almost to my death."

"Oh! How?" he asked defiantly.

"By a very simple process. I have merely to place the police in possession of the true facts regarding the crime which startled Paris not long ago. You shall not escape me now."

He stood erect, glaring at her, his mouth twitching, his face pale, with a murderous expression upon it.

"So those are your tactics, miss?" he cried, with rage, springing upon her, and clutching with both hands at her throat. "You are the only person who knows our secret."

"Help! police!" she shouted in alarm, noticing his determined manner.

Her cries echoed through the great empty church, but no assistance came.

His fingers tightened their hold upon her throat. He was strangling her.

The light had died away from above, and the shadows mingled in a shapeless mass.

"Help! help!" she screamed again; but her voice was fainter, for she was choking.

"Silence!" he hissed. "It's you—you who would brand me as a murderer, and send me to the gallows! Do you think I'm going to allow you to do that! By heaven, you shan't do it!"

She attempted to scream, but he placed his hand over her mouth.

His face was blanched, and his eyes gleamed with murderous hate as he glanced quickly around. His gaze fell upon the altar. Releasing her, he bounded towards it, and snatched up a heavy brass vase.

She saw his intention, but was powerless to recede.

"Help!" she shrieked.

Upon her throat she felt a hot hand; she saw the heavy vase uplifted above her.

"Take that!" he cried, as he brought it down upon her head with a crushing blow, and she fell senseless upon the stone pavement.

For a second or two he looked at her, wondering if she were dead. Then tearing off his surplice, he rushed into the vestry, and, putting on his coat and hat, fled from the church, locking the door after him.

The upturned face of the prostrate girl was calm and deathlike. She lay motionless upon the cold grey flags. The sun shone out again, and the coloured light, streaming from the stained-glass window, fell full upon her handsome features. But its warmth did not rouse her; she gave no sign of life.

Late in the afternoon, however, she struggled back to consciousness, and sat for a long time on the pulpit steps trying to calm herself and decide how to act.

The excruciating pain in her head would not allow her thoughts to shape sufficiently, so she made a tour of the building to discover some mode of egress. It was not long before she found that in one of the main doors the key had been left, and, unlocking it, she stepped out into the bright, warm afternoon with a feeling that a strange, oppressive weight had suddenly clouded her brain.

That evening the city clerks, small shopkeepers, with their wives and relations, who comprise the majority of the congregation of St. Barnabas, Camberwell, were agog when it transpired that their popular spiritual guide, the Rev. Hubert Holt, had suddenly thrown up his curacy. The vicar took the service, and at the conclusion announced with regret that his assistant had written to him that afternoon resigning his appointment, stating that a pressing engagement made it imperative that he should leave England at once. He gave no reason, but when the vicar sent round to his lodgings to request him to call and wish him adieu, it was discovered that he had packed a few things hurriedly, and already departed.

Then a local sensation was produced in the district between Denmark Hill and Camberwell Gate, and the devout parishioners prayed for the preservation and well-being of their popular but absent curate.

Chapter Twenty Seven
Silken Sackcloth

The certificate of death is all we require.

"I have it here."

"Why, how did you obtain it?"

"By a most fortunate circumstance. We saw one day, in the *Indépendance Belge*, that an unknown Englishman, apparently a gentleman, had died at the Hôtel du Nord at Antwerp. Pierre at once suggested that he might identify him as Hugh Trethowen. He went to Antwerp and did so. The man was buried as my husband, and here is the certificate."

"A very smart stroke of business—very smart. But—er—don't talk quite so plainly; you—"

"What do you mean? Surely you have no qualm of conscience? The payment we agreed upon ought to counteract all that."

"Of course. Nevertheless, it is unnecessary to refer to the strategy too frequently. As long as we have an indisputable death certificate in the name of Hugh Trethowen, and you have your marriage certificate as his wife, there will not be the slightest difficulty."

"I know that. To me you appear afraid lest we should be exposed."

"You need not upbraid me for exercising due caution. The success of the plan you have been so long maturing depends upon it. Supposing we were unable to prove the will, in what position should we be?"

"In an awkward one—decidedly awkward. But why speak of failure when we are bound to succeed?"

"Are you quite sure the—er—dead man will never trouble us?"

"Positive. A sentence of fifteen years in New Caledonia means certain death. He might just as well have been buried at once, poor devil!"

This confidential conversation took place in Mr Bernard Graham's gloomy private office in Devereux Court. The old solicitor, with a serious, intense expression upon his countenance, was sitting at his littered writing-table with a short legal document, covering only half of the sheet of foolscap, spread out upon his blotting-pad. Its purport was that the testator, Hugh Trethowen, left all he possessed to his "dear wife, Valérie," and the date of the signatures showed that it had been completed only a few days before they left Coombe for Paris.

In the client's chair, opposite her legal adviser, sat Valérie. Attired in deep mourning, that became her well, her thin black veil scarcely hid the anxious expression upon her face. Assuming her part with an actress's regard to detail, she did not overlook the fact that pallor was becoming to a widow; therefore, since she had put on the garments of sorrow, she had refrained from adding those little touches of carmine to her cheeks which she knew always enhanced her beauty. Neither her face nor voice betrayed signs of nervousness. With the steady, dogged perseverance of the inveterate gambler she had been playing for heavy stakes, and now, at the last throw of the dice, she had determined to win.

Their interview had been by appointment in order to arrange the final details. Now that Graham was in possession of the death certificate, he was to proceed at once to obtain probate on the will, after which the estate would pass to her. For his services in this matter, and in various other little affairs to which she was indebted to him, he was to receive twelve thousand pounds. A munificent fee, indeed, for proving a will!

There was a silence while the old solicitor took up the certificate she had handed him, and carefully scrutinised it. The declaration was quite plain and straightforward. It stated that Hugh Trethowen, English subject, had died from syncope at the Hôtel du Nord, and had been buried at the cemetery of Stuivenberg.

"If he lived to complete his sentence?" hazarded Mr Graham in a low voice, putting down the slip of paper, and removing his pince-nez to polish them. "Imprisoned persons, you know, have an awkward knack of turning up at an inopportune moment."

"And supposing he did, what could he prove?" she asked. "Has he not left a will bequeathing everything to me?—am I not mourning for him as his widow? Besides, he knows nothing—he can never know."

"I admit your cleverness," he said. "Notwithstanding that, however, we cannot be too circumspect."

"We've absolutely nothing to fear, I tell you," she exclaimed impatiently. "Hugh is as safely out of the way as if he were in his grave."

"And what of the others—Egerton, for instance?"

"He dare not breathe a word. As a matter of fact, he is ignorant of the whereabouts of his friend."

"Is Holt to be relied upon?"

"Absolutely. He has left the country."

"Oh! Where is he?"

"In America Through some unexplained cause he took a passage to New York. I expect he is in disgrace."

"Does he share?"

"Of course. He has written me a long letter announcing his intention not to return to England at present, and giving an address in Chicago where I am to send the money."

"Very good," Graham said approvingly. "As long as we can safely rely upon the secret being preserved, we need apprehend nothing."

"It will be preserved, never fear," declared Valérie flippantly. "They know how essential is secrecy for the safety of their own necks."

"Don't be so unsentimental," urged the old man smiling. "You talk a little too plainly."

"Merely the truth," declared she laughing. "But never mind—you prove the will, and the twelve thousand pounds are yours."

"Agreed. I shall take preliminary steps to-morrow."

"The sooner the better, you know."

"Shan't you live at Coombe?"

"Oh, what an idea!" she exclaimed in ridicule. "How could I live there among all those country busy-bodies and old fogies? I should cut a nice figure as a widow, shouldn't I? No. When I get the money I shall set up a good house here in London, mourn for a little time, then cast off my sackcloth and ashes."

"Remember," he said, "I am to receive twelve thousand pounds. But, really, you make a most charming widow."

"And you bestow a little flattery upon me as a sort of recognition," she observed, a trifle piqued at the point of his remark. Then, laughing again, she said lightly, "Well, if I really am so charming as some people tell me, I suppose I ought to be able to keep my head above water in the social vortex. At all events I mean to try."

"You cannot fail. Your beauty is always fatal to those who oppose you," he remarked pleasantly.

"We shall see!" she exclaimed, with a merry little peal of laughter. Rising and stretching forth her hand, she added, "I must be going. I consign the certificate to your care, and if you want me you know my address. I shall remain in London till the matter is settled."

The old man rose, and grasped the hand offered to him. Bidding her adieu, he again assured her that he would give his prompt attention to the business on hand, and, as his clerk entered at that moment, he ceremoniously bowed her out.

During the time Valérie had been in conversation with Mr Graham, a woman had been standing on the opposite side of the Strand, against the railings of the Law Courts, intently watching the persons emerging from Devereux Court. She was young and not bad-looking, but her wan face betrayed the pinch of poverty, and her dress, although rather shabby, was nevertheless fashionable. Her dark features were refined, and her bright eyes had an earnest, intense look in them as she stood in watchful expectancy.

After she had kept the narrow passage under observation for nearly an hour, the object of her diligent investigation suddenly came into view. It was Valérie, who, when she gained the thoroughfare, hesitated for a moment whether she should walk or take a cab to the Prince of Wales' Club. Deciding upon the former course, as she wanted to call at a shop on the way, she turned and walked along the Strand in the direction of Charing Cross.

When the woman who had been waiting caught sight of her she gave vent to an imprecation, the fingers of her gloveless hands twitched nervously, and her sharp nails buried themselves in the flesh of her palms.

As she started to walk in the same direction she muttered aloud to herself, in mixed French and English—

"Then I was not mistaken. To think I have waited for so long, and I find you here! You little dream that I am here! Ah, you fancy you have been clever; that your secret is safe; that the police here in London will not know Valérie Dedieu! You have yet to discover your mistake. Ha, ha! what a tableau that will be when you and I are quits! *Bien*, for the present I will wait and ascertain what is going on."

Throughout the whole length of the Strand the strange woman walked on the opposite pavement, always keeping Valérie in sight—a difficult task sometimes, owing to the crowded state of the thoroughfare. At a jeweller's near Charing Cross, Mrs Trethowen stopped for a few minutes, then, resuming her walk, crossed Trafalgar Square, and went up the Haymarket to the Prince of Wales' Club, calmly unconscious of the woman who was following and taking such intense interest in her movements.

Muttering to herself sentences in French, interspersed by many epithets and imprecations, she waited for Valérie's reappearance, and then continued to follow her down the Haymarket and through St. James's Park to her flat in Victoria Street.

She saw her enter the building, and, after allowing her a few moments to ascend the stairs, returned and ascertained the number of the suite.

Then she turned away and walked in the direction of Westminster Bridge, smiling and evidently on very good terms with herself. Indeed, she had made a discovery which meant almost more to her than she could realise.

Chapter Twenty Eight
At La Nouvelle

A wide, vast expanse of glassy sapphire sea.

The giant mountains rose in the west, sheer and steep—purple barriers between the land and the setting sun. A golden fire edging their white crests, that grew from their own dense, sombre shadows to the crimson light which flooded their heads, solemn and silent. And the calm Pacific Ocean lay unruffled in the brilliant blood-red afterglow.

Seated upon a great lichen-covered boulder on the outskirts of a dense forest, a solitary man gazed blankly and with unutterable sadness upon the magnificent scene. Above him the trees were hung with a drapery of vines and tropical creepers bearing red and purple flowers, and forming natural arches and bowers more beautiful than ever fashioned by man. Parrots and other birds of bright plumage were flying about among the trees— among them guacamayas, or great macaws, large, clothed in red, yellow, and green, and when on the wing displaying a splendid plumage. But there were also vultures and scorpions, and, running across the road to the beach and up the trees, innumerable iguanas. Great cocoanut and plantain trees jutted out and massed themselves to the right and to the left. A mountain torrent, sweeping swiftly over a moss-grown rocky ledge, seethed for a few moments in white foam, and then gurgled away down the bright shingles into the sea.

The man sat there stonily, voiceless, motionless, his chin fallen upon his chest, his hands clasped in front of him. Dressed in grey shirt and trousers that were ragged and covered with dust and dried clay, his appearance was scarcely prepossessing. On the back of his shirt was painted in large black numerals "3098," and his ankles were fettered by two oblong iron links. He was a convict.

Under the broad-brimmed, battered straw hat that protected his head from the tropical glare was a ruddy, auburn-bearded face, with sad blue eyes which at times turned anxiously up and down the beach path—the sun-tanned face of Hugh Trethowen.

His pickaxe lay on the ground before him, for he was resting after his long day's toil in the mine.

Toil! He shuddered when he thought of the weary monotony of his life. Down in the dark, dismal working he was compelled to hew and delve for twelve hours each day, and to satisfactorily perform the task set him by his warder before he was allowed his ration of food. Half an hour's relaxation when leaving the mine was all that the discipline allowed, after which the convicts were compelled to return to the prison to their evening meal, and afterwards to work at various trades for two hours longer before they were sent to their cells. The French Republic shows no leniency towards prisoners condemned to *travaux forces*, and transported to the penal settlement in New Caledonia, consequently the latter live under a régime that is terribly harsh and oft-times absolutely inhuman.

Instead of chattering with the *forcats*, assassins, robbers, and scoundrels of all denominations and varieties of crime who were his fellow-prisoners, Hugh, in the brief half-hour's respite, usually came daily to the same spot, to reflect upon his position, and try to devise some means of escape.

His conviction and transportation had been so rapid that only a confused recollection of it existed in his memory. He remembered the Assize Court — how the sun insolently, ironically, cast his joyous, sparkling beams into the gloomy, densely packed apartment. The hall, dismal and smoke-begrimed, is anything but imposing at best, but it was filled with the foetid exhalations from the crowd that had long taken up every vacant space. The gendarmes at his side looked at one another and smiled. The evidence was given — what it was he did not thoroughly understand — yet he, an upright man, resolute, honest to the very soul, and good-natured to simplicity, found himself accused of complicity in the murder of a man he had never heard of. Despondent at Valérie's desertion, he took no steps to defend himself; he was heedless of everything.

Then the verdict was pronounced, and the sentence — fifteen years' penal servitude!

He heard it, but in his apathetic frame of mind he was unaffected by it. He smiled as he recognised how mean was this noted Criminal Court of the Seine, with its paltry chandelier, the smoky ceiling, and the battered crucifix that hung over the bench on which the judges sat in their scarlet robes. Suddenly he thought of Valérie. Surely she would know through the newspapers that his trial was fixed for that day? Why did she not come forward and assist him in proving his innocence.

He strained his eyes among the sea of faces that were turned towards him with the same inquisitive look. She was not there.

"Prisoner, have you anything to say?" asked the presiding judge, when he delivered sentence.

The question fell upon Hugh's ears and roused him. The thought that Valérie had made no sign since his arrest, although he had written to her, again recurred to him. The die was cast. What probability, what hope, was there of liberty? For the twentieth time, perhaps, this cruel agony, this doubt as to Valérie's faithfulness, returned to him. She was absent; she had forsaken him.

"Will you answer me, prisoner? Have you anything to say?" repeated the judge sternly.

"I wish to say nothing, except that I am entirely innocent."

Then they hurried him back to his cell.

He had a hazy recollection of a brief incarceration in the Toulon convict prison, after which came the long voyage to La Nouvelle, and the settlement into the dull, hopeless existence he was now leading—a life so terrible that more than once he longed for death instead.

Sitting there that evening, he was thinking of his wife, refusing even then to believe that she had willingly held aloof from him. He felt confident that by some unfortunate freak of fate she had been unaware of his arrest, and might still be searching for him in vain. Perhaps the letters he wrote to her to the hotel and to Coombe might never have been posted. If they had not, there was now no chance of sending a message home, for one of the rules observed most strictly in the penal colony is that letters from convicts to their friends are forbidden. The unfortunate ones are completely isolated from the world. The families of French prisoners sent out to the Pacific Islands can obtain news of them at the Bureau of Prisons in Paris, but nowhere else. When convicts are handed over to the governor of the colony, their names are not given; they are known henceforth by numbers only.

Convict number 3098 knew that it was useless to hope any longer, yet it was almost incredible, he told himself, that he, an innocent man and an English subject, should be sent there to a living tomb for an offence that he did not commit—for the murder of a person whose name he had never before heard.

"I wonder where Valérie is now?" he said aloud, giving vent to a long-drawn sigh. "I wonder whether she ever thinks about me? Perhaps she does; perhaps she is wearing her heart out scouring every continental city in a futile endeavour to find me; perhaps—perhaps she'll think I'm dead, and after a year or two of mourning marry some one else."

He uttered the words in a low voice, more marked by suffering than by resignation. He preferred the companionship of his own thoughts, sad as they were; his mind always turned to Valérie, to the sad ruin of all his hopes.

"And Jack Egerton," he continued, resting his chin upon his hands; "he must know, too, that I have disappeared. Will he seek me? Yet, what's the use of hoping—trusting in the impossible—no one would dream of finding me in a French convict prison. No," he added bitterly, "I must abandon hope, which at best is but a phantom pursued by eager fools. I must cast aside all thought of returning to civilisation, to home—to Valérie. I've seen her—seen her for the last time! No, it can't be that we shall ever meet—that I shall ever set eyes again upon the woman who is more to me than life itself!"

He paused. In his ears there seemed to ring a little peal of Valérie's silvery laughter, which mocked the chill, dead despair that had buried itself so deeply in his heart.

The tears sprang to his eyes, but he wiped them away with a brusque movement, and looked about abstractedly. The sun had set behind the crags, and had been succeeded by the soft tropical twilight. A faint breeze was abroad. The sough of the leaves above was lost in the gurgling of the mountain torrent as it rushed over its rocky bed. The palms, played upon by the wind, made a sound of their own. It was silence in the midst of sound, and sound in the midst of silence—majestic, contradictory, although natural.

"And I shall never see her again!" he murmured. "I shall remain here working and living from day to day, a blank, aimless existence until I die. I've heard it said that Fate puts her mark on those she intends to strike, and the truth of that I've never recognised until now. I remember what a strange apprehensive feeling came over me on the night we left London for Paris—a kind of foreboding that misfortune was upon me, a strange presage of evil. Again, that warning of Dolly's was curious. I wonder what was contained in that newspaper report that she so particularly desired me to see? I'm sure Dolly loved me. If I had married her, perhaps, after all, I should have been happier. It was inflicting an absolute cruelty upon her when I cast her aside and married Valérie. Yet she bore it silently, without complaint, although I'm confident it almost broke her heart, poor girl!"

Sighing heavily, he passed his grimy, blistered hand wearily across his forehead.

"To think that I'm dead to them; that we shall never again meet! It seems impossible, although it's the plain, undisguised truth. That canting old priest told me yesterday that God would extend His mercy to those of us who sought it. Bah! I don't believe it. If the circumstances of our lives were controlled by the Almighty, He would never allow an innocent man like myself to suffer such punishment unjustly. No," he declared in a wild outburst of despair, "the belief that God is Master of the world is an exploded fallacy. What proof have we of the existence of a Supreme Being? None. What proof of a life hereafter? None. Religion is a mere sentimental pastime for women and fools. For priests to try and convert convicts is a sorry, miserable farce. There is no God!"

Several minutes elapsed, during which he thought seriously upon the mad words that had escaped him. The recollection of the religious teaching he had received at his mother's knee came back to him. He had often jested at holy things, but never before had he been smitten by conscience as now.

"Suppose—suppose, after all, there is an Almighty Power," he said thoughtfully, in an awed voice. "Suppose it is enabled to direct circumstances and control destiny. In that case God could give me freedom. He could give Valérie back to me, and I should return home and resume the perfect happiness that was so brief and so suddenly dispelled. Ah! if such things could be! And—why not? My mother—did she not believe in God? Were not the words she uttered with her dying breath a declaration of implicit trust in Him? Did she not die peacefully because of her firm, unshaken faith?"

Jumping to his feet with a sudden resolution, he stretched forth his hands in supplication to heaven, exclaiming, in a hoarse, half-choked whisper—

"I—I believe—yes, I believe there's a Ruling Power. No! I'll not abandon all hope yet."

His arms dropped listlessly to his side again, and he sank upon the boulder where he had been sitting, silent and thoughtful, wondering whether freedom would ever again be his.

"Hulloa," exclaimed a voice in French. "Why, what's the matter? Any one watching you from a distance, as I've been doing, would think you'd taken leave of your senses."

Glancing up quickly, he saw it was a bearded, unkempt prisoner who, condemned to a sentence *à perpétuité*, worked in the mine in the same labour gang as himself.

"I hope you've enjoyed the entertainment," he said, in annoyance.

"Entertainment," echoed the other. "There is scarcely entertainment in the *mauvais quart-d'heure*, is there? Bah! we all of us in this malarial death-trap have periods of melancholy, more or less. For myself, I'm never troubled with them. When you've been here a few years you'll see the folly of giving way to gloomy thoughts, and the utter uselessness of entertaining any anticipation of either escape or release."

"But we may still hope."

"Hope! What's the use? What can we hope for—except death?" he asked bitterly. Then, without waiting for a reply, he said, "Let's forget it all; we shall die some day, and then we shall obtain rest and peace, perhaps."

"We cannot all forget so easily."

"There, don't talk so dismally. Come, we must be going."

"Where?"

"To the cage," he replied, indicating the prison by the sobriquet bestowed upon it by the convicts. "The gun has sounded. Did you not hear it? Come, we must hasten, or you know the penalty."

Hugh sighed again, rose to his feet, took up his pickaxe, and, placing it upon his shoulder, walked with heavy wearied steps beside his companion in misfortune. Both trudged on in dogged silence, broken only by the clanking of their leg-irons, for nearly a quarter of a mile along the rough beach path, until they came to a broader path leading inland, with dense forests on either side.

Here they were met by two armed warders, who roundly abused them for their tardy appearance, and who escorted them within the grim portals of the long, low stone building which stood upon the side of the bare, rugged mountain overlooking Noumea.

Chapter Twenty Nine
Gilded Sorrow

"Good heavens! Why, it can't be true."

The exclamation escaped Jack Egerton's lips as he sat in his studio enjoying his matutinal pipe, and glancing through the *Daily News* prior to commencing work.

The paragraph he had read contained nothing startling to the ordinary newspaper reader. It was merely an announcement that the will had been proved of the late Mr Hugh Trethowen, of Coombe Hall, Cornwall, who died suddenly at the Hôtel du Nord, Antwerp, and that the whole of the estate, valued at 112,000 pounds, had been left to his wife Valérie.

"Dead! Dead! And I knew nothing of it, poor fellow!" he cried, starting up, and, after re-reading the words, standing motionless. "Died suddenly," he reflected bitterly. "An ominous expression where Valérie Dedieu is concerned. More than one person who has enjoyed her acquaintance has *died suddenly*. If I thought he had met with foul play, and could prove it, by Heaven! I'd do so—even at the risk of my own liberty. Poor Hugh," he added in a low, broken voice. "We have been almost brothers. God! shall I ever forgive myself for not warning him of his danger? Yet I did tell him she was not fit to be his wife, but he took no heed. No; he was infatuated by her fatally seductive smiles and accursed beauty."

Pushing the hair from his forehead he flung the paper from him with a gesture of despair.

"Dead," he murmured. "How much I owe to him. In the days when I scarcely earned enough to keep body and soul together, we shared one another's luck, Bohemians that we were, often living from hand to mouth, and not knowing whence the next half-crown was to come. Always my warmest friend from that time until his marriage: he was an irrepressible, genial, good fellow, whom everybody held in high esteem. Always merry, always light-hearted; in many a dark hour, when I've been on the verge of despair, it has been his perfect indifference to melancholy that has cheered and given me heart; nay, it was by his advice and encouragement that, instead of going out to the Transvaal as I intended, I remained here to work and win fame."

He sighed deeply, and tears welled in his eyes.

"I have no brother; he was one—and—and I've lost him. I should have liked to have been at the funeral to have paid a last tribute to his memory. Had I placed a wreath upon the grave, it would have been with hands more tender than any of those persons who showed outward bereavement. Where was the widow, I wonder?"

As he paused, his face grew stern and he clenched his hands.

"Bah! The widow who, by his death, has gained one hundred and twelve thousand pounds—the woman who, staking life for gold, held him in her fatal toils until death severed the bond. I wonder—I wonder, if I went to Antwerp, whether I could discover evidence of foul play? Is it not my duty to try? If he has met the same terrible fate as—"

"Good-morning, Jack!" exclaimed Dolly Vivian brightly, tripping into the room.

"Good-morning," he assented sullenly, without looking up at her.

"How disagreeable you are to-day," she observed, as she commenced unbuttoning her glove. "Anything wrong?"

"Yes, a good deal. I shan't want you; I can't work to-day," he replied sadly.

"What's the matter?" she asked in alarm, advancing towards him and placing her hand upon his arm.

Turning with a sigh, he looked into her face and said, in a low, earnest tone—

"Dolly, I've received bad news."

"What is it—tell me? Don't keep me in suspense."

"It is about some one you know."

"News of Hugh?" she cried, her thoughts at once reverting to the man she loved.

He nodded, but did not reply.

"What of him? Where is he?"

"Dolly," he said hesitatingly,—"he is dead."

"Dead!" she gasped, clutching at a chair for support.

She would have fallen had he not rushed to her and placed his arm around her waist. In a few moments, however, she recovered herself.

"You—you tell me he is dead. How do you know?"

"By the newspaper."

"Dead! Hugh dead! I can't—no, I won't believe it," she cried wildly. "There must be some mistake."

"He died suddenly at Antwerp," Jack said mechanically.

"You mean he has been killed—that his wife is a murderess."

"Hush, Dolly," he exclaimed quickly; "you cannot prove that, remember."

"Oh, can't I? If he has been murdered, I will discover the truth. Her past is better known to me than she imagines. I'll denounce Valérie Duvauchel as the woman who—"

"Why, how did you know that was her name?" he asked in amazement and undisguised alarm.

"What was I saying? Forgive me if I made any unjust remark, but I could not help it," she urged. "It is all so sudden—and—and he is dead."

She knew she had said too much, and tried to hide her confusion in the intense grief which his announcement had caused.

"You said her name was Duvauchel?" he said quietly.

"Did I? Well, what of that?"

"You are acquainted with incidents of her past. What is it you know? Tell me."

She hesitated. Her face was white and agitated, but she had shed no tears. Her heart was stricken with grief, yet she strove to conceal her intense love for the man who was reported dead.

"Why," she answered slowly, "I know that she—but—indeed, I know nothing," she added hysterically.

"That's not the truth," he said reproachfully.

"Perhaps not. Nevertheless, what I know I shall keep secret. The time may come when I shall have my revenge upon the woman who has robbed me of the man I love—the vile, heartless woman who has killed him."

"You cannot prove that he met with his death by foul means," he said reflectively. "The report says he died suddenly—nothing more. Read for yourself," and he handed her the paper, at the same time pointing to the paragraph.

"Then she has obtained all his money?" Dolly observed mechanically, after she had glanced at it. "Is not that sufficient motive for his death?"

The artist admitted that it was. The unutterable sadness of ten minutes before had given place to a strange apprehensive dread. It was clear that Dolly was in possession of some facts connected with the hidden pages of the Frenchwoman's history. In that case, he told himself, it was more than probable she would ultimately discover his own secret—the secret which fettered him to this clever, handsome adventuress, even if she were not acquainted with it already. His heart sank within him as he recognised that alienation and loathing would be the inevitable result Dolly would shrink from his touch as from some unclean thing. She would regard him as a debased criminal.

He tried to fix upon some means by which to ascertain the extent of her information. The thought suggested itself that he should tell her something of Valérie's history, and lead her on to divulge what she knew. Such a course, however, did not commend itself to him. He was bound to preserve the secret, for full well he knew that Valérie's threats were never idle—that she would show him no mercy if he divulged.

Thus he was as powerless as before. The maddening thought flashed through his mind that a plain, straightforward statement of facts to Hugh when first he had met her would have obviated his ruin and prevented his death.

To and fro he paced the studio in a frenzy of grief and despair.

The pretty model watched him for a moment, then, sinking upon a couch, and covering her face with her hands, burst into a torrent of tears. Unable to control her bitter sorrow, her pent-up feelings obtained vent in a manner that was heart-rending to the kind, sensitive man who stood before her.

"Dolly, I know what a terrible blow this is to you," said he sympathetically, removing her hat, and tenderly stroking her hair. "You loved him?"

She did not answer at once, hesitating even then to admit the truth.

"Yes," she sobbed at last, "I did. You little know what I have endured for his sake."

"Ah! I can well understand. You loved him dearly, yet he left you for the woman who exercised a fatal fascination upon him. With scarcely a word of farewell, he cast your love aside and offered Valérie marriage. I know the depth of your disappointment and terrible sorrow. Don't think that because I have never made love to you that I am utterly devoid of affection. I loved—once—and it brought me grief quite as poignant as yours; therefore I can sympathise with you."

He spoke with sadness, and with a heavy sigh passed his hand with aweary gesture across his care-lined brow.

"It's so foolish of me," she murmured apologetically, in a low, broken voice. "I ought not to have made this confession."

"Why not? I had noticed it long ago. Love always betrays itself."

Lifting her sad, tear-stained face, she looked earnestly into his eyes.

"What can you think of me, Jack?" she asked.

"Think of you?" he repeated. "Why, the same as I have always done—that you are an upright, honest woman. Neither blame nor dishonour attaches to you. When he left you so cruelly, you bore your sorrow bravely, thinking, no doubt, that some day he might return and make you happy. Was not that so?"

She nodded an affirmative. Her gaze was fixed thoughtfully on the canvas which stood on an easel behind him; her slim, white hands were crossed in front of her.

"Since we parted," she said, in a strained, broken voice, as if speaking to herself, "he has been uppermost in my thoughts. Often when I have been alone, indulging in dreamy musings, I have looked up and seemed to see him standing contemplating me. Then all the regret has fled from my heart, and paradise has stolen in. He has spoken to me, smiled at me, as he did in those pleasant days when first we knew each other. Yet next moment the vision would fade before my eyes, and I have found myself deceived by a mere chimera, tricked by an idle fancy. But now he is dead: gone from me never to return—never."

And she again gave way to tears, sobbing bitterly.

"Come, come, Dolly," said the artist, again passing his hand lightly over her hair, endeavouring to soothe her; "don't be downhearted. Yours is a cruel and heavy sorrow, I know; but try to bear up against it, try to think that perhaps, as you suggested, he is not dead. Even if you have lost your lover, you have in me a true and trusted friend."

"Yes, I know," she sobbed brokenly. "You are my only friend. It is extremely kind of you to talk like this; yet you cannot know the extent of my love for him."

"I quite realise how much you cared for him," he said slowly, in a pained voice. "If he had married you, his life would have been peaceful and happy. Fate, however, decreed different, and, that being the case, you must try to forget him."

"Forget him! Never!" she cried. Then recovering herself, she added: "Excuse what I say; I hardly know what I've been telling you."

"Whatever has passed between us will always be kept secret," he assured her.

"Ah! I feel sure you will tell no one; you are always loyal to a woman."

"Now, promise to think less about him," he urged, looking down into her grief-stricken face.

"I cannot," she replied firmly. "Somehow, I don't believe that he is dead. I shall endeavour to clear up the mystery and ascertain the truth."

"And I will render you what assistance I can. Count upon my help," he said enthusiastically. "We'll get at the real facts somehow or other."

"You are very kind," she answered, drying her tears, and putting on her veil before the mirror. "I have a terrible headache, and am fit for nothing to-day, so I'll go home."

To this proposal the artist offered no objection. Her inconsolable grief pained him, and he wanted to be alone to think; so, grasping her hand warmly, he again urged her to bear up under her burden, and watched her walk slowly out, with bowed head and uneven steps.

Chapter Thirty
The Englishman of the Boulevard Haussmann

A calm, boundless waste of sunlit sea. Three men, haggard, blear-eyed, and staring, sat in dejected attitudes in a small, open boat. The blazing noonday sun beat down mercilessly upon their uncovered heads, reflecting from the water's unruffled surface, blinding them by its intense glare.

There was not the faintest breath of wind, not a speck upon the clearly-defined horizon—nothing but the wide, brilliant expanse of the Pacific. Long ago all hope of rescue had been abandoned. One of the ragged, unkempt trio was lashed tightly to the thwarts for, having slaked his thirst with sea water, he had developed insanity, and his companions had bound him fast where he sat, wide-eyed and dishevelled, giving vent at frequent intervals to the drivel of an idiot, plentifully punctuated with horrible imprecations.

The two others, thin-faced, careworn, and anxious, sat silent, motionless, in blank, unutterable despair. Ever and anon their aching, bloodshot eyes wandered wearily around in search of a passing sail, but never once had a mast been sighted, for they were out of the track of the ships. In dress each bore a resemblance to the other, inasmuch as numbers were painted conspicuously on their backs, while the wrists of the one who had become demented were still in bracelets of rusted steel, although the connecting link had been broken. They were three bearded, dirty, repulsive-looking criminals, who, having been so far successful as to escape from New Caledonia, had discovered, to their dismay and horror, that their bold dash for liberty had been in vain—that they had escaped their taskmasters only to be ultimately overcome by thirst and starvation.

The heat was awful. The blazing sun parched their mouths, and set their brains aflame with fever. Though now and then they sucked the horn hilts of their knives in an endeavour to alleviate the all-consuming thirst, yet their throats were too dry to utter scarcely a syllable. Rowing was useless, conversation was useless, hope was useless. Abandoned to despair, they were patiently awaiting the moment when body and soul would part. They suffered most because they still remained sane.

Six days ago Hugh Trethowen and two fellow-prisoners had been told off from the labour gang to convey stones from the seashore to a spot several miles distant, where a road was being made through the forest. Unaccompanied by the warder, they had made several journeys with the ox-cart, when, on returning to the beach, they observed, to their surprise and satisfaction, that a boat had been run ashore from a ship lying on the opposite side of the headland, and that the crew had left it, evidently proceeding inland in search of provisions.

The prospect of escape immediately suggested itself, and ten minutes later the three men had embarked, and were rowing swiftly round another headland, so as to avoid being observed by those on the ship. After proceeding a couple of miles along a shore they well knew was deserted, they turned the boat's head and made straight for the open sea. Excited at the prospect of freedom, all three bent to the oars, exerting every muscle, for they were compelled to get out of sight before their absence was discovered, otherwise they would be pursued and most probably shot down.

Onward they pulled, until the island was only just visible, a dark blue line upon the far-off horizon: then after pausing for half-an-hour's rest, they resumed rowing with courage and confidence inspired by thoughts of the free life that lay before them.

The cool breeze of evening refreshed them, and through the long night they struggled on, bending to their oars with a will, even singing snatches of songs to the rhythm of the oars in the rowlocks. Never since their transportation had they experienced such joy as during those first few hours of freedom on the wide silent sea. But happiness does not allay hunger, and when about midnight they thought of food, they discovered to their dismay that there was not a morsel of anything eatable or a drop of fresh water in the boat.

Deep gloomy forebodings succeeded their brief period of happiness, and just before dawn the hungry, adventurous fugitives threw themselves down in the bottom of the boat and slept. In the morning the wind dropped, and there was a dead, breathless calm, that had since been unbroken.

Hugh Trethowen sat motionless and helpless, enduring in silence agony indescribable. Whither they were drifting he knew not, cared not. He knew his fate was sealed.

His companion was the man who had spoken to him on that evening when he was hesitating whether he should abandon belief in an Almighty Power, and now, as he leaned beside his fellow-convict, he was wondering which of them would die first. His brain was on fire; he could not move his eyes without acute pain, for their sockets felt as if they had been filled with molten lead. The pains through his cramped limbs were excruciating, yet he was in a drowsy lethargy—conscious and alive to the fact that the bodily torture was fast sapping his life; that ere the sun went down he would be dead.

The hours of furnace heat wore on more slowly than before: hunger, thirst, and madness waxed fiercer.

With that strange faculty possessed by dying persons he seemed to live the chief incidents of his career over again, each vividly and in rapid succession. But in all his wife was the central figure. The thought that he should never see her again—that now, when within an ace of regaining freedom and returning to her, he was to be cut off—roused him. Struggling against these gloomy apprehensions, he ground his teeth and, resting his elbows on his knees, determined to conquer pain and cheat the Avenger.

Taking the handkerchief from his forehead, he dipped it into the sea and again bandaged his head.

The other man looked up and moaned. He had passed the active stage of suffering. All grew more and more like a confused dream, in which he saw nothing clearly, except, at intervals, the grave sadness of Trethowen's face, as he sat awaiting insanity or death.

The groans of his fellow-sufferer did not escape Hugh. He groped about and found a small piece of canvas to lay under the man's head; it was all he could do to make him comfortable.

There was but little difference in the condition of all three now. Even the madman's fit had passed away, and he was lying back motionless, with bright, fevered eyes gazing aimlessly upward into the cloudless vault of blue.

After a long silence, broken only by the gasps and agonised groans of the suffering men, the convict by whose side Hugh was lying stirred uneasily, and turned his wide-open, glassy eyes towards his companion. "Tre—Tre—thowen!" he gasped hoarsely.

Hugh started up in surprise. All his strength came back to him in that moment. It was the first time he had been addressed by name since his transportation.

"How do you know me?" he inquired in French, regarding the prostrate man with a new interest.

The other sighed as he pressed his hand to his burning brow.

"*Dieu!*" he cried, "this awful heat will drive me mad." Then, looking round with wolfish eyes, he asked: "What was I saying? Ah, yes, you—you don't recognise me? I cannot hide my identity any longer. I'm dying. Does a beard make such a great alteration in a man's countenance?"

"Recognise you! How should I?" asked Hugh, now thoroughly aroused from his lethargy.

"Then you don't—remember—the Comte Chaulin-Servinière—at Spa?"

"Count Lucien!—Valérie's cousin!" cried Hugh, in incredulous astonishment, as he suddenly recognised the man's features. "Why—good God! yes. Only imagine, we have been comrades so long, yet I failed to recognise you. How came you to be sent to this infernal doom?"

"It was *her* doing."

"Whose?"

"Valérie's."

He ground his teeth viciously, and his bright eyes flashed as he uttered her name.

"How is that? Remember she is my wife?" Hugh exclaimed with wrath.

"Yes—alas for you?"

"What do you mean?" asked he, gazing at him fixedly, half inclined to accept his words as the manifestation of approaching madness.

"You—you married her. Ah! I know how it was all brought about. It was an evil hour, an accursed day, when you tied yourself to her, for her murderous clique have made us both their victims. I meant to live and escape, so that I could bring upon her that merciless judgment she richly deserves, but I—I'm dying. *Dieu!* Give me water! Just one drop!" he implored piteously. "For the love of heaven give me Something to drink. My throat's on fire. Can't you see I'm choking?" he added in a husky, intense voice.

Hugh looked into the dying man's face and shook his head sadly.

"Ah! none. I comprehend," he moaned. Then, with a sudden fierceness, he cried: "I'm dying—dying. *Ciel!* I shall never have the satisfaction of witnessing her degradation, of seeing her white neck severed by Monsieur Deibler at La Roquette!"

"Tell me. What do you mean by victims?" inquired Trethowen breathlessly.

The astonishment at discovering the identity of his comrade had given him renewed strength.

Again the man passed his hand across his drawn, haggard face, and wiped the death-sweat from his brow.

"I haven't the strength—to tell you all. Ah! water—for God's sake give me water!"

His tongue, swollen and red, was protruding from his mouth as he lay panting for breath and clutching at his parched throat in a paroxysm of pain.

When this had subsided, he continued—

"Now—now, before it's too late, swear—swear by all you hold sacred to do my bidding."

"What do you mean? I don't understand."

"If—if I tell you the secret and you escape from this, you'll be able to take my place as a living witness of her guilt—you'll be able to wreak vengeance upon her in my stead; to end a career, dark and dishonourable, shadowed by a terrible crime."

"Relate the facts," urged the younger man impatiently, for he well knew that the other's strength was fast failing, and feared lest the end should come before he could narrate the story.

"You have not sworn. Take an oath to deliver her up to justice should you escape, then I will show you the full extent of her villainy."

The dying man's terrible earnestness alarmed him.

"How can I do so until I am convinced?" he argued. What proof was there, he reflected, that Valérie had been false to him? After all, perhaps these wild words were the irresponsible expressions of a person whose mind was unhinged.

At that moment the madman in the boat's stern started up with a fearful oath, afterwards laughing, fiendishly, and keeping up a hideous gibbering which added to the horror of Trethowen's surroundings.

"Answer me," said his companion, in a low, guttural voice. "Will you take the oath?"

He hesitated, remembering that she was his wife, the woman he trusted implicitly, and whom he still adored, believing her to be good and pure. Yet here was a chance to ascertain something about her past, the secret of which had been so strangely preserved by Egerton. The temptation proved too great. To humour an imbecile, he thought, was justifiable.

Turning to the dying man, he exclaimed suddenly—"I swear."

The anxious wearied expression on the man's face almost momentarily disappeared on obtaining a decisive answer from his comrade, and after a few moments' silence he grew calmer, and his breathing became more easy.

In obedience to a motion from him, Hugh placed his ear closer, at the same time passing his arm gently under the sufferer's head.

"A few years ago," he said feebly, "three English students lived in Paris, on the first floor of a dingy old house in the Quai Montabello, facing Notre Dame. Their names were Holt, Glanville, and Egerton. They were—"

"Egerton! I have a friend of that name!"

"Yes, it was he! Like many other hare-brained denizens of the Quartier Latin, they frequently passed their evenings at the Bal Bullier. One night while dancing there, Egerton met a young and handsome woman. Her charms were irresistible, and he fell madly in love with her, young fool that he was! She was poor when these men first knew her, and, discovering that she was in the chorus at the Chatelet, they bestowed upon her the name of 'La Petite Hirondelle.' She was a clever woman, and not to be easily overtaken by adverse fortune. Indeed, hers had already been an adventurous career, and she had few scruples—"

"What was the woman's name?" asked Hugh anxiously.

"She had many. But—I was telling you. The man with whom she lived was an expert thief, and she, a *voleuse* also, was his accomplice, being an adept at abstracting jewellery from counter-trays in shops she visited on pretence of making a purchase. The money upon which they had been living was the proceeds of an extensive plate robbery at a mansion at Asnières, which had been perpetrated by this man and a youthful assistant; the man you know as Adolphe Chavoix."

"Chavoix! Your friend!"

The other nodded. He had spoken in broken sentences, without looking up and his breath now came with hard laboured gasps in the intervals, as if speaking and keeping silence were alike a pain to him. The stronger man felt touched with a reverent pity for the weak one at his side.

Again the swelling in the dying man's throat increased his agony. His thoughts wandered, and he uttered fierce imprecations with words that had neither meaning nor context.

"Valérie! Valérie!" he cried in deep guttural tones, after giving vent to a volley of fearful oaths. "It's you—your accursed treachery that has brought me to this! I die—I die in horrible torture the death of a dog, while you laugh, take your ease, and congratulate yourself upon getting rid of me so easily. *Diable!*" he screamed, making a desperate but futile effort to raise himself, "Trethowen shall know all—everything, and if he lives you will—ha, ha! you'll die in greater degradation than myself. You shall suffer—by Heaven you shall—"

His hands were clenched and his face distorted by an expression of intense hatred and dogged revenge. He closed his eyes, as if to shape his thoughts, and lay for some time motionless, while Trethowen, who had watched the changes of his countenance and listened to the wild allegations against his wife, whom he thought so pure, sat regarding him anxiously, awaiting the convict's further revelations.

Egerton and Valérie had met in Paris, he reflected. He had not been mistaken when jealousy had taken possession of him on that day he found them together in the studio. This truth cut short his resolution not to prejudge her without a full knowledge of the facts. It rose suddenly in his mind and covered every thought with a veil. His resolution broke down, and he argued with himself against it.

Clutching his arm, Bérard turned his fevered eyes again upon him, with an expression of terrible earnestness.

"I want," he said, articulating with difficulty—"I want to tell you something more."

"Concerning her?"

Making a gesture in the affirmative, he raised his head and glanced with eager eyes over the gunwale at the dear, calm sea.

"Water!" he implored piteously. "I—I must have some—some of that. My throat! Ah! I can't breathe."

Hugh noticed his effort to dip his hand into the sea, and arrested his arm, exclaiming in a calm voice—

"No, by Heaven! you shan't. That means death. Hope on; we may both live yet."

"Ah," he replied mechanically, his head sinking slowly back upon his companion's arm. Presently he resumed, in low, broken tones, sometimes so feeble that the anxious listener could scarcely catch them. "I told you that when these students first met this woman she was poor. Cruel in her coquetry as was her wont by nature, she encouraged the attentions of Egerton, although his pocket was light as his heart. The artist adored her, with the same passionate ardour that dozens of men have done, yourself included—"

"Do you mean that Valérie was a thief's mistress?" he cried in amazement, as the truth flashed upon him.

"Yes."

"I don't—I can't believe it. How can you prove it? What was this man's name?" he demanded.

"Victor Bérard," and he hesitated for a second. "The unfortunate devil who afterwards, in order to assist her in a nefarious plot which has been only too successful, assumed the name of the Comte Lucien Chaulin-Servinière!"

"What! You!" cried Trethowen, scarcely believing his ears, and withdrawing his hand from the prostrate man's head with a feeling of repulsion. "You were her lover!"

"Yes," he continued, unmoved by his companion's astonishment. "Remember when Egerton met her he believed she lived at home with her mother, who kept a little *estaminet*. He told her of his love, and she made pretence of entertaining true, honest affection for him. It was not long, however, before he discovered that she was no better than the rest of the women who sipped *sirops* at the Bullier. He found that in a handsome suite of rooms in the Boulevard Haussmann there resided a rich Englishman, named Nicholson. With this man she had a *liaison*, and when the artist charged her with it she admitted the truth, telling him that the Englishman held such power over her that she dare not refuse to visit him."

"Was that the truth?"

"Judge for yourself by subsequent events. This man Nicholson was a diamond merchant, and the safe in his rooms frequently contained gems worth large sums. Egerton fostered a murderous hatred towards this man, whom he had never seen, but who was the only obstacle to his happiness. One day he met them both in the Bois, and she introduced him. On subsequent occasions the two men met, and the artist ingratiated himself with his rival. Ah!"

He paused, and gasped for breath. Then, resuming, said—

"I—I needn't go into details. It is sufficient to say that she grew tired of Nicholson, and announced the fact to Egerton, remarking that if she could free herself from the odious bond she would become his mistress. This—this had the—desired effect. A few days later Nicholson was found dead in his room. He had been murdered by Egerton—"

"Jack Egerton a murderer?"

"Yes. And the safe, which had contained a quantity of valuable uncut stones, had been ransacked."

"Great heavens! you cannot be speaking the truth! Do you mean to say that this Nicholson was killed by my friend Egerton?"

"Yes. Stabbed to the heart," he replied faintly, with closed eyes.

"Do you expect me to accept this without proof?" asked Trethowen.

The prostrate man opened his eyes. In them the film of death had already gathered.

"I—I—can—prove it. He killed Nicholson because—because he loved Valérie?"

"Was she aware of his intentions?"

"No, no—*mon Dieu!*—no!" he gasped.

"Tell me all the circumstances which led to the tragedy," demanded Hugh, with fierce impatience.

"It's a long story. The whole facts would astonish you. You remember—your brother—was murdered? Ah! *Dieu!* My throat! I'm choking! My head! It's all so strange! Yet now I—I feel quite well again—quite—well!"

The colour had left his lips, and his eyes, although wide-open, were dim. The death-rattle was in his throat.

"For God's sake, tell me more before you die?" implored Hugh, bending over him.

But the convict took no heed.

"Valérie! Valérie!" he moaned in a hoarse, feeble voice.

His jaw suddenly dropped, and the light went out of his face.

Trethowen placed his hand upon his heart, but there was no movement. The spark of life had fled.

Scrambling along to where the madman lay silent and motionless, he touched him on the shoulder. A second later, however, he started back, as he became conscious that to the thwarts was bound a corpse.

Hugh Trethowen was left alone with two bodies to suffer death by slow torture, the horrors of which he had already witnessed.

Shading his aching eyes with his hand, he struggled back and gazed around.

No sign of assistance—only a wide stretch of horizon unrelieved by a single hope-inspiring speck.

The revelations made by the dead man had killed all desire for life within him. With a heart bursting with grief at finding the woman he loved so well guilty of such vile dishonour, he cast himself into the bottom of the boat and lay awaiting his end, praying that his agony might not be protracted.

Chapter Thirty One
A Wanderer

A wet winter's night in London.

Heedless of the heavy rain and biting east wind that swept in violent gusts along the dismal, deserted Strand, Hugh Trethowen, with bent head, plodded doggedly on towards Westminster. His scanty clothes, or rather the patched and ragged remains of what once were garments, were saturated and clung to him, while the icy wind blew through him, chilling him to the bone. Although unprotected by either umbrella or overcoat, he neither hesitated nor sought shelter, but, apparently quite unconscious of the inclement weather, continued to walk as briskly as his tired limbs would allow. Trudging onward, without glancing either to right or left, he splashed with heavy, careless steps through the muddy street, absorbed in his own sad thoughts.

Weary, hungry, and penniless, he nevertheless experienced a feeling of satisfaction, not unmingled with surprise, at finding himself again treading the well-remembered London streets, after escaping death so narrowly.

The two years' absence had aged him considerably. The hard lines on his still handsome features told of the privations and sufferings he had undergone, and he no longer carried himself erect, but with a stoop which was now habitual, the result of hard toil in the mine.

His rescue had been almost providential.

The shock at finding both his companions dead, combined with the agony of mind caused by the revelations made by Bérard, overwhelmed him. In despair he felt that his end was near, and as a natural consequence soon lapsed into unconsciousness. For hours, days, he may have remained in that condition, for aught he knew. When he recovered his senses he was astonished at finding himself lying in a berth in a clean, cool cabin. A man was bending over him—a big, bearded, kindly-looking seaman, who smoothed his pillow, and uttered some words in an unfamiliar language. By using French, however, both men were able to converse, and it was then he learnt that he had been picked up by the Norwegian steamer *Naes*, which was on a voyage from Sydney to San Francisco. The utmost kindness was shown to him by the captain, to whom he told the story of his imprisonment and escape, and after an uneventful voyage he landed at the American port. Utterly destitute, with only two dollars in his pocket, which had been given to him by a passenger for rendering some little services, he at once sought work, intending to earn enough to enable him to cross America and return to England.

Bérard's allegations against Valérie and Egerton were mysterious and incomprehensible, and, with the sole object of getting to London and seeking a full explanation, he toiled diligently at various menial occupations, always moving from town to town in the direction of the Atlantic. Successively he pursued the vocations of cattle drover, watchman, farm labourer, and railway stoker, until at length, after many months of anxious work, he arrived at New York, and shipped on board a steamer bound for London, giving his services as fireman in return for the passage home.

Thus he had reached the Metropolis that evening without possessing a single penny, and was therefore compelled to tramp the whole distance from the docks through the steadily-falling rain.

Had he written to Egerton for money to pay his passage he knew he should have obtained it, but he was determined to make his reappearance in London unexpectedly. He intended to descend suddenly upon both his friend and Valérie, to ascertain how much truth was contained in the dying confession of the convict. If he sent for money, he told himself that he might be asking a favour of his wife's lover, hence he decided to work his own way towards his goal, if slowly, nevertheless with effect.

Once only he raised his head. He was passing the entrance of Terry's Theatre, where upon the step there stood two young men in evening dress, who were smoking during the *entr'acte*. Looking up he recognised them as bachelor acquaintances, but desirous of being unobserved in that plight, he quickly bent his head again, and continued his dreary walk. The keen wind blew through his scanty garments, causing him to shiver, yet the atmospheric change from the hot, stifling stokehold to the midwinter blast troubled him not. He merely drew his wet jacket closer around him, quickened his pace, and strode across Trafalgar Square, turning in the direction of Victoria Street.

Indeed, he had little upon which to congratulate himself. True, he had escaped a terrible death; yet even this was counterbalanced by the fact that all that was nearest and dearest to him had been swept away. His idol had been thrown from her pedestal; the woman he had trusted and loved, turning a deaf ear to warning and entreaty alike, had been denounced as a crafty, shameless adventuress. Nevertheless, even in the depths of his despair he refused to give entire credence to the words of his dead comrade, and, arguing against himself, resolved to face her before judging her.

Strange it is how we men cling to the belief that the woman we love is pure, notwithstanding the most obvious proofs of infamy are thrust under our very noses. The moment we regard a woman as our ideal, we at once close our eyes to her every fault; and the more beautiful and kind-mannered she is, the less prone are we to accept what is told us of her past. It is so in every case of passionate affection. Woman always holds the whip-hand, while her adorer is weak and helpless as a child, easily misled, deceived with impunity, and made the shuttlecock of feminine caprice.

After marriage, when the glamour fails and man's natural caution asserts itself, then follows remorse—and frequently divorce.

Hugh had little difficulty in discovering Victoria Mansions, in which Valérie's flat was situated. Shortly before their marriage he had renewed the lease of the suite in order that they might have a place of their own in town; therefore he felt certain that he should find her there. With anxious feelings he ascended the broad staircase, and rang the bell of the outer door.

There was neither response nor sound of movement within, and although he repeated his summons several times it was evident no one was at home.

As he stood before the door the porter ascended, and, noticing his attire, inquired gruffly what his business was.

"I want Mrs Trethowen," he replied.

"She's away."

"Where is she?"

"How should I know?"

"When did she leave?"

"A week ago. She and the gentleman and the two maids went away together. I believe they've gone to their country place."

"The gentleman! Who's he?" asked Hugh in surprise.

"Why, madame's husband, I suppose. But there—I don't know anything about people's business in this place. Got enough to do to look after my own," he added, with a sardonic grin.

"What sort of man is this gentleman?" inquired Trethowen excitedly.

"Find out," replied the man in uniform arrogantly. "I don't want any of your cross-examination. She's gone away, and that's enough for you."

Then he turned and ascended the stairs to the next floor, leaving Hugh disconcerted and perplexed.

The gentleman! Madame's husband! Could it be that Valérie had already forgotten him? It was clearly useless to remain there, so he quickly resolved to go to Egerton, seek what information he could afford, and endeavour to obtain an explanation of the terrible allegations made by Bérard.

With this object he descended into the street, and with hastening steps pursued his way to Chelsea.

The artist was sitting alone before the studio fire, lazily smoking, and reading a novel, when Mrs O'Shea opened the door for Hugh to enter.

Unaware of the presence of a visitor, he did not glance up from his book for a few seconds, but when his eyes suddenly fell upon the gaunt, ragged figure before him, he was speechless with amazement.

"Good God!—Hugh!" he cried, springing to his feet, and making a movement as if to grasp his friend's hand.

But his visitor calmly put his hand behind his back, and, in a deep, earnest tone, he replied coldly—

"Yes, Jack. Before we shake hands, however, I have some questions to put to you."

"Questions!" exclaimed the artist. "Why, what's the matter?" Then, noticing the state of his clothing, he added. "You were reported dead. Where have you been; what's the reason of your long silence?"

"I've been in prison."

"In prison!"

The other nodded an affirmative, and briefly described how he had been arrested and transported, and the manner in which he had effected his escape.

The artist listened in dumb amazement.

"But what was your crime?" he asked, when Hugh had concluded his narrative. "Surely there must have been some very serious mistake."

"No, none. I have been the victim of a foul conspiracy, in which you, my old and best friend, have assisted," he replied bitterly.

"Why, Hugh, what do you mean? Of what do you accuse me?"

"Valérie was your mistress!"

"Valérie!" he cried, starting up. "I—indeed, I—"

"It is useless to deny it," interrupted Hugh coolly. "Your villainy has been exposed to me. Perhaps in your endeavour to prove your innocence you will disclaim acquaintance with Victor Bérard, with 'La Petite Hirondelle' or with a diamond-dealer named Nicholson, who—"

The colour left the artist's countenance at the mention of the latter name.

"Stop!" he cried hoarsely, clutching his companion's arm, and gazing earnestly into his eyes. "What is this you say? What do you allege?"

"That the police are still seeking for the perpetrator of the murder in the Boulevard Haussmann!"

Egerton raised his head quickly. The keen eyes of his friend were fixed upon him searchingly. Under that piercing gaze he tried to look as if the words had not disturbed him.

"How have you discovered that, pray?" he asked, with a calmness that was forced.

"Bérard has confessed."

"God! Hugh! Then—*then you know my secret!*" he gasped hoarsely, looking at his companion with wild, staring eyes.

"I do—at least, a portion of it," was the calm reply. "But you and I, Jack, are friends, and before believing anything base of you I seek an explanation from your own lips."

The artist paced up and down his studio with quick, short steps, endeavouring to control his agitation. Suddenly he halted and raised his head; his face was flushed, and the small mouth was closed firmly.

"I will trust you, Hugh. My life will depend upon your silence," he said in a low, distinct voice.

"I shall observe your confidence; if you doubt me, do not speak."

"I do not doubt you—I only doubt myself."

And he began to pace the room again, with head bent and hands clasped behind him.

Hugh waited.

"I know you will loathe me—that you will never again clasp my hand in friendship," said Egerton, as he walked up and down, with an agitation in his manner which increased as he went on. "You may tell me so, too, if you like, for I hate myself. There were no extenuating circumstances in the crime which I committed—none—"

"Hush!" cried Trethowen. "Don't speak so loud. We may be overheard."

Heedless of the warning, the artist continued—

"Does it not seem absurd that a man's whole life and ambition should be overthrown by a mere passion for a woman?" he said bitterly. "Yet this has been my case. You remember that soon after we first became acquainted I went to study in Paris—but there, perhaps Bérard has told you?"

"No; I wish to hear the true facts," replied Hugh. "Tell me all."

"Ah! the story is not an enticing one to relate," the artist resumed, with a subdued, feverish agitation. "There were three of us—Holt, Glanville, and myself—and in the Quartier Latin we led a reckless existence, with feast and jubilee one day, and starvation the next. We were a free-and-easy trio in our *atelier* on the Quai Montabello, happy in to-day and heedless of to-morrow, caring nothing for those bonds of conventionality which degrade men into money-grubs. I had freedom, liberty, happiness, until one night at a *bal masque* at the Bullier I met a woman. Ah, I see you are smiling already. Well, smile on. I would laugh were it not that I feel the pain."

There was an intense bitterness in his tone, which showed how very keenly he felt.

"Nay," interrupted Hugh coolly, "you mistake the meaning of my smile."

"No matter; you have every reason to smile, for it was contemptible weakness, and that weakness was mine. I had seen many women whom the world called beauties, and I could look upon them with indifference. At last—"

He paused; a lump rose in his throat, and his hands were clasped behind him convulsively.

"At last," he went on, with a fierce passion—"at last I saw her—our eyes met. It was no fancy, no boyish imagination—it was reality. I stood before her, dumb, trembling, spellbound. I could not speak, I could not move, the power of life seemed to have gone from me."

Again he paused—he was now standing before his friend—the bright eyes gleamed with the intensity of his passion, his lips were quivering, and his breast rose and fell with the emotion which the painful memory called forth.

"Laugh, sneer, if you will," he continued wildly; "but even as I have seen lightning strike a man dead to earth, her eyes flashed upon me, and reft me of heart, of reason, of soul."

He paused, and drew a deep sigh.

"I was mad—mad," he went on, with suppressed emotion, "and could not help myself. She absorbed all thought, all mind, and I was false to my true mistress, Art. Brush and easel were forgotten that I might seek this woman, and with my eyes drink in her beauty that filled my veins with poison. Her features and form were the perfection of beauty. Ah! but there—you know too well. Valérie's beauty is that of a divine statue, and only a statue. A very goddess of loveliness, but carven in cold stone. There is no heart, no life, no soul within. I saw this then clearly, as I see it now, yet still I loved her—I loved her!"

He flung himself into a chair, and, leaning his elbows upon the table, hid his face in his hands.

"Is that all?" inquired Trethowen, looking up from beneath his heavy brows.

"No, no—would to heaven that had been all. I scarcely know how, but we became friends. We were both poor, many of our tastes were in common, and at length I prevailed upon her to visit our shabby *atelier*, where I painted her portrait. It was my best work; I have done nothing to equal it since. She was pleased with it, and favoured me. In my madness I cared not how the favour was obtained. I was in a mad, drunken delirium of joy, and abandoned myself to destruction. Alas! it came. I was dashed from the threshold of paradise into the abyss of despair. I learned that this woman whom I worshipped as an idol was no better than the painted and powdered women who frequented the Bal Bullier and the Moulin Rouge— that she had a lover!"

He laughed a hard, bitter laugh, and then was silent.

Chapter Thirty Two
Gabrielle Debriège

A few moments' pause, and the artist resumed.

"She had admitted that she loved me," he said, in a low quivering tone of anguish. "But the fact of her relations with the rich Englishman, Nicholson, was forced on me with proof so damning that I could not shut my eyes, even despite myself."

Pressing his hands upon his brow as if to stay the wild throbbing of his brain, he sat in dejection, while his breath came with difficulty. The confession was wrung from his heart, and the haggard expression of anxiety and despair upon his face told of the mental agony it caused him.

"My jealous nature somehow prompted me to seek acquaintance with this man. Unknown to her I obtained an introduction to him, and with my fellow-student, Glanville, spent several evenings in his rooms in the Boulevard Haussmann. We drank, smoked and played cards together. He and I often dined at the Café Riche, and gradually I ingratiated myself with him. I really don't know why I did so; it must have been due to the devil's promptings. Holt and Glanville admired her, and I was flattered by their envy at the favour she bestowed upon me. Ah! poor fools, they did not know the blackness of her heart. Thus things went on for six months. Though I never looked upon Valérie with other thoughts than those of pure, honest love, we met almost daily, sometimes walking in the Bois, and frequently taking long excursions into the country, to Argenteuil, to Lagny, or Choisy-le-Roi, where we could be alone to indulge in those confidential conversations in which lovers delight."

"Was she aware that you had discovered her intrigue with this man Nicholson?" asked Hugh moodily.

"Yes. One day we had taken the train to Vincennes, and we were walking back through the wood near the Porte de Picpus, when I taxed her with it. At first she denied it; but recognising that I knew too much, burst into tears, and admitted all. Imploring pity, she kissed my hand, assuring me that she had been the victim of circumstances, that she hated him and loved me alone. My first impulse was to abandon her, and never look upon her face again. Yet, how could I? She was a woman after all, and that cold, calm exterior which chilled one, despite her beauty, might be only the mask of some fierce inward aching. She was a woman, with a woman's heart, a woman's sympathies and yearnings. I felt confident that she was bearing some heavy burden of guilt or sorrow, and that with agony she wore a mask that hid her secret from the world."

"A pity that, under such circumstances, you did not put an end to the acquaintanceship," Trethowen observed, without raising his head.

"Ah!" he sighed, "I was like you yourself have been, powerless in the influence of her presence. I knew I was a miserable fool, undeserving of pity; I knew that it was worse than madness to love her—yet still I loved. I felt that she had been wronged, and sympathised with her. On the one side my reason—calm, cold, and just—pointed to the insanity of my affection; and on the other my heart and Soul. Under the attraction of her beauty, dragged me towards her. I was determined to conquer; nevertheless, when she was near me I was a mere automaton, moving as she indicated, and executing her every desire. It was this inability to resist her that caused me to commit the crime—the crime of murder."

"Then you admit you stained your hands with blood?" Trethowen exclaimed anxiously.

"Yes, yes; but don't shrink from me," he cried, in a beseeching tone. "It was for her sake—for Valérie's sake. Prompted by the beautiful woman, whose loveliness maddened me, I took my rival's life. You will keep my secret, I know, so I will tell you how it came about. We were seated late one night in the Chat Noir, when she told me she had discovered that Nicholson and I were friends. I was not surprised, for I had anticipated that sooner or later she would find this out: but in the conversation which ensued I reproached her for continuing her intrigue with him. The words I uttered appeared to cause her a fit of remorse, for she protested that it was through no fault of hers, but under absolute compulsion. She declared that this man was in possession of a secret which, if divulged, would ruin her, and hence he held power over her which made it imperative that she should continue the relationship even against her will. We went out and wandered along the deserted streets. With such terrible earnestness did she speak, entreating pity, and asserting her affection for me, that, like a blind, trusting imbecile that I was, I believed her. Indeed, it was evident that whatever love she had entertained for Nicholson had turned to hate. The remembrance of that night is so confused that I can scarce recollect the words I uttered. However, it was she who suggested the crime, for she assured me that if he died she would be willing to marry me. What greater incentive could a jealous lover have to kill the man who barred his happiness? In the few days that followed I tried to tear myself away from her; yet still I was drawn towards her, and at last Valérie—your wife—and I sat together one night actually plotting his death. Blindly I resigned myself to a fate worse than that of the doomed. I promised to murder him!"

He spoke in low, hoarse tones, and gazed around the dimly-lit studio with a bewildered, frightened expression in his haggard eyes.

Trethowen stood by him in silent wonder, waiting for him to continue.

"I deemed that by striking the blow I should be rendering her a service as well as securing our mutual felicity. I did not know that I was preparing a living torture for myself, that I was resigning every hope, joy, and sentiment that makes life precious. No; in my frame of mind, with my intense hatred excited by the words of the woman I loved, I thought naught of the enormity of the crime, and only regarded the deed as a justifiable means of ridding her of an obnoxious and unholy tie. She planned the crime with care and forethought, even arranging the day, the hour, the moment, that it should be committed. But there—why should I blame her when it is I who was the coward, the criminal? You will understand when I say that at ten o'clock one night I softly ascended the stairs from the boulevard, and cautiously entered Nicholson's apartments by means of a key provided by Valérie. Passing along a short, dark passage, I saw a light coming through the chinks of the door which led into the front room that he used as a library and office. In this room was the safe in which he kept his gems, cunningly concealed behind a mock bookcase, so that anyone entering saw nothing of the great green iron doors with shining brass handles. Scarcely daring to breathe, I pushed open the door of this room, and saw my victim seated at his writing-table with his back towards me. The cosy apartment was in comparative darkness, except for the shaded reading-lamp which shed a subdued light in the vicinity of the table. My rival had evidently only just come in, for he had not removed his Inverness coat, and was apparently engrossed in a sheet of accounts he had spread out before him. At first I faltered, but my hand struck the handle of the long, keen, surgeon's knife with which I had armed myself. Its touch gave me courage; in a moment I remembered all that I should gain by striking the fatal blow. It was enough! I crept up behind him stealthily, and, lifting the knife, buried it almost up to the hilt in his back! He fell forward dead, without a groan."

The artist sat pale and trembling, with a clammy moisture upon his brow.

"Only for a moment I stood regarding my foul handiwork, then I turned and made my way cautiously out, descending to the boulevard and walking as fast as I could to a small café on the other side of the Seine, where I spent the remainder of the evening in drinking cognac."

"And what of Valérie?" asked Hugh, eager to learn the whole of this almost incredible story. "Did she keep her promise?"

"No, curse her! Two days later, when all Paris was discussing what the papers called the 'Mystery of the Boulevard Haussmann.' I met her, and asked her to redeem her promise and become mine. But she only laughed and treated me with scorn, urging me to leave the city, and announcing her own departure, saying that she was afraid that the police would ascertain her relations with the murdered man, and interrogate her. In vain I implored her to allow me to accompany her, but she refused, and with a cold, formal farewell left me. The sudden change which had come over her was extraordinary, as likewise was the mysterious manner in which she afterwards disappeared. With a broken heart and a heavy burden of guilt, I, too, fled from Paris—anywhere—everywhere. By-and-by I found consolation in my Art—but no ambition. There was a gloomy, morbid pleasure in trying to catch and reproduce those divine lineaments which hid so bad a spirit. And so I wandered from place to place in Italy, in Spain, in Germany, until I returned to London."

"When did you next meet her?" inquired Trethowen.

"Though I heard of her, discovered further proofs of her infamy, and ascertained that at the time she was pretending to love me she was living under the protection of Victor Bérard, a notorious thief, I never set eyes upon her until we met her together that afternoon at Eastbourne. Then I found that she had assumed the name of Dedieu instead of Duvauchel, and that she had managed to acquire sufficient money to live in affluence."

"But why did you not warn me?" asked Hugh, with bitter reproach.

"I told you all I dared. As soon as she knew that you admired her she came to me, and threatened that if I divulged anything she would give me up to the police. Therefore I was powerless to save you, and could only give vague warnings which were worse than useless. Don't you think that the knowledge of your blind implicit trust in such a woman caused me anxiety, especially when I knew that ruin only could be the ultimate result?"

The men looked at one another earnestly; each pitied the other.

"Ah! I understand Jack," exclaimed Trethowen. "Your explanation shows that you did your best to prevent me from falling a victim. We have both been duped; but she shall not go unpunished."

"What! You mean to denounce her?" he cried, in alarm.

"Why not?"

"Because—because—I am a murderer, and she will have me arrested and tried for taking the life of her lover! Cannot you see that for my own safety we must preserve silence?"

Trethowen started as this truth flashed across his mind. He had not before thought of that contingency, and with a sinking heart was compelled to admit the truth of the assertion.

The fetters of matrimony which bound him to this woman were irrevocably welded around his life, unless, perchance, by divorce he could free himself. The "gentleman" of whom the hall-porter had spoken, who was he?

"I have a strong suspicion that it was by her plotting you were sent to New Caledonia," continued Egerton. "Depend upon it, sooner or later, we shall discover that 'La Belle Hirondelle' has had a hand in it."

"What causes you to think so?" his companion asked, in amazement.

"It was to her interest that you should be imprisoned. When you were safely out of the way, with a long sentence before you, her course was quite clear."

"How?"

"Simply this: A man who died at a hotel in Antwerp was identified as yourself, a death certificate was obtained in your name, and—"

"And what then?" cried Hugh, astonished.

"Your will was proved."

"My will?"

"Yes; you left everything unreservedly to your wife, and consequently she has obtained possession of it."

"How did you know?" asked the other, dumbfounded.

The artist, without replying, went to his secretaire and took out a newspaper, which he handed to his companion.

Then he flung himself into his chair again, and sat staring blankly into the fire, his face wearing an expression of abject despair.

As Hugh read the paragraph indicated, he uttered an imprecation under his breath, and savagely flung the paper from him. Presently he placed his hand upon his friend's shoulder, exclaiming in a sad, sympathetic, voice:

"Jack, forgive me! I have judged you unjustly, for before my marriage I was jealous of you, and from the day I found Valérie here in your studio I confess I distrusted; now, however, I find you are my companion in misfortune—that you have also been duped by her. I clearly understand your inability to warn me by relating the terrible story I have just heard from your lips; I know you were powerless to prevent me falling into her cunningly-baited trap. The discovery of her infamy and exposure of her real character is, indeed, a cruel shock to me. Nevertheless, why should our friendship be any the less sincere? Come, let's shake hands."

"No, Hugh," he replied despondently, shaking his head. "I'm unworthy to grasp the hand of any honest man."

"Why not?"

"I'm a murderer."

"M'sieur Jack does not speak the truth," interrupted a shrill, musical voice in French.

Both men started and turned in astonishment. Standing in the deep shadow at the opposite end of the studio was a tall female form, which had apparently been concealed behind a large canvas fixed upon an easel. She had been admitted by Mrs O'Shea, and her presence had remained unnoticed by the men, so engrossed had they been in their conversation.

They glanced at one another apprehensively, and as she advanced the artist sprang to his feet in indignation and alarm.

A moment later, when the lamplight revealed her features, he drew back in amazement.

"You—Gabrielle?" he cried.

"*Oui*, I am that unfortunate personage," she replied, with an air of nonchalance. "And, moreover, I have been an unintentional eavesdropper."

"You heard my confession?" he asked hoarsely.

"Well—yes. It was an interesting story, yet scarcely novel—at least, to one who is better acquainted with the real facts than yourself."

"Then you knew of my crime?"

"Yes. A combination of circumstances revealed to me who it was who committed the murder."

"Ah! It was I—I who killed him," he cried wildly, glaring with haggard eyes.

Hugh stood staring at the strange visitor. Amazed at her sudden appearance, he was speechless. About twenty-eight, tall, dark, with features that were decidedly foreign, she was well-dressed, wearing a smart little sealskin cape, the collar of which was turned up around her neck, while upon her head was perched a coquettish little bonnet.

Jack Egerton recovered himself quickly, and, apologising for neglecting to introduce them, presented her to his friend as Mademoiselle Gabrielle Debriège. Then offering her his chair, he stood before her, and commenced a series of inquiries as to her movements since they last met, and what had induced her to seek him.

"This world is a very little place," she replied in broken English, and with a winning smile. "An artist is one of the easiest men to find. Let's see, I believe it's five years ago since we last saw one another. On the Pont de la Concorde, if I remember aright, and on the morning you left Paris so suddenly without bidding us farewell, you—"

"How is Glanville?" interrupted the artist. "Have you met him since he forsook the Quartier Latin?"

"Forsook! Bah!" exclaimed the voluble Frenchwoman, shrugging her shoulders deprecatingly. Without answering the question, she continued: "At the time your departure caused some surprise among us, but we little dreamed that you had any connection with the affair of the Boulevard Haussmann. It was only afterwards that the reason of your flight was discovered—"

"By whom?" he asked anxiously.

"By me alone. Never fear, I shall act with circumspection," she added, noticing his look of anxiety and alarm. "My life has been as adventurous as yours, and since that occurrence I have learnt wisdom. I have sought you for two reasons."

"What are they?"

"Firstly, your friend here, M'sieur Trethowen, and yourself have both been the victims of Valérie Duvauchel. You drank of her love philtre, and succumbed to her beauty. You desire revenge—eh?"

Hugh bent his head in acquiescence.

"I, too, have been cruelly wronged by her. I have waited long in order to repay the debt I owe, and the hour of her retribution is now at hand."

"What has she done to you?" asked Hugh anxiously.

"I will explain everything when in your presence, I meet her face to face. Till then I keep my own secret, fully confident that after the revelations I shall make she will not dare to trouble you again with her presence."

"But you must not—you shall not—do this!" cried Egerton excitedly. "She will wreak her vengeance upon me."

"Entertain no such gloomy apprehensions," urged Gabrielle, with a smile of assurance. "Before I have done with 'La Belle Hirondelle' she will implore for mercy upon her knees. But will I extend any to her? No. *Grand Dieu*! She shall suffer for her crime, as I have done."

She spoke determinedly, her dark eyes emitting a fierce gleam of hatred.

"How do you propose to do that?" inquired Hugh breathlessly.

"Ask no questions at present, m'sieur. Your wife and her lover have obtained your fortune and are spending it recklessly. At present this—what you call leader of the *demi-monde*—is entertaining a party at your château. My proposal is that we three go down there to-morrow and in the midst of the festivities, we will produce an interesting tableau. Do you agree?"

"You spoke of my wife's lover," gasped Hugh. "Tell me, who is he?"

"Pierre Rouillier—the man you know as Adolphe Chavoix."

"Chavoix!"

"Yes. Accompany me to-morrow, and you shall see."

There was a brief silence, followed by some protests from Egerton, but after considerable argument it was eventually agreed that mademoiselle's suggestion should be carried out.

The artist produced some wine and glasses, and they drank together. Soon afterwards Gabrielle, urging her old friend to be of good cheer, took her departure. As she opened the door to take her leave, she exclaimed, with an exultant laugh—

"La Belle little dreams how near is Nemesis. You do not anticipate how complete my revenge will be. Her future is in my hands. *Mon Dieu*! We shall triumph and crush her. Nevertheless she richly deserves her punishment, and she shall receive it, never fear."

Chapter Thirty Three
La Petite Hirondelle

The fine old banqueting hall at Coombe, with its dark oak panelling and polished floor, transformed for the nonce into a ballroom presented an animated and pleasing spectacle.

In the decorations, flags and palms had been used, and the ferns and evergreens ornamenting the walls contrasted well with the bright dresses of the dancers. The myriad lights in the magnificent chandeliers re fleeting in the mirrors multiplied and increased in effect; the air was heavy with the perfume of exotics; and the strains of tripping music from the band, now loud and fast, and again soft and low, resounded through the mansion. At the farther end of the hall a large square window stood open and gave exit to the garden, every bush and tree of which was illuminated by fairy lamps, notwithstanding that the night was frosty and moonlit.

Valérie's outward and visible signs of lamentation had been of brief duration. Within a year of her husband's reported demise she threw off the trammels of widowhood, cast aside her weeds, and at once set herself to lead the unconventional set into which she had entered during her former residence in London. With a Parisienne's love of admiration, her ambition for several years had been to outvie the other women who comprised her circle; and now, with wealth at her command and an establishment as fine as any in the county, she was enabled to indulge every whim and entertain her guests in a lavish manner which caused them envy.

For the most part her acquaintances were women who were shunned by the disciples of Mother Grundy; some cigarette-smoking Bohemians whose only offence against society's unwritten laws was that they exhibited their un-conventionalities openly; others pure adventuresses almost as fair and fascinating as herself. During the year she lived in England immediately before meeting Hugh, she had come into contact with these people, and after her sudden acquisition of fortune she had lost no time in renewing their acquaintance.

It is astonishing what a large number of friends a wealthy women can command, even though she be placed beyond the pale of society and has never bowed before her august Sovereign. If she be handsome and fashionable, she can easily conquer the prejudices of the hypercritical followers of Dame Straightlace. Thus, although the magnates of North Cornwall and their wives and daughters were somewhat shocked and scandalised by her brief period of mourning, and the apparent levity with which she regarded her bereavement, nevertheless many retained a visiting intimacy with the widow of the once popular young owner of Coombe.

Assessing the value of her personal charms correctly, her attempt to shine as the leader of a smart set had not failed. Aware that should her connection with Pierre become known it would be to her detriment, she had arranged with him to keep apart from her as much as possible; therefore the direction of her affections was suspected only by one or two of her oldest friends. Her fêtes were characterised by their extravagance and profuse display, for she spared no effort to ensure the enjoyment of those who accepted her hospitality; nevertheless, on this particular night she had eclipsed the *menu* of pleasures previously provided.

An entertainment so novel could scarcely fail to be a success. Possibly it might have stirred feelings of pain and indignation within the breasts of the pharasaical, but as none of that order were included in the company, a satisfactory issue of the terpsichorean novelty was assured.

It was nothing less than a reproduction of that strange spectacle which was originated at Ootacamund by the Governor and his select circle, and which caused so much excitement and comment in Madras, the Demon's Dance.

The ball had opened with two extras and two valses, after which came the feature of the evening.

As the first discordant crash of music was heard, eight men rushed into the room. The attire of these imitators of his Satanic majesty was in itself remarkable. Long black-forked tails, tufts of hair on either side of the head, gave the idea of pointed ears; black coats, with a kind of bat's wing under the arm and joined at the side; black bands of silk across the shirt front covering all gleams of white, knee-breeches, silk stockings, and pumps. Each in his rush along the room seized a reluctant angel, and dragged her to a place in the set. Their fair partners were most becomingly attired in soft flowing robes of white, with silver girdles, stars in their hair, flowing wing sleeves, and a big spray of lilies in their hands.

No one but the eight from above and the subterranean eight took part in this dance, the rest being content to watch the curious sight. They danced with wonderful fiendish grace and agility, dragging their partners, whirling them round and pirouetting around them. Some angels appeared to dance easily while others, feigning reluctance, unwillingly went through the set. Valérie, in the arms of a tall demoniacal partner, almost flew about, her feet scarcely touching the ground, and her face bearing an expression of intense satisfaction and enjoyment.

The bright spirits, with their sable lords, having finished the Lancers, concluded with a wild rapid waltz.

The radiant hostess, flushed by excitement, had been led to her seat, and was receiving the congratulations of her guests on the success of the entertainment, when Jacob crossed the room and deferentially accosted her.

"Well, what's the matter?" she inquired, scanning the servitor sharply.

"A gentleman in the library wishes to speak to you, madame. He will not give his card," said the old man.

"I can't be troubled now to see anyone," she replied petulantly.

"Excuse me, madame," he exclaimed, bowing. "But I think he desires to see you on very urgent business."

"Do you know what it is? Haven't I told you often to always ask strangers what they want to see me about?"

"I have asked him, madame, but he refused to tell me," said Jacob, undisturbed by her impatience. "He said he wished to see you at once and alone."

"Alone," she repeated, in surprise. "I wonder who it can be?"

Then reflecting that any business at that hour must be of importance, she directed the servant to take her to where the stranger was in waiting.

The library, a small, quaint old room, was situated in a wing of the building, at some distance from where the ball was in progress, and was virtually shut off from the rest of the house by baize doors placed halfway down the corridor.

Jacob led the way, and, ceremoniously throwing open the door of the apartment, announced the advent of his mistress. The two shaded candles which stood upon the writing-table threw such a dim light over the sombre room that when she entered she did not for the moment recognise her visitor.

The door had closed.

He rose slowly from a chair near the fire, and walked towards her.

"*Dieu*! Jack! Why, what means this?" she cried in amazement, when she recognised him.

"You have company to-night," observed the artist, without offering to shake hands. "I thought it probable that, under the circumstances, you would not grant an interview to an old friend."

"How absurd! Why, you must know you are always a welcome guest here," and she beamed upon him one of her sweetest smiles.

As she stood before him in the subdued light he gazed upon her in hesitation. Her costume was perfect, enhanced as it was by a sparkling diamond star in her hair and a necklet of exquisite brilliants. Her dress was of white silk, with very high sleeves, mounted in a sort of ball at the shoulder, hanging draperies from the arms representing wings, which expanded as she moved, and silver bands around a very high waist and under and across each arm.

"The welcome you accord me is somewhat premature," he observed meaningly. "No doubt you have a morbid satisfaction in seeing the man who is under your thrall—the miserable, deluded fool who stained his hands with a terrible crime for your sake, yet you—"

"Why refer to that horrid affair?", she asked, shuddering slightly. "Let's forget it."

"No doubt you wish that dark page in your history to be closed," he said ominously; "but, strangely enough, it is upon that very subject I have sought this interview."

"What do you want, pray?" she asked quickly.

"Merely to introduce two persons to you—old friends."

"Old friends!" she echoed. "Who are they?"

For answer, Egerton crossed the apartment and opened the door communicating with an ante-chamber. As he did so two persons advanced into the library.

"Gabrielle! Hugh!" she gasped, a look of sudden terror overspreading her countenance.

The tableau was well arranged and striking.

Valérie's glance shifted in alarm from one to the other, while her three visitors looked upon her in silence, with expressions of calm, confident determination.

Hugh Trethowen's countenance was careworn and pale; his whole appearance was that of a man weighed down by profound grief. The sufferings and privations had aged him considerably, yet there were in his face traces of some new feeling. His mouth, as a rule so serious, actually smiled; his look had more animation than it was wont to have, and altogether he had somewhat about him which was at once sad, malevolent, and self-satisfied.

"I—I did not expect this pleasure," the adventuress stammered, with bitter sarcasm, without asking them to be seated.

The icy reception did not astonish them. They were fully prepared to meet the passionate wrath which they knew would be stirred within her.

"We are unwelcome, no doubt," said Gabrielle Debriège, with a cynical smile. "Nevertheless, it is a long time, madame, since you and I met."

"And what have I to do with you, pray?" cried Hugh's wife, drawing herself up to her full height, and standing erect before them. "It is gross impudence for a woman of such reputation as yourself to claim my acquaintance. I do not forget what you were in Paris."

"Oh, indeed!" replied mademoiselle. "Before you asperse my character, think of your own."

"Who dares to defame me?" she asked indignantly.

"I do," declared mademoiselle.

This bold reply caused the colour to flee from her cheeks, for the object of their visit began to dawn upon her.

"I have come here, madame," continued Gabrielle, "to bring your lost husband before you, so that he may hear the true story of your perfidy; I have—"

"By Heaven! I'll strangle you!" Valérie hissed, stepping forward threateningly, with clenched hands and flashing eyes.

The two women were, however, separated by the writing-table.

"First, listen to what I have to say," the other replied coolly. "I alone know the truth, and it is useless to protest your innocence or deny your guilt—"

"The truth of what?"

"Victor has confessed," said Gabrielle, without answering the question.

"Confessed!" she repeated, betraying increased alarm.

"By your treachery he was sent to penal servitude, but your plan proved rather too ingenious, for, strangely enough, he denounced you to a fellow-convict, who chanced to be your husband!"

Valérie glanced sharply at Hugh, with unwavering gaze.

"Yes," he said, in a tone of disgust, speaking for the first time. "Your lover told me the horrible story, how—like myself—he had been tricked and wronged by you. I can scarcely believe that I ever loved a woman so vile and despicable, so depraved by sin as yourself."

"Vile and despicable!" she echoed, in anger. "What have I done that you, too, should turn against me?"

"If you forget," interposed Gabrielle, "I'll refresh your memory."

"I desire to hear none of the vilifying denunciations. Let me get back to my guests."

"No," said Egerton, turning the key in the door, and placing it in his pocket. "You don't leave here yet. We have not finished."

She turned upon him like an infuriated animal brought to bay.

"You," she cried, scanning him from head to toe in exasperation. "Do you consider it wise for you—of all men—to interfere with my liberty? Remember the affair of the Boulevard Haussmann!"

The speech had its desired effect. The artist shrank from her.

"At the same time," exclaimed Gabrielle, addressing her, "remember there are other sentences in the Penal Code besides imprisonment."

"I don't understand you," answered Valérie, giving her shoulders a shrug indicative of unconcern.

"There is death for those who take the lives of their fellow-creatures."

The adventuress shuddered. Then resuming her air of indifference, said—

"You are talking enigmas."

"You wish me to speak more plainly. Very well. Perhaps you have forgotten that night we met at my rooms in the Boulevard St. Michel, when, after your taunts and threats, I prophesied that a day would come when I would hold your life in my hands, and compel you to beg for mercy. That day has dawned."

"I'll not stay here to be insulted in my own house," cried Valérie fiercely.

"We shall compel you," remarked her husband abruptly.

"This is some infamous plot against me," she said, boldly facing him. "You are unworthy the name of husband if you do not protect me from this pair of criminals."

"We've had enough of heroic talk," interrupted Gabrielle impatiently. "It will be as well to get to the business of our visit at once."

"If your business is only to insult me, I'll ring for the servants and have you turned out."

"In that case we should embrace the opportunity of relating to your guests a story which would no doubt interest them," answered Gabrielle calmly.

"Bah! you are cowards," she said, with face blanched by rage. "Three of you against one defenceless woman!"

"Ah; do not malign us," urged the other, in a tone of banter. "I know that the sight of your husband is somewhat embarrassing, especially when you and your adored Pierre very ingeniously proved his demise." With a smile she added: "I should feel a trifle disconcerted myself under such distressing circumstances. Indeed, it is a most awkward *contretemps*, is it not?"

"*Sacré*! keep your sympathies to yourself," screamed Valérie, with a sudden outburst of terrible passion.

Then, panting with excitement, she stood supporting herself by a chair, and facing her traducers. She saw plainly that the result of the conflict must be either complete annihilation, or a triumphant vindication of the character which Hugh had hitherto considered immaculate.

Drawing a deep breath, she braced herself up for the ordeal, and stood ready to hurl back the accusation into the teeth of her enemies.

Chapter Thirty Four
Dregs of Life

"If you two men would understand how you both have been ensnared and betrayed, listen to the facts I will relate," said Gabrielle, leaning on the table before her.

"Lies," observed Valérie, as if speaking to herself.

"A few years ago in Paris," continued Mademoiselle Debriège, turning to her companions, "there lived, as you know, three artists, named Holt, Glanville, and Egerton. At that time I, too, lived in the Quartier Latin and became acquainted with them by meeting them frequently at the Chat Noir, whither I sometimes went in company with the man who had promised me marriage. The latter, however, forsook me—bah! it was the usual story—a woman's foolish trust in a man who cast her off like a frayed glove. You understand?"

She paused, and the colour mounted to her cheeks.

"Ruin came," she went on; "my father, a small tradesman, turned me from his door, and I found myself wandering friendless, forsaken, and homeless in the great city. Eventually I obtained an engagement as a *figurante* at the Opera, and while there I first met the woman before you, Valérie Duvauchel. Although a gay coquette, she confided in me the fact that she was living under the protection of Victor Bérard, a convicted thief. I was poor, earning scarcely enough to keep body and soul together, when she asked me to assist her and her lover in their various schemes of robbery. This temptation proved too great, for I was to receive a fair share of the plunder. The first occasion on which I participated in the crusade against riches was at a burglary at Auteuil. We were successful, and I received a thousand francs for my services. During the nine months I was connected with them I assisted at a number of robberies of jewellery and plate, sometimes as a decoy, at others pilfering myself."

"I never knew you allied yourself in that manner with them," remarked the artist in surprise, "although I often thought the dresses you wore cost you more than you obtained at the Opera."

"In order to carry out our plans, I was compelled to dress well," she replied. "But that has little to do with the events that followed. While assisting Bérard, I frequently spent days about the *ateliers*, and Glanville, the student of the Quai Montabello, and I became enamoured of one another. He had more money at his command than the average denizen of the Ile de la Cité, therefore I was not averse to accompanying him to cafés, balls, and theatres, especially as I had given up my engagement of the Opera, and was dependent entirely upon the proceeds of Victor's depredations. After a few months at this life I discovered, by mere accident, that my English lover was not so devoted as I believed, and—that he knew Valérie. The affection between this woman and Egerton was a matter of comment among the students living on the Quai, but no one suspected that she favoured Glanville, whom everybody believed idolised me."

"I didn't encourage him. I couldn't help your lover admiring me, could I?" protested Valérie scornfully.

"My awakening was a cruel one," Gabrielle continued, speaking slowly and distinctly. "I taxed him with faithlessness, but he denied it so earnestly that at length I became convinced of his firm affection for me alone. A few days later a calamity befell us. I had stored in my rooms a quantity of stolen property previous to disposing of it. One evening, while I was out, Glanville called, and, entering with his key, sat down to await me. Hardly a quarter of an hour elapsed before two detectives and half a dozen policemen entered the place, armed with a warrant. They searched and quickly found several valuable articles, descriptions of which had been circulated. Then they arrested and charged him with perpetrating the robberies."

"Were you arrested also?" asked Hugh, greatly interested in the narrative.

"No; fortunately Victor got wind of the affair, and warned me not to return. I was present, however, at the trial. The police had unfortunately discovered that the property was the proceeds of several extensive burglaries, and the court sentenced him to ten years' transportation. The first few months he spent in performing hard labour at Brest, and at the end of that period I received a letter from him. It was long and earnest, reminding me of how he was suffering for my sake, and declaring his passionate love. To this I replied, and, after the lapse of a few weeks I received another, urging me to marry him. He said that he was sailing for New Caledonia that day, therefore if I consented I should be compelled to follow him out there. To meet this contingency he gave me the address of a bank, where I was to call and obtain money for my journey; and, further, he stated that in the event of my consenting to become his wife, he had given orders that three thousand francs were to be paid annually to me until his liberation. Naturally, such a proposal caused me grave doubts, especially as I had discovered a few days previous to his arrest a fresh and most striking proof of his love for this vile woman who stands now before you."

"Did you marry him after all?" inquired the artist impatiently, for he had been in ignorance of all this.

"Yes, Valérie and Victor, having suspicions that the police had scented them, fled from Paris: consequently I was without means. Although I was fond of Glanville, and admired his courage in shielding me, yet I did not love him so well as another man I had lately met. However, finding myself almost destitute, I drew the money from the bank, and sailed for 'La Nouvelle' where, after a few weeks' residence, the Governor gave us permission to marry. The ceremony was duly performed, and I have here the lines which prove it," she added, exhibiting a small strip of paper which she had taken from her pocket.

"Your honey noon was scarcely pleasant, I should think," observed Hugh sympathetically.

"Its brevity did not allow either of us to become bored," she said. "I parted from him at the chapel door, and I have not seen him since."

"Not seen him!" repeated Egerton. "Why, has he not yet obtained his freedom?"

"Yes; he escaped before he had been there two years. However, we never met."

"But why did you marry him?" the artist asked. "A convict was hardly a desirable husband."

"Ah! you wonder. Well, there were several reasons," she said. "Firstly, I was afraid lest he should expose me with regard to a certain incident which occurred at Passy, in which Bérard and I were implicated. We were on a midnight expedition, and a policeman who proved troublesome received an ugly dig with a knife; therefore I was confident that if this were divulged I should be arrested and sentenced as one of Victor's accessories. Then, again, I had been told by an Englishman who knew him that Glanville had an ample income, and this was confirmed by his offer to provide me with money until his release. Besides, he, on the other hand, was anxious to marry me in order to secure my silence, because he knew I had discovered a secret of his which, if not preserved, might bring dire consequences. It may have been for the best that we parted so quickly, for as soon as the marriage ceremony was performed I regretted the rash step, inasmuch as the recollection of my discovery regarding his alliance with this woman came back to me in all its hideous reality."

"What alliance?" inquired Valérie, whose firm, set face was as colourless as the dress she wore.

"It is well you should feign ignorance," Gabrielle replied angrily. Then, turning to the two men, she said: "In order that you shall understand matters aright, I shall be compelled to describe the scene. It took place in a suite of rooms in the Boulevard Haussmann tenanted by an English dealer in gems named Nicholson."

"What do you know of him?" cried Valérie in a husky voice.

"Have patience and you shall hear," she answered with a sarcastic smile. Again addressing her companions, she continued her narrative, saying: "While this woman was living with Victor, she had enchanted Egerton and Glanville. Both, unaware of one another's feelings, were ecstatic over her face and figure; both worshipped her, and both were prepared to do anything to secure her favour."

"That is true," admitted the artist moodily. "I was a brainless fool. Yet I did not know until now that Glanville had also been smitten by her fatal beauty."

"He had, nevertheless, as you will see. This woman—who afterwards assumed the name of Dedieu—with her usual crafty far-sightedness saw that it was possible to turn the mad impetuosity of you and your fellow-student to her advantage, and did not fail to embrace the opportunity. The scheme she concocted was indeed a fiendish one, which she carried out unaided, and the secret would have been safe even now had I not been the witness of her crime."

"You—you saw me?" shrieked Valérie in dismay. "You lie! You saw nothing."

"Her crime! What was it? Tell us quickly," urged Hugh.

"The facts are almost incredible, but they are simply as follows: Nicholson was her lover, and the safe in his room contained a quantity of cut and uncut gems. She devised an ingenious plan by which she could get rid of her lover, obtain the stones, and throw the guilt upon the two men who were infatuated with her."

"Bah! don't believe her!—she's telling you a pretty romance!" declared Valérie, striving to appear unconcerned.

But Gabrielle took no notice of her interruptions.

"The way she set about it," she went on, "was, to say the least, skilful and heartless. Showing favour to each, unknown to the other, she told them that Nicholson held her enthralled by means of a secret, and that she was unable to break from him in consequence. An insinuating proposal she made was likely to lead to but one result—a promise from each that they would take Nicholson's life."

"Wretch?" hissed the unhappy woman, under her breath.

"She arranged the details of the assassination with both, instructing each in the manner by which the Englishman was to be killed. Both were in ignorance of each other's intention, for she gave them strict injunctions to preserve the secret as they valued their lives. These facts I afterwards learnt, but I must tell you now how I became aware of the plot. Glanville had gone to London for a week, and I also had been away in the country for a few days. It was about half-past nine at night when I arrived at the St. Lazare Station, and while passing down the Boulevard Haussmann it suddenly occurred to me that Nicholson, being a very intimate friend of Glanville's, would most probably be aware whether he had returned from England. I scarcely know what prompted me, but I halted before the house and ascended the stairs. The concierge was absent, and the staircase was in darkness, he having omitted to light the gas."

"Of course, you knew Nicholson," observed the artist. "I remember it was I who introduced you."

"Yes; I had frequently met him with Glanville, and had been to his rooms before. Without much difficulty I found the door. It was ajar, and I pushed it open noiselessly. As I did so I heard loud excited talking, and recognised one of the voices as that of Valérie. The discovery that she had called upon this man excited my curiosity, and I resolved to watch them. They were in a room upon the left of the passage, the door of which was almost closed. Passing with scarcely a sound, I entered the sitting-room, and glanced round for some place of concealment. There were several, but the one I decided upon was behind the heavy crimson curtains that were drawn across the window overlooking the boulevard. Scarcely had I retired into my hiding-place when I heard the Englishman walk to the outer door and close it. Then he returned to the room in a frenzy of passion, invoking terrible curses upon her. They spoke in English, which at that time I did not understand; yet it was evident she had done something to arouse his hatred, for a few moments later she screamed for mercy, and rushed headlong into the room where I was. He followed at her heels, and, clutching her by the throat, flung her backwards upon the sofa. His face was livid with passion, and for several minutes they struggled together. Then, almost before I was aware of her intention, I heard a loud report. A puff of smoke curled between them as he relaxed his hold and grasped convulsively at his breast. 'Dieu! Valérie! You—you've shot—me!' were the only words that he uttered, for he reeled and fell backwards, striking his head violently upon the corner of the table."

"Did she really murder him?" asked the artist breathlessly.

"Yes; the revolver with which, as I afterwards found, she had shot him through the heart, was still smoking in her hand. Flinging it from her to the opposite end of the room, she bent over the body of her lover and extracted the keys from his pocket. Crossing to the mock bookcase, she pressed a button and opened it, revealing the ponderous iron doors of the safe. Without hesitation she quickly applied the keys, and the handles yielded. In a few moments she had cleared the two iron drawers of the white paper packets they contained. Satisfying herself that she had not overlooked anything of value, she quickly closed the safe and transferred the plunder to the pockets of her dress and jacket."

"*Ciel!* She *does* know!" escaped Valérie's lips involuntarily, as she stood trembling and leaning heavily upon the chair, her distended eyes glaring at the trio before her with a terrible fire of hatred.

"But what of Nicholson?" asked Hugh. "Was he dead?"

"Quite. Death had been almost instantaneous," Gabrielle replied, speaking in the same distinct, mechanical tones in which she had recounted the strange incidents. "When the murderess had concluded her search for the gems, she turned her attention to the body. First, she bent and satisfied herself that there was no movement of the heart, then, by dint of exerting every muscle, she managed to drag the body up and seat it in the chair at the writing-table. The limbs being not yet rigid, it was an easy task to place it in a natural position, with the arms leaning upon the table and head bending over, as if reading the papers, which she spread out upon the blotting-pad. After she had rearranged the room, she glanced at the watch she wore in a bangle upon her wrist. Lighting the reading-lamp and turning out the gas, she left the room with only a dim, subdued light. She had just completed this when she started at the click of a latchkey in the outer door, and concealed herself quickly behind a high screen which stood near the fireplace. Barely had she time to do this before Egerton entered, and, creeping up cautiously behind the dead man's chair, struck him a terrible, murderous blow in the back with a long sharp knife he carried in his hand. The force he used caused the body to overbalance and roll, with the chair, upon the floor. With scarcely a second look at the result of his horrible work, he turned and stole out as noiselessly as he had entered. In a few minutes Valérie, having convinced herself of his departure, emerged from her hiding-place, and again reseated the corpse in its chair, at the same time removing the blood from the clothes with a cloth she obtained from a drawer. For a few minutes she was engaged in staunching the blood, and prevented it from flowing over his coat after she had withdrawn the knife from the wound.

Subsequently she went into the adjoining apartment, and was absent about ten minutes. When she re-entered, Glanville accompanied her. He, too, was also armed with a knife, the blade of which gleamed in the ray of lamplight which fell upon it. The murderess crept stealthily behind the corpse and, bending over, placed her arms around its neck, as if caressing it, while at that moment, in obedience to a motion from her, the student rushed up and struck it a violent blow with the knife full in the chest. Valérie released her hold and again the body lolled upon the floor. The woman snatched up her hat, and, without casting a glance at the murdered man or uttering a word, both went out and closed the door after them. Five minutes later I followed, hardly daring to breathe until I had reached the boulevard and mingled with the people."

"Good God! Is it really true?" demanded Egerton excitedly.

"True? Bah! Surely you are not such an imbecile as to believe the foul lies of that woman?" shouted Hugh's wife. "She has no proof."

"I'll convince you before I have finished," answered Gabrielle. "The strangest phase of the affair yet remains to be narrated—"

"*Diable!*" cried the trembling woman passionately. "Ah! you would crush me, would you not?" she said, with a hollow laugh. "You—you would hurry me off to pay the penalty without a moment's pity. But I shall be out of your reach. You see well enough that you can't succeed; bah! you are vanquished."

Gabrielle took no heed of this sudden outburst of fury. Drawing from her pocket a crumpled newspaper, she said—

"This is a copy of the *Gaulois*, containing a full report of the discovery of the body, and if you read it you will find the three distinct wounds described as I have explained."

"Then, after all, I am not a murderer?" cried the artist, suddenly recognising how he had been tricked by the woman who had so artfully cast her toils about him and bound him to do her bidding.

"No; you are innocent."

"Ah, Gabrielle," he cried earnestly, "how shall I ever thank you enough for clearing up the awful mystery and removing the guilty burden from my conscience?"

"Before you thank me, hear the end," she said calmly. "I told you how I married Glanville. Well, at that time I believed him to be a student of whose conviction I had unfortunately been the cause. Yet after his escape he wrote to me, making an appointment for me to meet him in London, and admitting that Glanville was only a name he had assumed in order that his friends should not discover that he had entered Bohemia. It was his hobby to study Art—"

"Who was he, then?" inquired Hugh, interrupting.

"Your brother."

"Douglas?" he ejaculated, in abject amazement.

"Yes."

"Surely you must be mistaken," cried Egerton incredulously.

"I said I would convince you. Here is the letter," and she handed the missive for their inspection.

"Did you meet as arranged?" Hugh asked breathlessly, recognising his brother's handwriting.

"No. Long before the enactment of the tragedy, this woman and her myrmidons, Victor Bérard and Pierre Rouillier, *alias* Chavoix, had discovered who Glanville was, and also that he had a brother who would inherit the estate in the event of his decease. Yet the plot does not seem to have occurred to them until after his imprisonment. My husband arrived in England several days earlier than I expected—"

"And they murdered him?"

"Yes. From place to place they followed him until a fitting opportunity occurred, and, as you are aware, they carried out their evil design in an omnibus in a clever, audacious manner that baffled the police. The murder remained a mystery, and it was not until several months afterwards that I succeeded in obtaining conclusive evidence proving that either Valérie or her accomplice, Bérard, assassinated him. They were unaware that I had married him, for I had returned to Paris and gone upon the stage again. But I afterwards accepted a London engagement, and set myself to watch the development of their skilfully concocted plans."

"But what was their object in taking his life?" Hugh inquired, bewildered by the extraordinary narrative.

"It was quite plain. Immediately after our marriage, before we left the chapel, I told Douglas that it was Valérie who had killed Nicholson, and not himself, as he believed. The reason I did so was in order that he should see how he had been tricked, and the announcement, I feel sure, transformed his love for her into deadly hate. Before he left 'La Nouvelle' I believe he managed to write to her explaining that he had discovered her treachery, and announcing his intention of seeking revenge. It was the knowledge that he had discovered her secret that first prompted them to murder him. Their design was a deep one, to ultimately obtain your money. They saw that it was impossible for Valérie to marry Douglas after what had occurred, while on the other hand it was obvious that if they killed him the estate would pass to you, and Valérie could afterwards marry you for the sole object of obtaining possession of the money. They believed, too, that if Douglas died, Valérie's secret would be safe, therefore what greater incentive to commit the murder could there have been?"

"Could they not have obtained his money without taking his life?" asked Hugh.

"No. The preservation of the secret of Valérie's guilt was to them of vital importance, for while Douglas lived he would always have her in his power. She little thought, however, that it was I who had witnessed her crime and told Douglas the truth. She felt confident that by killing him she would be free."

"And that she did, alas!" Trethowen added bitterly. "Ah! you have little idea of the terrible extremities to which they resorted in order to ensure the success of their nefarious plot. Indeed, the conspiracy was a devilish one; they hesitated at nothing. They had no money when Valérie commenced to allure you by her crafty smiles, and you would never imagine how they obtained sufficient to make you believe she was wealthy."

"How did they? Tell me."

"Rouillier—whom you know as Chavoix—is an adroit swindler, and to his ingenuity the credit for it is due. Some months previously he had insured his life for a large amount, and having made a holograph will bequeathing the money to an imaginary person named Chavoix, he then succeeded in finding a poor, destitute Frenchman in Soho who slightly resembled himself. Aided by Bérard and Holt he drugged his victim, placed his own card-case and letters in his pocket, and flung him from a train on the District Railway. The insensible man was run over and killed. The body was discovered much mutilated, and the insurance company, believing that he had fallen from the train, paid the money over to Pierre, who was already living in a secluded village in Belgium, and who had taken the name of Chavoix."

"How horrible to sacrifice a life for a paltry sum!" Hugh exclaimed, unable even then to fully realise the truth of the extraordinary story of conspiracy and crime.

"The manner in which they got rid of you was quite as ingenious as their dealings with that old scoundrel Graham, and all their other plans. You remember, you were in Paris when arrested?"

"Yes."

"Well, it was your wife who informed the police. She represented that you were Douglas Trethowen, who had escaped from 'La Nouvelle.' You were identified by the photograph in the *dossier* at Monsieur Goron's bureau, hence your arrest. The police had already discovered Valérie's *liaison* with the murdered man Nicholson, and when you were interrogated you admitted that you were her husband. This strengthened their suspicions that you were guilty of complicity in the murder, even if you did not actually kill your wife's lover. Again, they had previously obtained evidence that Douglas Trethowen was seen to leave the house on the night of the tragedy accompanied by Valérie, therefore it was not surprising that the heavy sentence was passed upon you, especially as Pierre Rouillier gave damning information against you in secret."

"This is all so strange, mademoiselle, that I can scarcely believe it," Trethowen remarked. "Yet my brother's connection with this woman— this murderess—accounts for the picture and letters of hers which I found among his papers. I remember now that one of the letters contained the words 'Boulevard' and 'Montabello.' Yes," he cried, suddenly realising the truth; "what you have told me tallies with the facts. My brother has been murdered, and I have been victimised by this vile, debased creature, in a manner that has almost cost me my life. I believe you have spoken the truth. My lifelong thanks are due to you for your self-denial in watching the complicated game of these wretches, and rest assured I shall not overlook your claim upon me as my poor brother's widow." Turning to Valérie, who still stood ashen pale and trembling, he paused, looking straight into her unflinching eyes with a terrible expression of loathing and hatred.

"You!" he cried. "As for you—you know what punishment a murderess deserves! I little dreamed that such a fair form could hide so black a heart; yet it seems that while pretending to reciprocate my love you were planning my destruction—"

"No," she cried wildly. "I—I loved you—once," and she stretched out her hand as if to grasp his arm. He stepped back quickly, saying—

"Keep away! Your touch is polluting!"

Her submissive and resigned attitude instantly changed as he uttered this reproach. Her look was menacing and full of hate. She turned furiously upon Gabrielle, and poured forth a torrent of abuse.

But she exposed herself to terrible reprisals.

Mdlle. Debriège was not a woman to be cowed by the vindictive insults heaped upon her. She had nourished a natural and bitter hatred against this woman who had robbed her of her husband, and now the opportunity for revenge had come she did not fail to take advantage of it.

In plain, pointed words she addressed her, without sparing one cause of complaint or a single reproach, and in their full hideousness casting in her teeth the enormity of her sins. She repaid with interest in that moment all the countless sufferings the guilty woman had caused, completely overwhelming her with vituperation. Valérie heard her out with but little interruption, and when at length Gabrielle concluded, there was a moment's silence.

"Now, madame," exclaimed Hugh sternly, addressing his wife, "we will end this our last interview, for you and I will never meet again. From the bottom of my heart I hate you, hoping that a just retribution will be yours. When it comes, you will probably recollect the words of a man who loved you dearer than his life. Coombe never before gave shelter to a murderess, and it shall do so no longer. The hour is late, therefore I will grant you until to-morrow, but if you have not left here by midday I shall call in the police and give you up to justice. You understand—I shall not depart from my word. The tie which bound us has been broken, and I curse the day when I was so blindly infatuated as to link my life with yours."

"Hugh! Hugh! I—I am penitent. Have pity."

"You had none for me. I have none."

"Hugh! Forgive!"

"Never!"

As he turned from her, Egerton unlocked the door, and in silence they went out, while the unhappy woman tottered forward, and in despair cast herself upon the couch, burying her face in the silken cushions.

Chapter Thirty Five
Devil's Dice

Alone in her dainty little boudoir, Valérie was standing deep in thought.

In the ballroom, the excited revellers continued their antics, and the fair gleeful angels, now thoroughly resigned to their sable attendant spirits, allowed themselves to be whirled wildly up and down the room amid the applause of the gay assembly, who were too amused and absorbed with the novelty of the scene to notice the absence of their hostess. Had they seen her at that moment they would scarce have recognised her as the woman who, only an hour before, was so radiant and reckless, and who had headed the Demon's Dance with so light a heart.

Nanette, having entered unexpectedly without knocking, had been surprised to find her mistress crouching by the fire in the cosy, luxuriant room, and noticing her pallor and agitation, asked with alarm what ailed her.

"It's a mere trifle," was the abrupt reply. "I—I'm not very well. Should any of the people ask for me, tell them—tell them I have a bad headache—say anything, only don't let them disturb me. I must be alone—you understand?"

"Yes, madame," said the girl. "This came for you by to-night's post. You have been so worried about the dance, I thought I would not give it to you before you came upstairs," she added, handing her mistress a letter.

Valérie glanced hastily at the envelope.

"You may go, Nanette," she said calmly. "I shall require nothing more to-night. Perhaps to-morrow I shall leave for London."

"Very well, madame," and rather pleased at this early release from her duties, the maid discreetly withdrew, closing the door noiselessly.

Going over to the corner where stood a tall lamp, the light of which was tempered by a shade of amber silk, she tore open the letter eagerly, and read its contents.

"Ah!" she cried, staggering as if she had been dealt a crushing blow, and staring wildly at the open note in her hand. "He, too—he has deserted me! I am forsaken!"

The letter, indeed, completed the retribution which had fallen so suddenly and mercilessly upon her. It was a short, curt note from Pierre Rouillier, whom she had left in London, stating that, having discovered that Gabrielle had instituted inquiries, and fearing the exposure that must inevitably follow, he had taken the money she had entrusted to him to deposit in the bank, and was leaving England that night. The communication concluded with a cold, heartless declaration that he had grown tired of her caprices, and therefore he had resolved that they should never meet again.

Wounded to the quick, she tore the letter in half, and cast it upon the fire.

"Miserable coward!" she hissed. "Afraid of your own safety, you run away and leave me to meet them alone."

Sublime in her indignation, she paced the room impatiently. In her despair she pushed the thick hair from her hot, fevered brow. It came unloosened, and fell in profuse luxuriance over her bare heaving breast, while at the same time the diamond star dropped upon the floor, and lay glistening in the fitful firelight.

Mad with passion, she crushed it under the heel of her tiny satin shoe.

Ignominious defeat, combined with the desertion of the only man for whom she entertained a spark of genuine affection, had completely corroded her soul. At first she thought only of revenge, and strode up and down muttering fearful imprecations upon those who had been the cause of her downfall. With a sudden ebullition of passion she unclasped the bracelet from her wrist, and flinging it down, treated it in the same manner as the other ornament. Then hooking her thin white fingers in the lace of her bodice, she tore it to shreds, casting the fragments heedlessly about her.

She caught sight of her reflection in a mirror; a shudder passed over her graceful form, and her slim hands trembled violently.

"*Dieu!*" she wailed. "What shall I do? Enemies on every side await their opportunity to overthrow me, and jeer at my discomfiture! Ah! what a fate!"

Pale as the gown she wore, she reeled, and would have fallen had she not clutched the table for support.

Her passion was succeeded by blank, poignant despair. The bloodless lips were compressed firmly as she made a vain effort to shake off the terrible fear which had taken possession of her; but the soft, smooth brow contracted, and the handsome face became dark and gloomy. She could not put away the black forebodings; they clung to her; they clutched her mind with a desperate grasp, and she was powerless to resist them. Her whole frame shook with a feverish tremor, for she was conscious that fate was against her, and that the spirit of evil was hovering about her ready to drag her down to destruction.

Her lips quivered, but she stood motionless and mute in contemplation.

The strains of a dreamy waltz penetrating into the room jarred upon her nerves. She covered her ears with her hands to shut out the sound of gaiety, and waited patiently until it had ceased.

"If I leave here what will be my future?" she asked aloud in desperation. "I can do nothing—nothing. Hugh knows all—everything! I am already branded as a murderess—a woman who should be hunted down and delivered to justice! And what then? Suppose that cursed Gabrielle gave me up to the police?" She paused, and drew a long breath before continuing.

"La Roquette! The *lunette!*" she cried hoarsely. "I see them! I know how justice would punish me, and how my enemies, those who are jealous of my success, would triumph. No—no! *Dieu!* I couldn't bear it—I—!"

A deep-drawn sob burst from her, and she hid her agonised face in her hands.

The stillness was only broken by the ticking of the tiny Dresden dock, the chimes of which, as it struck the hour, mingled with the sighs of the dejected woman.—Presently she raised her blanched face.

"Death!" she exclaimed in a husky whisper, looking half fearfully around, as if startled at the sound of her own voice. "Nothing else remains for me. There is no hope—no mercy—I am guilty—*guilty*! Sooner or later death will be the punishment of my crime, so why not now? If I escape from here, I shall only plunge into poverty and be tracked by the bloodhounds of the law. Ah! no! *Sapristi!* I prefer death!" With wild, wearied eyes she gazed slowly around, bewildered by her own suggestion.

"Yet am I so much to blame after all?" she soliloquised. "It was Victor's suggestion—he taught me to commit robbery. He compelled me to commit murder. Dazzled by the prospect of wealth and luxury he held constantly before my eyes, I submitted. He made me his cat's-paw to perpetrate crimes which he was too great a coward to commit himself, and when he found himself cornered he exposed me in order to deprive me of liberty and life. Had I never met the mean, contemptible scoundrel, I should have led as blameless a life as ordinary women, and remained the dutiful wife of Percy Willoughby, notwithstanding his ill-treatment."

Across her aching forehead she passed her hand quickly, brushing her hair back from her face.

"Bah!" she continued, with bitterness. "What's the use of thinking of things as they might have been? Victor's companionship made me callous, and I stained my hands with crime in order to gain riches. I abandoned every womanly feeling and instinct, and carried out the plot without regard for those who stood in my way. Therefore, there are no extenuating circumstances. No. I staked my life upon the game, but, my usual luck having deserted me, I have lost—lost irretrievably. I must pay."

Her frenzy of passion had been succeeded by a calm thoughtful mood, and she was silently reviewing her past, recognising for the first time how vile and hideous were her sins.

"God," she cried, in an intense, pitiful voice, "I would give all—everything I possess—if it were possible to atone—if I could obtain Hugh's forgiveness! He loved me so dearly, lavished all his affection and money upon me, and closed his ears to the truth, which he thought calumnies, yet—I killed his brother—stabbed him—afterwards sending Hugh himself to penal servitude. And for what? Merely for my own aggrandisement—in order that I might become mistress of this place, and live in luxury and ease. It was a foul, horrible plot," she added, shuddering. "Repentance is useless, forgiveness hopeless; I can only—die—*die!*"

As she uttered these words her eyes fell upon the davenport which stood on the opposite side of the room. A thought suddenly occurred to her. She crossed the boudoir, and, seating herself, took up a pen and commenced to write rapidly.

The letter was long and rambling, devoid of any endearing terms. It commenced with an admission of her marriage with Willoughby and the subsequent divorce, followed by a full confession of the murder of Douglas Trethowen. She wrote:

I was walking along Pall Mall alone, about ten o'clock at night, when I encountered him, not by accident but by design. He quickly recognised me, and appeared pleased that we had met. For nearly a quarter of an hour we stood talking, until he told me he had an appointment at Liverpool Street Station. At that moment an omnibus slackened speed opposite us to allow two men to alight. I suggested we should go to the City together in the 'bus, and we entered it. There was no conductor, and we were alone. Scarcely had we entered the vehicle when his manner suddenly changed, and he spoke of the affair of the Boulevard Haussmann. His attitude was threatening, and he said that now I was there with him without any chance of escape, he intended to give me up to the police as a murderess when the conveyance arrived at its destination. I grew frightened, for I was convinced from his manner that he meant what he said. It was not by accident, but by intention, that I had met him, and I was fully prepared. I saw the time had come, and, drawing from my pocket the handkerchief I had prepared, I soon quieted him. Then I struck the blow. I drove the knife in hard; it killed him. It all happened in a few moments, and while the omnibus was still in motion and about to enter the Strand I jumped out quickly and made my escape.

The remainder of the letter was a confused and disjointed declaration of love, combined with a penitent entreaty for forgiveness, without any attempt at palliation.

Blotting the tears that had fallen and blurred the words as she wrote, she placed it in an envelope and addressed it with a nervous, shaky hand "To Hugh."

"Ah, well," she murmured, sighing heavily.

Again she opened the davenport, and from under some papers took a little morocco case. Rigid and determined, she rose, more calm than before. Her lips were thin and white, her teeth tightly clenched, and in her eyes was a fixed, stony look. Walking with firm steps to the door, she locked it, afterwards flinging herself upon a chair beside the small bamboo table in the centre of the room.

Overwhelmed by despair, she had no longer any desire for life. Insanity, begotten of despondency and fear, prompted with headlong wilfulness, an ardent longing for death.

Opening the case, she extracted from its blue velvet interior a tiny silver hypodermic syringe and a small glass phial. Examining the latter in the dim light, she saw it was labelled "Chloral." This was not the drug she desired. She was in the habit of injecting this for the purpose of soothing her nerves, and knew that it was too weak to produce fatal effect.

Her breath came and went in short uneven gasps, while her half-uncovered breast heaved and fell with the excitement of her temporary madness.

Staggering to her feet, she returned swiftly to the davenport, from which, after a few moments' search, she abstracted a small dark-blue bottle containing morphia, afterwards reseating herself, and, uncorking it, placed it upon the table.

Taking up the syringe, she tried its needle-point with her finger. It pricked her, and she cast it from her with an exclamation of repugnance.

"Dieu!" she gasped hoarsely. "I have no courage. Bah! I am still a coward!"

Yet, as it lay upon the table she fixed her strained eyes upon it, for as an instrument of death it possessed a fatal fascination for her.

Slowly she stretched forth her hand, and again took it between her cold fingers. Then, with a sudden resolve, she filled it to its utmost capacity with the drug from the bottle.

"A certain remedy for mental ailments," she remarked to herself, smiling bitterly as she held it up contemplatively. "Who will regret my death or shed a tear? No one. I have no adieux to make—none. As a friendless, sinful wretch, I adopt the preferable mode of speedy death rather than undergo the ordeal of a criminal trial, with its inevitable result. I would live and atone for the past if I could, but that is impossible. Ah! too late, alas! Pierre has forsaken me, and I am alone. Forgiveness! Bah! A mere mockery to set the conscience at rest. What use? I—I can never be forgiven—never!"

While speaking she had, with a feeble, trembling hand, applied the sharp point of the syringe to her bare white arm. Unflinchingly she ran the needle deep into the flesh, and thrice slowly emptied the liquid into the puncture.

She watched the bead of dark blood oozing from the wound when she withdrew the instrument, and quickly covered it with her thumb in order that the injection should be fully absorbed in her veins.

"Ah!" she gasped, in sudden terror a moment later, as the syringe dropped from her nerveless grasp, "I—I feel so giddy! I can't breathe! I'm choking! The poison's killing me. Ha, ha, I'm dying!" she laughed hysterically. "They thought to triumph over me, the vultures! but, after all, I've cheated them. They'll find that Valérie Duvauchel was neither coward nor fool when run to earth!"

Springing to her feet she clutched convulsively at her throat, tearing the flesh with her nails in a horrible paroxysm of pain.

The injection had swiftly accomplished its work.

"Pierre! Pierre!" she articulated with difficulty, in a fierce, hoarse whisper, "where are you? Ah! I see! You—you've returned. Why did you leave me in their merciless clutches when you knew that—that I always—loved you? Kiss me—*mon cher!* Kiss me—darling,—kiss me, Pierre—"

The words choked her.

Blindly she staggered forward a few steps, vainly endeavouring to steady herself.

With a short, shrill scream she wheeled slowly round, as if on a pivot, then tottered, and fell backwards, inert, and lifeless!

A dead, unbroken silence followed. The spirit of Valérie Duvauchel had departed, leaving the body as that of a dishevelled fallen angel.

In a few moments the strains of another plaintive waltz penetrated into the chamber of death, forming a strange incongruous dirge.

When, a few hours later, the yellow winter's dawn crept in through the window, the dull, uncertain light fell upon the calm, upturned countenance.

It was beautiful—very beautiful. Before the last breath had departed, the drawn, haggard features had relaxed and resumed their enchanting smile.

Yet there was something in the expression of the blanched face which cast a chill upon the admiration of its loveliness—the brand of guilt was there.

Chapter Thirty Six
Conclusion

When the door of the boudoir was forced open, old Jacob was the first to enter and find his mistress rigid in death. While Nanette and two of the domestics were endeavouring to raise her, his quick eyes caught sight of the letter addressed to his master which lay upon the blotting-pad, and unnoticed he slipped it into his pocket.

By this a scandal was avoided, for a coroner's jury at the inquest subsequently held returned a verdict of "Accidental death, due to an overdose of morphia." There was not the least suspicion of suicide in the minds of the twelve respectable tradesmen, for, prior to the room being visited by the bucolic constable, Jacob had picked up the remains of the diamond ornaments, and carefully obliterated other traces of her passion. The jury expressed an opinion that the sudden appearance of Mrs Trethowen's husband, who was believed to be dead, had caused a violent shock to the nervous system, and that, being in the habit of injecting narcotics, she had accidentally administered to herself an overdose.

Hugh, in order to further allay any conjecture that she had taken her own life, put on deep mourning and attended the funeral. He endured the mournful ceremony, the nasal mumbling of the clergyman, and the torture of the service, with feelings of disgust at his own hypocrisy. He affected inconsolable grief, and his friends, ignorant of the truth, sympathised with him. Yet his generous nature asserted itself. The letter she had addressed to him had softened his heart towards her, and as he stood watching the coffin being consigned to the grave in the churchyard at Bude, tears welled in his eyes.

He had forgiven her, endeavouring to believe that she had been more sinned against than sinning.

Contrary to the expectations of his friends, he did not leave Coombe after the funeral, but took what appealed to many to be a sad, bitter pleasure in remaining amid surroundings that reminded him of his late wife. Scarcely uttering a word to any one save his faithful servant Jacob, he grew cynical and morose, while his face wore a fixed expression of gloom.

People thought that Valérie's death had been a terrible blow to him, and that he cherished everything which brought her to his memory. In truth, however, it was quite the opposite. He was gradually removing every trace of her occupancy. Her photographs, several of which stood about in the rooms, he destroyed with his own hands. Cushion-covers that she had embroidered, and a mantel fringe she had made, he ruthlessly tore off and threw into the fire.

When he had destroyed all the small articles, the sight of which was repugnant, he called in a furniture dealer from Bude, and for a mere trifle sold the whole of the contents of the boudoir which she had furnished so extravagantly. The rooms were dismantled to the curtains and blinds, and after it had been repainted and redecorated, he gave orders to a London firm to refurnish it as a boudoir in a style even more costly than before.

The servants marvelled greatly at what they considered their master's folly, and even the discreet Jacob was puzzled at his irony and resolution.

Bright spring days succeeded the boisterous, gloomy ones of winter on the wild Cornish coast, still Hugh Trethowen continued to live in semi-seclusion. The greater part of each day he spent in the library with his books, and for recreation took long, lonely walks along the seashore, or over the moorlands, swept by the invigorating Atlantic breeze.

Suddenly his habitual sullenness left him, and one day in July he announced to Jacob that he expected visitors. Thenceforward there was a complete change in his demeanour. Resuming his normal lightheartedness, he greeted his friends with that thoroughness and *bonhomie* that were characteristic of him in the old days, and personally looked after their comfort.

His guests, a pleasant, merry party, consisting of Jack Egerton, Dolly Vivian, and Gabrielle Debriège, had no reason to complain of the cordiality of their host's welcome, or of the efforts he made to entertain them with the various pleasurable pursuits which the neighbourhood afforded.

The close of a hot summer's day.

A charming little hollow, fringed with hazels and ferns, on a green hillside overlooking the shining sea. A long stretch of bay lies in the mellow light, curved like a crescent moon, while behind rise hills that are somewhat low but steep, scalloped by dells clad in silver birches, hazels, graceful ferns, and golden gorse. Nearly at the centre of this picturesque amphitheatre of green slopes and rocky buttresses snugly nestles a quaint old-world village, a community of pretty cottages clustered around the ancient church, and deeply set in the verdure of the hillside like a handful of snow-white shells in a green dell of the sea.

Not only the crimson-tinted ocean, but the land also, is strangely transfigured in the glow of twilight. The long stretches of cliff, with the precipitous Raven's Crag towering high above the rocks on either side, which, in the fierce glare of noonday, stood out like bastions, centres of strength and power, and now rounded by the softening shadows of the gloaming hour. The mantling grass with which they are crowned has lost its emerald colour, and assumes a subdued preternatural tint, while the softened sea in its violet light comes up to the deep shadows of the overhanging crags, lustrous, pure, serene.

Hugh had driven with his visitors from Coombe, and they had left the carriage at the village inn, and set out on foot to explore the beauties of the district. Dolly and he had wandered away from Egerton and Gabrielle, and walked upon the top of the cliffs towards the great perpendicular Crag.

While they had been strolling along, she had been telling him of the vile plot to keep them apart while Valérie exerted her irresistible charms upon him. She showed him the dark red scar upon her throat, now concealed by a narrow band of black velvet, and explained how she had made the discovery while imprisoned in the strange house near Twickenham, her escape, her visit to the church on the morning of his marriage, and her denunciation of Holt. To all this he listened with incredulous amazement.

When, on their return, they arrived at the stile at the entrance of the wooded hollow through which they had to pass to reach the village, they both paused. Hugh stood leaning with his back against the rails, thoughtfully puffing his cigarette. The manner in which Dolly had told the story puzzled him. True, they were still friends, and since her arrival at Coombe had often spoken confidentially; nevertheless, he did not forget that on the last occasion they strolled together alone on the Cornish cliffs, he ridiculed her warning, and openly professed his preference for Valérie.

He glanced at her handsome face. Her head was turned seaward; her soft brown eyes wore a thoughtful, serious look, and a ray of fading sunlight tinted her hair. The cool, flimsy blue dress fitted her lithesome figure with scarcely a wrinkle, and the wide-brimmed hat set off to advantage the fair countenance beneath.

"Dolly," he said earnestly, after a short silence, taking her gloved hand in his at the same time, "all this you have just told me adds increased horror to Valérie's terrible crimes. I now understand the reason you wrote that warning—it was because you entertained some sort of affection for me. Ah, had I fully understood you before I allied myself with that woman—had I seen her in her true light as an adventuress, and summoned sufficient strength to cast her off—I should not have been instrumental in bringing such a calamity upon you. I alone am to blame for all the misery that has fallen upon you, and must ask your forgiveness."

"There is nothing to forgive, for I consider you are in no way to blame, Hugh—I mean, Mr Trethowen."

"No, no; call me Hugh, as you did in the old days. Why need there be any formalities?"

"You are not to blame, Hugh," she repeated ingenuously. "That woman fascinated you as she enmeshed many other men, all of whom paid dearly for the privilege of bestowing their affections upon her. Think of Jack—of your brother, Douglas! Did she not entice them both into her coils, so that she might use them for her own ends? Hubert Holt she ensnared in the same manner, she—"

"Why was he so obedient to her will?" asked Hugh interrupting.

"Gabrielle told me all about it a few days ago. It appears that when he was a fellow-student with Jack he also admired Valérie. In order to supply her with money he forged a cheque at her instigation, the proceeds of which, amounting to something like twenty thousand francs, he handed over to her, thinking thereby to secure her good graces. But she treated him the same as the others. Though he abandoned Art and entered the church, she did not allow the crime to fade from his memory, for at intervals she compelled him to perform services for her which were revolting to one who was trying to atone and lead a better life. Now, fearing exposure and detection, he has fled to South America, where, I believe, he has been joined by that old scoundrel, Graham, whom Valérie paid handsomely for his services. It is not likely that they will ever return to England."

"And you really forgive me for all the trials and torture I have brought upon you?" he asked earnestly, with a slight pressure on the little hand he held.

"Of course I do," she said frankly, raising her fine, wide-open eyes to his.

"Before I met that woman I flirted with you, Dolly," he said, in a low, intense tone. "You were not averse to flattery or sly whispers in the studio when Jack's back was turned, and I, having nothing else to do, amused myself in your company. Indeed, it was not before that night when, being on the verge of ruin, I came to wish you farewell, that I discovered you really cared for me. Then I blamed myself for being so cruel as to let you see that I loved you—"

"Hugh!" she cried in astonishment. "Why, what do you mean?"

"Listen, and I'll tell you, dearest," he answered, looking earnestly into her eyes. "It was soon after my brother's death that I met Valérie. Prior to that, however, I had grown to love you, because I knew that, although you lived in an atmosphere that was somewhat questionable as regards morals, you were nevertheless pure and good. I was on the point of asking you to become my wife when Valérie crossed my path. You know the rest. She was no fairer, no better-looking than you are at this moment, but with that fatal, irresistible power she possessed she drew me to her, and I became her slave and as helpless as a child. Now and then you and I met, and as you did not appear to notice the coldness I exhibited, I congratulated myself that you no longer entertained any affection for me."

"What caused you to think that?" she demanded in dismay.

"To tell the truth," he responded hesitatingly, "I believed those repeated warnings you gave me against Valérie were merely the rancorous fictions of a jealous heart, and that is why I took no heed of them."

"Ah!" she exclaimed, with sadness, "I tried hard but could never bring you to understand that my woman's power of perception was keener than yours. You were so credulous, and did not suspect treachery. Although Jack's secret sealed his lips, yet I knew from the manner in which he spoke that if you attached yourself to her, ruin would quickly follow."

"Yes," he admitted gloomily, "you told me so, but I was too blind an idiot to believe it. Had I taken your advice how much pain and sorrow would have been avoided!"

"Of what use is regret? She is dead—and you free!"

"Free—free to marry you!" he said in a deep, earnest voice, pressing her hand to his lips at the same moment.

She glanced inquiringly at him, as if unable to grasp his meaning, and tried to withdraw her hand.

"To marry me?" she repeated.

"Yes. Will you be my wife, Dolly?" he urged passionately. "We have been friends for so long that we ought to know each other's peculiarities of temperament by this time. I know I have no right to make this request after the heartless manner in which I cast you aside. On the other hand, you have passed the ordeal and been true to me, trying to rescue me from ignominy and ruin, even when I ridiculed your affection. For that reason I love you now more than ever, and I cannot refrain from asking you to make me happy."

"It is true that you left me, preferring Valérie," she said reflectively. "But you should not forget that you thought her a woman in your own sphere, whereas I was only an artist's model. It was but natural you should consider her a more fitting wife than myself; and, although I loved you so well!"

"Did you love me, then?"

She blushed.

"But do you still care for me?" he asked with earnestness, putting his arm around her slim waist and pressing her to his breast. "Promise me, Dolly," he pleaded—"promise me that you will be my wife!"

"Do you love me sufficiently?"

"Can you doubt me?"

"No," she replied, in a tremulous voice; "I do not doubt you, Hugh. I will be your wife."

Then she bent her fair head, and hid from him her tears of happiness. The only light that can show us the road to better things is that which shines within us. The words he uttered were tender and reassuring, and for a long time they stood together talking of the new, bright, and unclouded life that lay before them.

Meanwhile the exquisite gradations of colour on sea and land had faded, the glow upon the horizon had disappeared, the wind had fallen, and all was calm and still in the mystic gloom of the dying day.

Startled by hearing voices behind them, they turned and faced Jack and Gabrielle, who had approached unnoticed.

After a hearty laugh and some good-natured chaff in English, the purport of which was not thoroughly understood by mademoiselle, Hugh grasped the artist's hand, and, wringing it warmly exclaimed—

"Congratulate me, old fellow! I'm beginning life afresh from to-day. Dolly has consented to become my wife."

"By Jove, is that so?" Egerton cried, in pleasant surprise. "Well, you have my heartiest wishes, Hugh." Then he added, after a moment's hesitation: "Strangely enough, I, too, have to make a similar announcement."

"What?" cried Hugh and Dolly simultaneously. "Gabrielle has resolved to give up the stage and become Mrs Egerton," he answered, with a happy smile. "We knew one another years ago in Paris, and although no word of affection was then spoken, we have to-day discovered that we love one another."

"Yes," added Gabrielle, her accent making her voice sound pleasant to English ears. "Having released him from the thrall of 'La Petite Hirondelle,' and proving that he was not guilty of the crime he believed he had committed, I am going to many him. It is as it should be—eh?"

And she laughed contentedly.

After many mutual congratulations and expressions of surprise, they crossed the stile, and continued their stroll through the dell towards the village, where the scattered lights had already commenced to twinkle.

The two men walked together at a little distance behind.

"Hugh, old fellow," the artist remarked confidentially, "I'm glad Dolly is to be your wife. I feel confident that you'll never regret the step; for I know, perhaps better than any one, how pure and honest she is, how dearly she loves you, and how acutely she suffered when you forsook her."

"Don't mention the past again, Jack, old fellow. We both played dice with the devil, expecting to throw sixes," said Hugh, as they stepped out upon the broad highway. Then he added, "I feel assured we shall now be happy and contented. Let us look only to a bright and prosperous future, and let us forget forever the grim shadow that fell upon us, the shadow of The Temptress."